COLOUR
for
LIVING

HOW *to* CHANGE
YOUR LIFE *with*
COLOUR

COLOUR
FOR
LIVING

HOW *to* CHANGE
YOUR LIFE *with*
COLOUR

TINA DUNNE

MERLIN
PUBLISHING

First published in 2008 by
Merlin Publishing
Newmarket Hall, St Luke's Avenue,
Cork Street, Dublin 8, Ireland
Tel: +353 1 4535866
Fax: +353 1 4535930
publishing@merlin.ie
www.merlinwolfhound.com

ISBN 978-1-903582-75-6

A CIP catalogue record for this book is available
from the British Library.

10 9 8 7 6 5 4 3 2 1

Cover Images: Front/lemon © Peter Vaclavek; Front/flower
© Steve Dibblee; Front flap © Robert Churchill; Back/pepper
© Pali Rao; Back/strawberries© Enrico Fianchini;
Back/apricots © Jorge Gonzalez.
Typeset by Carrigboy Typesetting Services.
Cover Design by Graham Thew Design.
Printed and bound in Slovenia.

Contents

ACKNOWLEDGEMENTS

I wholeheartedly appreciate and thank all my clients, mentors, family and friends who have shared their encouragement and belief with me, and who patiently supported me as I created *Colour for Living*. As a result of their colourful existence, generosity and love this book has been created.

Thank you also to Aoife, Laura, Chenile, Julie and Tony of Merlin Publishing and to Noelle who all dedicated so much time and energy to making this book a reality.

Picture Credits

Jack Puccio ii; Satu Knape iv, v; David Mason viii; Steve Dibblee 5, 49; Zoubin Zarin 5; Stuart Miles 7; Lise Gagne 10, 75, 213; Alex Bramwell 11; xyno6 11; Enrico Fianchini 12; Maria Bacarella 12; Sergei Didyk 12; Tomas Bercic 13, 81, 304; Skip ODonnell 13, 17, 225; Christine Balderas 14; Tom Hahn 15, 124; Dave White 18; Robyn Mackenzie 20, 21, 71, 296; Mike Bentley 22; Olga Lyubkina 23; eva serrabassa 24; pandapoo.com 25; M_Studio 26; Jennifer Daley 29; Damir Spanic 29; Ahmad Faizal Yahya 31; Alex Bramwell 32; Joan Vicent Cantó Roig 34, 62, 89; Rich Legg 37; Annett Vauteck 38; Effinity Stock Photography 38, 289; Ellen Sheppard 39; William Berry 39; Jorge Gonzalez 39; Yoko Bates 40; Tomo Jesenicnik 42; Anssi Ruuska 44; Paul Tessier 45; HD Connelly Photography 46; Barbara Sauder 49; Alexey Avdeev 51; Heiko Potthoff. 54; Manuela Krause 56; Pali Rao 56; KL Photography 57, 81; Michael Hill 57; Miranda Salia 58; Tony Campbell 61; Peter Mlekuž 61; Markus Guhl 62; Diane Rutt 62; Javier Fontanella 63; Kelly Cline 64, 83, 271; Dirk Richter 65; Jack Puccio 67; Jacqueline Hunkele 68; Oren Ariel 70; Jarek Szymanski 73; Duncan Walker 73; Nathan Gleave 77; Alison Stieglitz 80; Gabriel Nardelli Araujo 81; Jason Reekie 82; Steven Allan 82; Creacart 82; Steve Dibblee 83; Bluestocking 83, 245; Dušan Zidar 83; Diane Diederich 84; Stuart Pitkin 86; Brent Melton 88; Paul Cowan 90; Vladimir Vladimirov 91; Marc Dietrich 93; Evgeny Kuklev 93; Lucian 96; Ian McDonnell 98, 112; Dariusz Sas 98; Erik Reis 100; Richard Gunion 101; Forest Woodward 101; Manfred Konrad 103; Ben Blankenburg 105; Kriss Russell 107; Sawayasu Tsuji 109; Marianne Fitzgerald 109; Dan Chippendale 110, 216, 224; Carol Gering 115; Lisa Thornberg 117; Andreas Karelias 117; McKevin Shaughnessy 119; Monika Adamczyk 121; Mark Weiss 123; Fuat Kose 127; Heiko Potthoff 127l; Mikhail Tolstoy 128; Anna Yu 128; Andrew Howe 128; Joe Gough 129; Ivan Mateev 131; SebastianKnight 132; bridgette braley 133; Cloki 135; Steve Goodwin 135; Amanda Rohde 137; Pederk 139; Rafal Fabrykiewicz 141; Matt Jeacock 141; Westmacott Photography 142; Ben Phillips 142; Tim Fan 143; ShyMan 144, 250; Scott Karcich 147; Elena Elisseeva 148; Lee Pettet 151; Martin McCarthy 151; Nadezda Firsova 154; Volker Kreinacke 155; Joanna Pecha 157; Roberto Adrian 160; David Ellis 160; Asher Welstead 160; Marcelo Wain 162, 164, 249; Michael-John Wolfe 162; Sawayasu Tsuji 163; Jason Wickens 163; Aleksandr Ugorenkov 164; Donna Franklin 166; Dóri O'Connell 167; Stocksnapper 168; Heidi Anglesey 169; Daniela Andreea Spyropoulos 170, 282; Olivier Le Moal 172; Christian Michael 174; Natalia Klenova 175; Denise Torres 177; Christopher Badzioch 178; Graça Victoria 180; Glen Teitell 181; Tomo Jesenicnik 182; Dobri Dobrinov 183; Liv Friis-Larsen 185; Martin Garnham 186; MKucova 187; eli_asenova 189; Eric Isselée 189; Juan Monino 190; Kristian Sekulic 194; Norman Pogson 195; Jasmin Awad 196; Heidi Morton 198; Adam Booth 199; Joselito Briones 201; Graça Victoria 203; Scott Karcich 206; MKucova 207; Dawna Stafford 209; Imo 211; Ben Blankenburg 211; John Pitcher 212; Oscar Durand 212; PMSI Web Hosting and Design 215; Christine Glade 215; Suzannah Skelton 215; Michael Hill 216; Nicola Stratford 216; Lior Filshteiner 217; Chris Beddoe 218; Mara Cole Mat Greiner 219; Curt Pickens 221; Benjamin Brandt 223; PMSI Web Hosting and Design 226; Alain Couillaud 227; Yoko Bates 228; Dane Steffes 231; Amanda Rohde 231; Yong Hian Lim 235; Rolf Weschke 236; Marie-france Bélanger 238; Feng Yu 239; Tobias Ott 240; Linda & Colin McKie 240; Joan Vicent Cantó Roig 240; Pawe Strykowski 241; Liv Friis-Larsen 242; Rolf Weschke 244; Brian Daly 247; Olga Lyubkina 248; Carlos Wigderowitz 252; Nick Provan 253; Olaru Radian-Alexandru 255; Alexander Chelmodeev 255; Mark Weiss 256; Ed O'Neil 263; Dušan Zidar 265; Yangshuo 267; Petr Vaclavek 271; Jane Norton 280, Sean Locke 281; James Pauls 284; konstantin32 292; Hazel Proudlove 294; Diana Lundin 295; Joanna Pecha 297; Esemelwe 298; Jason Reekie 304; Michael-John Wolfe 304; Christine Balderas 304

LIVING WITH COLOUR

The origin of *Colour for Living* dates back to 1998 when I took a trip to South America to investigate the foods and flavours of the continent but in many ways, the roots go back even further. On my twelfth birthday, an aunt of mine gave me a red top; it was a casual jersey style top, with the word 'Caracus' embroidered in orange thread on the label. I was fascinated with this word as it sounded so exotic and different – home to oil barons, Miss World and tropical fruits, I became fascinated with Caracas, capital of Venezuela, South America. I grabbed any possible opportunity to explore the magic this place stirred up in me, whether  selecting it as a topic for school projects or creating romantic stories about falling in love under the Angel Falls. Needless to say I did give Venezuela a lot of dream time and when I finally got the chance to go there in September 1998 I gladly took time off from my job as Food Advisor and set out on the adventure of a lifetime – a solo trip to South America. Adventures can inspire us to create a fresh life philosophy and change the way we live our lives forever.

I travelled for a full six months through nine South American countries, enveloped in the food, flavours and exotic passions of this continent for the entirety – from the colourful and bustling markets deep in the Andean regions and the remote areas of the Amazon to the sunny seashore regions of Columbia, Chile, Argentina and Brazil.

I had already envisaged putting together a recipe book with information on all the regions I travelled through and I kept a record as I went along, noting unusual ingredients and cooking techniques. I spent a lot of time at the market places, meandering and exploring the stalls which were filled with exotic and extraordinary goods. These stalls sold the richest of spices, the juiciest of pineapples, mango and acai (a Brazilian berry), the finest Brazil nuts in Bolivia and quinoa in Peru. I ingested sufficient quantities of iron from red meat in Argentina to keep me topped up for life. I ate in local restaurants keeping a watchful eye on the dishes and delicacies the local folk were eating and all the time I was gathering recipes and culinary tips.

As my trip continued, I became curious about other aspects of the South American lifestyle. I loved the vibrant music, the flamboyant rhythm at carnivals, the exquisite artefacts in the markets, the gem stones, fabrics and the positive disposition of the people. Their energy and passion captivated me; it was like a tonic for longevity. Travelling on, I gradually realised that the awe-inspiring ingredient for this happy way of living was one thing – colour.

The way they lived and enjoyed life prompted me to explore the contribution that colour plays in our daily lives, not only in food related activities but from the way we move, live and think. On my return, I started to explore the concept and sought out a course to learn and understand the scientific impact that colour has on our physical and psychological wellness, adaptability and attitude.

Since then I have not stopped exploring the role that colour plays in our daily lives. I decided the next step was to share the information I had accumulated – and *Colour for Living* was born. The contents of this book detail the dynamic power and role that colour plays in our lives. This impact extends to our health and diet. If you want to protect your health, the first crucial step is to take the decision to make the necessary life changes that will support your health in a positive way. There are up to 30,000 new cases of cancer diagnosed in Ireland each year and up to 70% of these could be prevented through a lifestyle change, whether it's by quitting smoking and/or drinking, lessening your exposure to the sun or by eating a healthy balanced diet!

Fruit markets in Argentina

It's vital that you make the connection between good food choices and good health. One of the simplest, most efficient and cost effective ways to improve your health, energy levels and mood is to eat fruits and vegetables and other foods that contain natural plant colours or phytonutrients. (See Glossary for more details.) The current dietary guidelines suggest eating at least five portions of fruits and vegetables per day. This book will encourage you and your family to eat five and more fruits and vegetables per day. There are so many ways you can serve healthy, colourful food and they will eliminate toxins from your body, making you look and feel magnificent. Even the pickiest eaters in your home will adore the creative and fun way to go about planning your weekly menu, using colour as your guide. All the fruits and vegetables mentioned in this book are readily available and are grown locally so that you can purchase them organically.

I sincerely hope you can embrace adventure and allow your life to lift with colour. It's simple. Give yourself the best chance of being the happiest, healthiest and calmest gem you can be.

Tina

THERAPEUTIC USES OF COLOUR

BOOST CIRCULATION, COMBAT ANAEMIA,
RELAX THE MUSCULAR SYSTEM,
PROMOTE VITALITY, STIMULATE APPETITE

BOOSTS IMMUNE SYSTEM, STIMULATES APPETITE,
ELIMINATES TOXINS, STIMULATES LUNG FUNCTION,
GOOD FOR HEALTHY HAIR, ENERGISES

GOOD FOR SKIN, NAILS AND HAIR,
STRENGTHENS NERVES, BOOSTS THE PANCREAS,
LIVER AND GALL BLADDER

HELPS HEART CONDITIONS, EXPANDS BREATHING,
LUNGS, ASTHMA, BRONCHITIS,
BOOSTS IMMUNE SYSTEM

RELIEVES STRESS,
PAINFUL MENSTRUATION,
EASES THROAT PROBLEMS

SORE THROATS, STIMULATE PARATHYROID,
KILLS BACTERIA
CHOLESTEROL CHECK

CONTROLS EXCESSIVE HUNGER,
SEDATES AND SUBDUES INSOMNIA

FERTILITY,
SELF-LOVE

SELF-VALUE,
EMBRACING THE GOLDEN YEARS

Your Colour Personality

Colour plays a vitally important role in the world in which we live. The psychological language of colour is universal as it is rooted in our biology. Colour is understood by the unconscious mind, whether the stimulus is applied directly to the skin or through the eyes. As a result of the judicious use of colour in your life, bodily response patterns can be shifted and harmony can be restored. For example, red stimulates the sympathetic nervous system which raises our readiness for action, whereas blue stimulates the complementary system, the parasympathetic nervous system, which lowers blood pressure and induces calm.

Colour can sway thinking; change actions and cause reactions. **Different colours can energise you, raise your blood pressure or suppress your appetite but if colour is used in the wrong ways, it can cause feelings of low self-esteem, poor decision-making and fatigue**. It is essential that you learn how to make colour work for you, as the use of colour in your life will have a significant impact on your mood and physical well being.

The connection between colour and energy goes back a long way. It has its roots in the ancient civilisations of Egypt, India and China. Many pioneers championed the use of colour in healing. In the 1500s, Paracelsus, a prominent physician and astrologer, practised forms of colour therapy based on colour analysis, using elixirs, gems and minerals. His therapy was dismissed by the medical establishment because of its unscientific findings. By the 20th century, however, there had been many investigations into the use of colour therapy to overturn this dismissal. **For example, in 1990 in the *American Association Journal for the Advancement of Science*, scientists published successful results on the use of colour therapy to treat cases of depression, impotence, addictions and eating disorders**. In recent years, babies born with neonatal jaundice are treated with blue light therapy in hospitals and dyslexia sufferers are now able to read comfortably with tinted glasses. Specialist optometrists use the Intuitive Colorimeter, invented by Dr Arnold Wilkins, to evaluate which individual colours are best for the tinted glasses to improve reading and also to help prevent migraines.

Along with investigations into colour therapy, the 20th century heralded a new interest in defining and identifying separate personality types, in close correlation with the field of psychology. Personality analysis or testing has been around since Hippocrates' time in the 4th century BC. It aims to discover and describe aspects of a person that remain stable throughout their lifetime – mapping the individual's character and behavioural patterns, thought processes and feelings. Several distinctive tests have emerged such as the Myers-Briggs Type Indicator. This is a sixteen type personality test based on theories of Carl Jung during World War II. Another model is the Big Five personality traits – now commonly referred to as the 'Five-Factor model' – that was originally devised by WT Norman.

WHAT IS YOUR COLOUR PERSONALITY?

To work out your colour personality, first write down your birth date in full. It is essential to have the four digits of the year you were born.

For example: your birth date is January 2, 1990 – 2/01/1990

Then add all the digits together to work out your birth number. There are only 9 numbers so 10 will work down to 1.

For example: 2 + 1 + 1990

$2 + 1 = 3$

$1 + 9 + 9 + 0 = 19$

$19 + 3 = 22$

Add 22 together as it is essential to have a single digit number

$2 + 2 = 4$

Your birth number is 4, which means your colour personality is Green.

Personality testing is used across the board today, from career guidance at post-primary level to human resource departments in major corporations. It is a universal tool, employed to help people understand more about themselves and to help businesses identify a person's suitability to fill a specific role.

Colour is a physical component that can help to expose your personality type and reveal the things in life that motivate you, assist self-expression or identify areas of your personality that may require attention, so that you can live your life with grace, ease and happiness. After working out your colour personality, using the formula on the previous page, have a look at the list below to reveal your individual colour personality.

COLOUR PERSONALITIES

NUMBER 1	RED
NUMBER 2	ORANGE
NUMBER 3	YELLOW
NUMBER 4	GREEN
NUMBER 5	BLUE
NUMBER 6	INDIGO
NUMBER 7	PURPLE
NUMBER 8	PINK
NUMBER 9	GOLD

Having discovered the colour of your personality, check out the personality profiles from pages 1 to 269 and find out what it reveals about your career choice, leisure activities and best/worst personality matches. It could promote a whole new way of thinking for you or you can simply have fun discovering your friend's, partner's or boss's personality profile!

THE COLOUR red

RED IS THE MOST EMOTIONALLY INTENSE COLOUR. IT SYMBOLISES ENERGY AND ACTION AND IS ASSOCIATED WITH POWER, LEADERSHIP, SEXUALITY AND HEAT. RED STIMULATES A FASTER HEARTBEAT AND FASTER BREATHING.

Introducing red into your life will also activate your muscular system and help to keep your feet and hands warmer by stimulating the circulation system and boosting vitality levels.

People who like red tend to be optimistic and extrovert. **BRIDES IN INDIA WEAR RED ON THEIR WEDDING DAY TO SYMBOLISE HAPPINESS AND PASSION.** Red is also the colour historically associated with kings and very important people. Think of the red carpet treatment stars get today. Red cars are popular targets for thieves. In decorating, red is usually used as an accent colour because of its intensity.

WHAT IS YOUR COLOUR PERSONALITY? TO FIND OUT TURN TO PAGE 2.

THE **RED COLOUR** PERSONALITY

- PASSIONATE
- AMBITIOUS
- EXTREMELY GENEROUS
- GOOD AT BUILDING GREAT THINGS FROM VERY LITTLE
- BORN STRATEGIST – LOVES PLANNING
- SELF-EMPLOYMENT SUITS THIS PERSONALITY
- THEY PUSH FORWARD AGAINST ALL ODDS
- SELF-PRESERVATION AND SURVIVAL ARE VITAL TO THEM
- THEY GET THEIR OWN WAY – NO MATTER WHAT

Mr Red

This is an energetic, go-getter type. He's got big ideas and no limits when it comes to getting what he wants. Mr Red can be restless, thoughtless and demanding but he is also generous and loving. 'Passion' was his invention! Sexiness oozes out of his veins. He will wine and dine, pamper and treat you.

Being around him is fun, action-packed and his unpredictability will keep you on your toes. Just make sure to 'recharge' yourself when he is not around. Siestas are a great thing to work into your day if you have a red man in your life. It will help keep your energies up for all the strenuous activities he's got planned.

Ms Red

The firecracker of all females, she knows what she wants and will stop at nothing until she gets it. She is straight-talking and no-nonsense in approach. Manipulation is not her style and Ms Red will get right to the point with no holes barred. A little minx in the bedroom, this red-hot babe pulsates passion. She is upfront and honest in relationships and won't mess you about but she will expect that respect in return. She is a fierce protector and, once she has figured out who her perfect partner is, she will treasure you and all your possessions.

Young Red

This is the 'live wire' child – the one that does not need to sleep at night. They are always eager to check out new adventures and make great leaders in their gang. They are constantly on the go, always exploring new avenues and never leave anyone bored. In teen life they can be very industrious – initiating anything from a car boot sale in the neighbourhood to sporting games – and the possibility for activities are limitless with young reds. They have big spending capacity so their pocket money will always be spent on the latest gizmo, gadget or rock festival ticket. They tend to love music and do not rule out the idea of them setting up a band of their own. You may even find your red child has a talent for playing the drums!

The Red Parent

The red parent is very adventurous. They have ambitious ideas for their children. They will help in any way possible to advance their child's potential and can be a little pushy. They will encourage a fighting spirit and the motto 'do not give up' was designed by them. They strive to make their children resilient and hardy and do not entertain emotionality. 'Let's get on with it' or 'That's the way the cookie crumbles' is an attitude that figures high in the red parent's approach.

Guide to Wearing Red

If you want to get noticed – wear red. Wearing red will get you motivated but be careful if you wear it in negotiations as red is an extreme colour and you could come across as threatening. In these situations choose lighter shades of red, as they are softer and less dramatic. Red is, however, a good colour to wear for sports events, as it will heighten your energy levels.

Red clothing lifts your mood and can encourage shy people to come out of themselves. Start by using a red lipstick/gloss as everyone will then pay attention to what you say. If you are on a date wearing red lipstick will give out a signal of love.

THE RED CAREER

Red workers are best suited to self-employment as they tend to be energetic go-getters. They adore a challenge and like to keep moving. If the red employee finds something that needs to be fixed, you are in for dynamic and ingenious solutions. They work long hours and will not stop until the contract or deal has been signed, sealed and delivered. The red personality is brilliant at carrying ideas through and will pull all the punches necessary to get the job done.

Strong, dynamic and pioneering are among the strengths attributed to this career person. Red careerists are so driven and ambitious that they must watch their mental and physical health, as they can tend to push themselves more than any of the other colour personalities, both physically and mentally. The red careerist has a highly competitive nature which must be given time to recuperate, so that their blood pressure does not go through the roof.

THE RED PERSON HAS AN AMAZING ZEST FOR LIFE. THEIR MOTIVATING FORCE IS DESIRE, WHICH IS MANIFEST IN A HUNGER FOR FULLNESS, EXPERIENCES AND LIVING.

THE KEY WORDS *associated* WITH **RED** *are* ACHIEVEMENT, INTENSITY, IMPULSIVENESS, DARING, AGGRESSION AND PASSION.

SHADES OF RED

CRIMSON: The blue-red tones include plum, berry and wine shades. These look great on fair-haired people. Wearing these shades will make you feel very assertive.

SCARLET: Pink-red tones are more flowery, like fuchsia and rose. They look great on fair/brown-haired people. Wearing them will make you feel very confident.

FLAME: Orange-red has brilliant and vibrant warmth about it. This looks great on darker toned skin. They will wash out people fair in tone. Wearing it you will feel hot and sassy.

RUSSET: Brown-reds are rich and chocolate-like. Wearing it you will feel strong, very passionate and appealing.

WHEN TO WEAR RED

When you are feeling sexy is a good time to wear red. It is the perfect colour to wear if you are already feeling confident and you feel like pepping up a gear. Wearing red will also help you keep your wits about you and have your feet firmly planted on the ground.

WHEN TO AVOID RED

Do not wear red when you are feeling tired or stressed out as this will only exacerbate these conditions. If this is the case you are better advised to choose blue or turquoise as these colours will help you to regain a calmness or sense of being centred.

Avoid wearing red if you have tendencies to overheat or if you feel agitated, angry, impatient or hyperactive.

A RED DAY PLAN

EXERCISE/BEAUTY – I WILL CHECK OUT MY LOCAL CYCLE TRAIL – CYCLING 30 MINUTES BURNS 310 CALORIES. POWER YOGA FOR ME TODAY – 30 MINUTES BURNS 100 CALORIES. I WILL GO FOR A RUN – GOOD FOR THE HEART AND 30 MINUTES BURNS 450 CALORIES.

CLOTHES – I WILL WEAR SOME RED UNDERWEAR TODAY AS I AM PASSIONATE.

PERSONALITY – I AM GROUNDED AND CAN STAND ON MY OWN TWO FEET.

RED EXERCISE AND LEISURE ACTIVITIES

Red personalities adore competitive sports. Dance will also excite them. They must be very careful to balance exercise with relaxation or they can run into problems with heart circulation and over-heating. A course of stress management, with relaxation techniques, would be a very well advised move for the red personality to explore. Massage will also help relax the body and mind of the red personality.

BEST COLOUR PERSONALITY MATCH

Green personalities suit red personalities the best. Both personalities enjoy the finer things in life and so they appreciate good food, fragrance and nature. The green personality can help the energetic red personality to get out in the open helping them to unwind, relax and recharge. The red personality is generally grounded and this is a quality that the green personality appreciates. Both can be extremely passionate and so they can enjoy both the adventurous and intimate activities of their relationship.

WORST COLOUR PERSONALITY MATCH

The red personality may be challenged in a relationship with a blue personality as blue personalities tend to be quite analytical and may take a little longer to initiate a change or take on a challenge. However, in business this pairing is very advantageous. The red personality's spontaneity may be a little stilted in a romantic relationship, however, as the reds tend to talk quickly, move quickly and have high energy expectations whereas blues talk and act slower and this can cause tension between the two.

⊕ Red Health

BOOST CIRCULATION + COMBAT ANAEMIA + RELAX THE MUSCULAR SYSTEM + PROMOTE VITALITY AND ENERGY + STIMULATES APPETITE

FATIGUE

FATIGUE IS ONE OF THE MOST INJURIOUS CONDITIONS to health and lack of energy is like a power failure in the body – your liver cannot function effectively, circulation and absorption will be poor and you will be prone to depression. A person's concentration will be weakened and they will look grey and worn. However there are ways of dealing with these challenges.

Check your energy level by considering the following questions:

1. On waking do you feel rested and ready to get into the day with vitality or take ages getting up, feeling sluggish and heavy?
2. After eating your lunch are you full of energy and eager to complete all your daily tasks or ready to call it a day?
3. By the end of the day, do you feel like the day has taken its toll and you are ready to get into bed or are you still on the go?

The Results

IF YOUR ANSWERS TO THESE QUESTIONS SHOW THAT YOU GENERALLY FEEL TIRED THEN HERE ARE SOME TIPS ON HOW TO INCREASE YOUR ENERGY LEVELS.

1. DRINK MORE WATER – DEHYDRATION IS A MAJOR CAUSE OF FATIGUE. SUFFICIENT WATER IS NEEDED IN ORDER TO FACILITATE BASIC METABOLIC PROCESSES WITHIN THE BODY.

2. EXERCISE – THE KEY TO REJUVENATION AND BETTER BLOOD CIRCULATION IS EXERCISE. IT IS EASY TO STOP EXERCISING WHEN YOU ARE FEELING SLUGGISH BUT DOING A LIGHT WORKOUT OR BRISK WALK WILL ENABLE YOU TO KEEP YOUR ENERGY LEVELS ELEVATED.

3. PRACTISING A DE-STRESSING TECHNIQUE ON A DAILY BASIS SETS UP THE RELAXATION RESPONSE WITHIN THE BODY. AFTER A BUSY DAY UNWIND IN A BUBBLE BATH WITH YOUR FAVOURITE SCENTED BATH FOAM. PUT ON YOUR FAVOURITE MUSIC AND TAKE SOME TIME OUT FOR YOURSELF. PLAY A GAME OF FOOTBALL OR JOIN IN A DANCE OR YOGA CLASS. THIS ALLOWS THE MUSCLES, INTERNAL ORGANS AND BRAIN TO TAKE A DEEP REST, RESULTING IN IMPROVED ENERGY LEVELS.

4. FOODS – EAT PROTEIN FOODS AND ENSURE THAT YOU EAT NUTS SUCH AS ALMONDS AND HAZELNUTS, ALSO FISH AT LEAST THREE TIMES EACH WEEK. SARDINES ARE AN IDEAL OPTION FOR LUNCHTIME. FOR EXTRA VITALITY EAT SPICY FOODS, SUCH AS CHILLIES AND GINGER.

5. AVOID SUGARS, ALCOHOL AND CAFFEINE AS THESE PRODUCTS DEPLETE YOUR ADRENAL GLANDS AND HAVE A DRAMATIC EFFECT ON ENERGY LEVELS. THEY CAN LEAVE YOU FEELING SLUGGISH AND IRRITABLE.

EAT RED FOODS

RED FOODS contain anthocyanins – powerful anti-oxidants that may reduce the risk of heart disease and stroke by inhibiting clot formation. Anthocyanins are technically known as flavonols and strengthen collagen which is the most abundant protein in the body and the powerful ingredient that helps keep skin young and elastic in composition.

A SELECTION OF RED FOODS AND DRINKS

SALSA

TOMATOES

BEEF

CHILLI PEPPERS

WATERMELONS

APPLES

STRAWBERRIES

REDCURRANTS

CRANBERRIES

RED CABBAGES

RED ONIONS

RED PEARS

WINE

PEPPERS

Red Onion

Make friends with pods of the **ONION** family. Add plenty of spring onion, onions, chives, leeks and shallots to your dishes for both flavour and their many health benefits.

Onions contain the enzyme allinase which is released when you slice the bulb. The release of allinase on sulphur compounds results in the chemicals that give onions their flavour and also make you cry.

Nutrition
- Very low in calories
- Vitamin C

Good For
- Removing free radicals from the body due to the presence of quercetin (only found in yellow and red onions, not in white).
- Boosting energy levels.
- Healthy skin.

How much to eat
A thick slice (20g/ 3/4 oz) as part of five to nine servings per day

Phytonutrients
- Allium compounds
- Flavonoids

did you know?

ONION IS REPUTED TO BE BOTH AN APHRODISIAC AND A REMEDY THAT STIMULATES THE GROWTH OF NEW HAIR. PARISIAN MYTHOLOGY MENTIONS ONIONS AS A STAR FOOD CONSUMED AT THE END OF A NIGHT ON THE TILES WHERE FRENCH ONION SOUP WOULD BE SERVED IN ORDER TO HELP GET THE COUPLE INTO THE MOOD FOR LOVING!

Strawberries

A native fruit of America, wild **STRAWBERRIES** are smaller than cultivated ones. They can help the body to deal with stress as the powerful anti-oxidants help eliminate damaging toxins from the body so that body functions can run effectively. In some cases strawberries can cause allergies, particularly skin rashes. They are an excellent source of Vitamin C, niacin and folate. Strawberries are also good for healthy skin and mucous membranes (the lining of the nose and respiratory tract).

Nutrition
- Vitamin A
- Iron
- 100g (3 $^1/_2$ oz) contain more Vitamin C than one orange
- High fibre
- Magnesium
- Niacin
- Folate
- Phosphorus

Good For
- Healthy skin
- Combating stress

How much to eat
- 8 strawberries weigh approx. 100g (3 $^1/_2$ oz)
- 20 strawberries (240g/8 oz) have proven effects on anti-oxidant levels in blood (eat as part of five to nine portions a day when in season)

Phytonutrients
- Salicylic acid
- Ellagic acid

Beef

Overcooking **BEEF** on the barbecue or under the grill leads to the greatest production of carcinogens. The highest levels are found in combination with the highest fat content.

Take care when purchasing lower cost sausages and burgers as they may have a higher fat content.

Nutrition
- Rich in protein
- Rich in iodine, manganese, zinc, cobalt, selenium, fluorine and chromium iron

Good For
- Easing stress
- Nervous disorders
- Anaemia

How Much To Eat
No more than a couple of times a month (as it is a dense food and can take some time to digest)

Phytonutrients
- None

did you know?

IN ARGENTINA AND SOUTHERN CHILE, OFFAL AND INTESTINES ARE CONSIDERED A DELICACY ON THE MENU.

Tomatoes

TOMATOES are probably one of the world's most important food crops and worldwide production is measured in tens of millions of tons each year. The ancestral home of the tomato is the western coastal region of South America, stretching from Ecuador to Peru and on to Chile. Even in the high mountains wild varieties abound.

Some tomatoes can cause allergic reactions.

Nutrition
- Vitamins C, E
- Folic Acid
- Low in sodium

Good For
- Skin challenges
- Fertility
- Protection against skin cancer (the powerful phytonutrient lycopene is said to be responsible for this as it prevents ultraviolet radiation absorption by the skin)

How Much To Eat
- Medium tomato weighs 85g (3 oz)
- Eat tomatoes regularly as part of your five to nine servings of fruit and vegetables daily

Phytonutrients
- Carotenoids
- Lycopene

Red Cabbage

As soon as the **CABBAGE** leaves are chopped, crushed or cooked, enzymes are released in the plant which convert its glucosinolates into anti-carcinogenic indoles.

By far the most exciting development in the history of cabbage is the discovery that it contains cancer protective enzymes. Population studies have shown that where people eat large quantities of red cabbage, some cancers (particularly lung, colon and breast cancer) are far less common. A high intake of raw red cabbage, however, may cause a condition known as goitre (a swelling of the thyroid gland).

Use it shredded in salads, soups, casseroles or stir-fries or make baked cabbage parcels.

Nutrition
- Rich in iron and Vitamin C
- High in folate (Great food for "mums-to-be" as folic acid is recommended)
- Rich in sulphur compounds (this is what causes a nasty smell in the kitchen when cooking it!)

Good For
- Helping improve skin complaints
- Helping with chest infections
- Protection against cancer

How Much To Eat
An average portion of red cabbage weighs 95g (3 $^1/_2$ oz). Eat as part of your five to nine servings of fruit and vegetables per day
- Red cabbage 19 kcal per serving
- White cabbage 24 kcal per serving

Phytonutrients
- Dithiolthiones
- Carotenoids (help the body eliminate free radicals and prevent disease)
- Flavonoids (may help to combat the development of cancer)
- Beta-carotene

Chilli Peppers

The spicy constituents of **CHILLI PEPPERS** are phytonutrient compounds called capsaicinoids. Capsaicinoids exerts strong anti-inflammatory effects on the body and stimulates thermogenesis so eating them does tend to raise body temperature. This causes people to sweat which ultimately lowers body temperature.

Red hot chilli peppers can add spice to your meal and a new zest for life. Many people believe, incorrectly, that all hot spices are irritants to the digestive system. However chillies and cayenne have the reverse effect. They are both beneficial to digestion and actually soothe the stomach. Since ancient times, healers have used chillies to cure a variety of ailments.

Nutrition
- Vitamin C

Good For
- Raising metabolic rate temporarily. This stimulates the adrenal glands to produce adrenaline. This helps the body burn stored body fat and sugars.
- Easing nasal congestion.

How Much To Eat
- A medium chilli weighs 10g ($^1/_4$ oz) – as part of your five to nine portions a day

Phytonutrients
- Carotenoids
- Flavonoids
- Capsaicin (helps relieve nasal congestion and acts as an anti-inflammatory)

TINA'S TIP

THE MORE MATURE THE PEPPER – THE HOTTER AND REDDER IT WILL BE SO A RED JALAPENO WILL BE HOTTER THAN A GREEN ONE. IF YOU FIND CHILLIES TOO HOT, REDUCE THE HOTNESS BY REMOVING THE SEEDS BEFORE COOKING.

A SINGLE PEPPER HAS BEEN FOUND TO CONTAIN A FULL DAY'S SUPPLY OF BETA-CAROTENE AND NEARLY TWICE THE RECOMMENDED DAILY ALLOWANCE OF VITAMIN C, WHICH MAKES THE CHILLI AN INVALUABLE FOOD IN AIDING WEIGHT LOSS AND SPEEDING UP METABOLISM.

Apples

APPLES are a wonderful addition to any food plan. They contain both soluble and insoluble fibre, about 5g per apple. The soluble fibre is called pectin and it has the power to decrease appetite. They do contain sugar but exert a stabilising effect on blood sugar due to the high fibre content. They also contain a special phytonutrient called phloretin, which is a flavenoid-type blood stabilising phytonutrient which is exclusive to apples.

Apple consumption has also been linked to helping respiratory and asthma conditions. This is due to the anti-inflammatory anti-oxidant activity of quercetin – a major component in apple peel.

Nutrition
- Rich in soluble fibre
- Phosphorus
- Potassium
- Sulphur
- Pectin
- Magnesium
- Manganese
- Malic and tartaric acid
- Pectin joins with metals such as lead and mercury and helps the body to get rid of them

Good For
- Easing hangovers
- Tummy upsets – grate apple and allow go brown, then drizzle with honey
- Boosting the body's own immune system
- Respiratory and asthma conditions
- Anti-inflammation
- Anti-oxidant

How Much To Eat
- A medium sized apple weighs 100g (3 $^1/_2$ oz) ex core
- Average glass apple juice 150 ml (4 $^1/_2$ oz) per day

Phytonutrients
- Flavonols – especially quercetin
- Phloretin

TYPES OF APPLES

Bramley Apples
Used only in cooking. Good for pie sauces and purées.

Cox Pippin
A dessert apple with a spicy smell. Also good for baking.

Golden Delicious
All-purpose apple. The yellow skinned types are best eaten raw.

Granny Smith
A good eating apple. Ideal for baking and stewing.

Crab Apples
Available briefly in autumn, this small, acidic apple fruit can be yellow or red in colour. High in pectin (a soluble fibre), it is widely used in making jellies and preserves.

COOKING WITH APPLES

There are few fruits more versatile than the common apple. They are the most useful as they can be eaten on their own, blended with other fruits and there is always a variety in season to give a diversity of flavour and taste to the diet. They are also excellent eaten raw at any time of the day, combine well with cheese, make homely pies or elegant desserts, and can also be cooked with meat, poultry and game.

Selecting the right apple for cooking is important if you do not want your pies to end up watery or your baked apples to collapse in the oven. When choosing apples avoid ones with bruises and soft spots but do not be put off by dull, rough, brown patches on sound apples. This is called russeting. Russet apples are splendid with cheese. Fragrance is really important when testing for ripeness and the fruit should be firm.

Apples continue to ripen after they have been picked so if they are to be stored they should be spread out so that they are not touching each other. Large quantities should be stored on special fibre apple trays in a cool, dry and dark place. A cool loft is the ideal place to store apples.

Apple purées – when making purées, choose crisp, juicy apples with plenty of acid, adding sugar towards the end. Tart apples give a sweet acid taste that is delicious with pork, pheasant or goose.

Apple slices: Tarts, turnovers and fritters depend on apples retaining their shape. Sugar and/or butter added at the beginning of cooking helps to prevent them from falling apart.

Stewing apples: Choose the same varieties as you would use for pies and tarts. To vary flavours add cloves, cinnamon, coriander seeds or grated lime peel.

Baking apples: These are cored and the cavity filled with sugar, butter, nuts or dried fruits. They are baked and possibly basted or flamed with calvados – a delicious liqueur distilled from apple juice. It is fabulous with pheasant, pork and veal dishes.

TINA'S TIP FOR ANYONE ON THE NO-SMOKING TRAIL EAT AN APPLE A DAY AND THEY WILL BE YOUR NEW BEST FRIEND AS THE POWERFUL ANTI-OXIDANTS CAN HELP SUPPORT HEALTHY LUNG FUNCTION.

RED BERRIES

Berries such as redcurrants are sold in clusters and are great in cooking. Dipped in lightly whisked egg white, then frosted with white sugar, they make a simple decoration for the table or dessert dish. Berries also make wonderful preserves, jams and jellies, as well as sauces and vinegars.

Select brightly coloured, tender fruit and turn punnets upside down to make sure the fruit is not squashed. Ripe berries are brightly coloured and plump, with a full aroma. Avoid those with green patches.

Remove the berries from the punnets and discard any soft or spoilt fruit. Wash berries quickly under running water and drain well. Dry with kitchen paper. Remove the hulls from strawberries after washing. If they are removed before washing the berries will absorb water. Cover with cling film and refrigerate. Eat within two days.

If serving them uncooked, remove from the refrigerator at least 30 minutes before serving to allow the flavours to develop.

CRANBERRIES

It has now been shown that a glass of cranberry juice a day is ten times as effective at killing urinary bacteria as conventional antibiotics. Cranberries contain a component that covers the walls of the kidneys, bladder and connecting tubing. This prevents bacteria from attaching themselves to these sensitive tissues, where they could normally live and multiply. A study of elderly women suggested a 50% reduction in infections in those who drank 300 ml (10 fl oz) of cranberry juice daily, over six months.

Fruit-sellers on the streets of El Bolson, Patagonia, Chile are devoted to the growing of fine fruits without the use of pesticides.

Tomato and Coriander Salsa

SERVES 4

4 RIPE TOMATOES – CHOPPED

1 RED ONION – CHOPPED

1 RED CHILLI – FINELY CHOPPED

2 TBSP OF CORIANDER – FRESHLY CHOPPED

SEA SALT & FRESHLY GROUND PEPPER TO TASTE

1 TSP SUGAR

Mix all the ingredients in a bowl and season to taste. This is nice served with fajitas.

Tiger Prawns in a Spicy Tomato Salsa

SERVES 2

1 MEDIUM ONION – FINELY CHOPPED

3 TBSP OLIVE OIL

450G (1 LB) FRESH PLUM TOMATOES – CHOPPED

1 KG (2 LB) PRAWNS

100 ML (3 FL OZ) RED WINE

2-3 GARLIC CLOVES – FINELY CHOPPED

3 TBSP CHOPPED ITALIAN PARSLEY

1 SMALL RED CHILLI – DE-SEEDED AND SLICED INTO ROUNDS

SALT AND PEPPER TO SEASON

Heat the olive oil in a large heavy based saucepan, over a moderate heat.

Add the onion and cook until soft. Stir in the parsley, garlic and chilli and cook for a further two minutes, stirring constantly, until the garlic is golden. Be careful not to burn the garlic.

Add the chopped tomatoes and increase the heat. Season with freshly milled salt and pepper.

Add the red wine and slowly bring to the boil.

Add the prawns and bring back to the boil, then reduce the heat and simmer until the prawns are firm and this should take about 8 minutes.

Remove from the heat and serve with steamed rice and toss in the chopped Italian parsley.

Red Cabbage and Beetroot Salad

SERVES 4

3 PLUMP GARLIC CLOVES – CRUSHED

1 TBSP DIJON MUSTARD

1 TBSP RED WINE VINEGAR

3 TBSP EXTRA-VIRGIN OLIVE OIL

450G (1 LB) RAW BABY BEETROOT

100G (3 ½ OZ) SHREDDED RED CABBAGE

1 SMALL BUNCH SPRING ONIONS – SHREDDED

2 TBSP CHOPPED FRESH PARSLEY

1 TBSP POPPY SEEDS

Add garlic, mustard and vinegar into a bowl and whisk well. Gradually whisk in the olive oil and season generously. Set aside.

Peel the beetroot and grate, using a grater or food processor. Put into a bowl with the shredded cabbage and spring onions, parsley and poppy seeds.

Drizzle over the dressing and toss together using two forks.

Tomatoes with Winter Squash and Gruyére Cheese

SERVES 4

1 1/4 KG (2 LB 9 OZ) SQUASH (SUCH AS CROWN PRINCE)

4 TBSP OLIVE OIL

1 SMALL RED ONION – FINELY CHOPPED

2 GARLIC CLOVES – CRUSHED

120 ML (4 FL OZ) WHITE WINE

1/2 TSP CASTER SUGAR

2-3 FRESH THYME SPRIGS, LEAVES PICKED, PLUS EXTRA TO GARNISH

1 BAY LEAF

1/2 RED CHILLI PEPPER – FINELY DICED

450G (1 LB) VINE-RIPENED TOMATOES – PEELED, DESEEDED AND CHOPPED

142 ML (4 FL OZ) CARTON DOUBLE CREAM

GRATED NUTMEG

100G (3 1/2 OZ) GRUYÉRE CHEESE – FINELY GRATED

Cut the squash into quarters and remove the peel, seeds and fibres. Cut into small, chunky pieces. You should have 750g (1 lb 10 oz).

Heat 2 tablespoons of the olive oil in a medium-size pan, and then add the red onion and garlic. Cook gently until the red onion is soft but not browned.

Add the wine and sugar and simmer until reduced by half. Add the thyme, fresh red chilli, bay leaf and tomatoes and leave to simmer gently for 15 minutes until reduced and thickened. Spoon the sauce onto the base of a shallow oven-proof dish.

Preheat the oven to 200°C (390°F) or gas mark 6. Heat the rest of the oil in a large pan; add the squash and sauté gently for 3–4 minutes, until lightly golden on both sides. Scatter the squash over the tomato sauce.

In a small pan, bring the cream, some seasoning and a little grated nutmeg to the boil; then remove from the heat. Sprinkle the cheese over the top of the squash, pour over the cream and bake for 30 minutes, until the squash is tender and the cheese is golden and bubbling.

Sprinkle with thyme leaves to garnish.

Chilli con Carne

SERVES 6

100G (3 ½ OZ) DRIED CANNELLONI OR
   KIDNEY BEANS – SOAKED OVERNIGHT,
   THEN DRAINED

1 KG (2 LB) CUBE CASSEROLE OR
   STEWING STEAK – LEAN

375 ML (12 FL OZ) RED WINE

4 SPRIGS FRESH ROSEMARY

1 TBSP OLIVE OIL

1 SMALL RED ONION – CHOPPED

2 LARGE GARLIC CLOVES – CHOPPED

4 RASHERS STREAKY BACON – CHOPPED

1 TSP CUMIN SEEDS

2 X 400G (2 X 12 OZ) CANS TOMATOES –
   CHOPPED

½ FRESH CHILLI PEPPER – FINELY DICED

1 TSP SMOKED PAPRIKA

142 ML (4 FL OZ) CARTON SOUR CREAM

FRESH CORIANDER AND SLICED RED CHILLI – TO GARNISH

SALT AND PEPPER

Soak the beans overnight.

Then put the steak in a large bowl with the red wine and rosemary. Set aside for an hour or two, stirring from time to time – this tenderises and flavours the meat.

Heat the oil in a large pan and cook the red onion, garlic and bacon for 3–4 minutes. Add the cumin seeds and cook for one minute more. Add the steak, wine and rosemary to the pan.

Stir in the chopped tomatoes then fill one of the empty tomato cans with water and add that to the pan too. Stir in the drained beans, chilli (1 tsp is quite fiery), paprika and some salt and pepper. Bring to the boil, allow to bubble rapidly for 10 minutes. Then lower the heat, cover and simmer for 1 hour. Remove the lid and cook gently for another hour until the meat and beans are tender. Divide between 6 bowls.

Serve with boiled rice and guacamole. This dish takes 40 minutes to make, plus 2 hours marinating and 2 hours cooking.

It's a real party starter and is ideal served with grated cheese, Greek style yoghurt or fresh slices of avocado.

Beef and Vegetable Rice Noodles

SERVES 4

250G (9 OZ) PACKET
    MEDIUM RICE
    NOODLES
500G (17 OZ) THIN
    BEEF FRYING STEAKS
1 TBSP VEGETABLE OIL
BUNCH SPRING
    ONIONS – TRIMMED
    AND SLICED
    DIAGONALLY
150G (5 ¹/₂ OZ)
    BEANSPROUTS
3 MEDIUM PAK CHOI –
    QUARTERED
    LENGTHWAYS
50G (2 OZ) CASHEW NUTS – CHOPPED
3 TBSP DARK SOY SAUCE, PLUS EXTRA TO SERVE
SMALL HANDFUL FRESH CORIANDER LEAVES – TO GARNISH

Put the noodles into a large, flat dish and cover with boiling water. Set aside for 2 minutes to soften, then drain and rinse under cold running water. Leave in cold water to prevent sticking.

Season the steaks. Heat a large wok or frying pan and sear for 1–2 minutes, so they're still pink in the middle. Rest them for 5 minutes; then slice.

Drain the noodles.

Heat the oil on the wok and stir-fry the spring onions, beansprouts and pak choi for 2–3 minutes. Toss in the noodles and most of the cashew nuts. Drizzle with soy sauce and stir-fry for 1 minute to heat through. Season to taste.

Divide the noodles between 4 bowls. Top with the beef, the remaining cashew nuts, coriander leaves and soy sauce.

This is a brilliant quick supper dish.

All-In-One Oven Curry

SERVES 6

600G (1LB 5 ¹/₂ OZ) TRIMMED LAMB NECK FILLETS CUT INTO BITE SIZE PIECES

1 ¹/₂ TBSP MEDIUM CURRY POWDER

2 TBSP OLIVE OIL

1 LARGE RED ONION – THINLY SLICED

500 ML (16 FL OZ) HOT VEGETABLE STOCK

400G (12 OZ) CAN TOMATOES IN NATURAL JUICE – CHOPPED

2 CINNAMON STICKS

4 GARLIC CLOVES – CRUSHED

4 DRIED CURRY LEAVES OR BAY LEAVES

450G (1LB) ORZO PASTA OR SIMILAR TINY PASTA SHAPES

Dried curry leaves are available from larger supermarkets, or use bay leaves instead.

Preheat the oven to 180°C (350°F) or gas mark 4. Toss the lamb in the curry powder. Heat half the oil in a large frying pan and brown the lamb in batches for 5 minutes and set aside.

Heat the remaining oil and add the onion and fry for 5 minutes. Spoon it into a 3 litre baking dish, along with the lamb and any juices. Stir in the stock, tomatoes, cinnamon, garlic and curry leaves, and season.

Cover with foil and bake for 20 minutes. Uncover, stir in the orzo pasta and return to the oven for 20 minutes, until most of the liquid has been absorbed.

Stir, season, then divide among plates and serve with pilau rice, naan bread, samosas, yoghurt and fresh coriander.

Strawberry and Raspberry Smoothie

SERVES 2

50G (2 OZ) STRAWBERRIES

50G (2 OZ) RASPBERRIES

150 ML (4 FL OZ) LIVE PRO-BIOTIC YOGHURT

Gently wash the strawberries; then dry with kitchen paper. Wipe raspberries in paper too.

Place all the ingredients into the blender and mix until creamy.

Sprinkle a little cinnamon for an extra zing.

Great as a snack as it will boost your stamina.

Strawberry Dressing

SERVES 4

MAKES 180ML (6 FL OZ)

100G (3 ½ OZ) STRAWBERRIES

2 TBSP LEMON JUICE

5 TBSP OLIVE OIL

PINCH SALT

GROUND BLACK PEPPER

Push strawberries through a plastic sieve. Whisk the lemon juice and olive oil together. Season with salt and black pepper, and drizzle over salad leaves.

Strawberry and White Chocolate Mousse

SERVES 4

150G (5 ¹/₂ OZ) WHITE
   CHOCOLATE

150 ML (4 FL OZ) CREAM

4 EGGS

250G (9 OZ) STRAWBERRIES

MINT LEAF

Melt chocolate in microwave or heatproof bowl over a pan of simmering water. Cool and stir in cream.

Separate 4 eggs. Stir yolks into chocolate. Whisk whites until light and fluffy. Fold into mixture.

Mash strawberries and stir in.

Divide into 4 serving glasses. Chill for at least 4 hours. Serve with a mint leaf from your herb garden.

Strawberry Muffins

MAKES 12

250G (9 OZ) SELF-RAISING FLOUR

175G (6 OZ) BROWN SUGAR

1 EGG

200G (7 OZ) FRESH STRAWBERRIES – CHOPPED

200 ML (6 ¹/₂ FL OZ) MILK

125 ML (4 FL OZ) VEGETABLE OIL

2 TBSP ICING SUGAR

Sieve flour into a bowl and add sugar. Break egg into a jug and whisk until it is all the same colour. Add the egg, fresh strawberries, milk and vegetable oil to the flour and sugar and mix well. Spoon the mixture into a greased muffin tin. Place in oven. Bake for 25 minutes at 190°C (375°F) or gas mark 5.

Sift icing sugar over the top before serving.

Red Apple and Almond Nut Cake

SERVES 5-6

2 COOKING APPLES

125G (4 ½ OZ) SUGAR

150G (5 ½ OZ) PLAIN FLOUR

1 LEVEL TSP BREAD SODA

1 TSP CINNAMON

1 TSP ALLSPICE

75G (2 ½ OZ) ALMONDS

1 EGG

125G (4 ½ OZ) MELTED BUTTER

ICING SUGAR – FOR DUSTING

Preheat oven to 170°C (325°F) or gas mark 3. Grease tin. Melt butter in a saucepan.

Peel, quarter and slice apples very thinly. Cover with sugar in a bowl. Sift flour, soda, cinnamon and allspice onto apples. Add almonds and mix.

Now beat egg; adding butter, and then mix in the apple.

Spoon into tin and bake for 45–50 minutes until it springs back to the touch. Dust with icing sugar.

Allow to cool on a wire tray and serve warm with cream as a dessert.

Baked Red Apples

SERVES 4

4 COOKING APPLES

50G (2 OZ) BUTTER

FILLING:

50G (2 OZ) SOFT BROWN SUGAR

2 TSP CINNAMON – GROUND

25G (1 OZ) ALMONDS CHOPPED

25G (1 OZ) APRICOT – CHOPPED

25G (1 OZ) DRIED FIGS – CHOPPED (IF DESIRED)

Core the apples and place each apple on a square of foil. Combine the filling ingredients in a bowl. Fill each apple with the mixture. Dot each apple with butter and wrap in foil.

Bake for about 45 minutes at 180°C (350°F) or gas mark 4.

Serve on their own with a dollop of ice-cream.

Apple and Cinnamon Cookies

MAKES 12

100G (3 ¹/₂ OZ) UNSALTED BUTTER –
    SOFTENED

70G (2 ¹/₂ OZ) GRANULATED SUGAR

50G (2 OZ) LIGHT MUSCAVADO SUGAR

1 LARGE EGG

140G (5 OZ) PLAIN FLOUR

50G (2 OZ) PORRIDGE OATS

1 TSP GROUND CINNAMON

100G (3 ¹/₂ OZ) DRIED READY-TO-EAT
    APPLES – ROUGHLY CHOPPED

ICING SUGAR – FOR DUSTING

¹/₂ TSP OF BICARBONATE OF SODA

Preheat the oven to 180°C (350°F) or gas mark 4.

Lightly grease 2–3 non-stick baking sheets.

Put the butter and sugars into a large bowl and cream together using an electric hand whisk until pale, light and fluffy. Gradually beat in the egg until mixed together.

In a small bowl, mix the flour, oats, cinnamon, bicarbonate of soda and a good pinch of salt. Lightly mix this into the butter and egg mixture, along with the dried apples, until just combined. Put 12 tbsps of the cookie dough onto the baking sheets; spaced apart to allow for some spreading. Bake for 12 minutes, and then remove from the oven. Leave on the baking sheets for 2 minutes, then transfer to a wire rack to cool.

Dust with icing sugar and eat immediately or store in an airtight container for up to 5 days.

Apple and Mint Jelly

SERVES 10

MAKES 675G (1LB 8OZ)

570 ML (19 FL OZ) UNSWEETENED CLEAR APPLE JUICE

20 ML (1 FL OZ) CIDER VINEGAR

570 ML (19 FL OZ) WATER

SMALL BUNCH CHOPPED FRESH MINT

675G (1LB 8OZ) SUGAR WITH ADDED PECTIN (TO AID SETTING)

Place the apple juice, vinegar, water and half the mint into a saucepan. Bring to the boil for 5 minutes. Strain through a sieve and return to a clean saucepan.

Stir in the sugar and heat gently until the sugar is dissolved. Boil rapidly for 5 minutes.

Remove from the heat and add the remaining mint.

Pour into hot sterilised jars. Seal and label.

Sticky Syrup Red Apple Sponge

SERVES 4

SYRUP MIX:

25G (1 OZ) BUTTER

25G (1 OZ) SOFT DARK BROWN SUGAR

TOPPING:

1 LARGE COOKING APPLE

SPONGE:

100G (3 ½ OZ) BUTTER

100G (3 ½ OZ) CASTER SUGAR

2 EGGS

100G (3 ½ OZ) SELF-RAISING FLOUR

SYRUP: Melt the butter and brown sugar in the dish on high for 1 minute. Swirl the melted butter around dish to coat. Peel, core and slice the apple thinly. Arrange the apple slices in a neat pattern in the syrup.

SPONGE: Beat the butter and sugar until light and fluffy, beat in the eggs, sieve flour and fold into the mixture. Spread gently over the topping.

Cook for 10 minutes at 180°C (350°F) or gas mark 4. Test with a knife or skewers as it will look uncooked on top but will be done on the inside.

Leave the pudding to stand for 8–10 minutes. Loosen the edges with a knife. Turn onto a plate. Serve with whipped cream.

THE COLOUR
orange

ORANGE IS ASSOCIATED WITH VIBRANCY AND LIFE. USE IT WHEN YOU NEED A SUDDEN BURST OF ENTHUSIASM AS THIS COLOUR STIMULATES ENERGY AND FLAMBOYANCE. ORANGE IS AN ENERGISING AND INVIGORATING COLOUR. AS A COMBINATION OF RED AND YELLOW, IT TAKES ON MANY CHARACTERISTICS OF BOTH COLOURS. IT IS DARING, UPFRONT AND LIGHTENS THE MOOD.

Orange and its shades coral, peach and amber, are vibrant and warm with the influence of red's physical force, but are less intense and more fun. **IT MAKES US THINK OF SUNSETS AND WARM, BLAZING WINTER LOG FIRES**. It is a colour for all seasons but is traditionally associated with autumn and Halloween.

Lovers of orange work hard, and spend their leisure time seeking adventure. Orange is also a favourite of design conscious and self-motivated individuals. It is for people who have a very good nature – sociable and extrovert. In some areas influential and independent people are said to be the strongest supporters of orange – people who are always looking for new worlds to conquer.

DID YOU KNOW?
FRANK SINATRA CONSIDERED ORANGE TO BE HIS HAPPY COLOUR.

THE ORANGE COLOUR PERSONALITY

- LOVES FREEDOM
- EXPLORER
- LOOKS AHEAD
- POSITIVE
- SELF-RELIANT
- SUBTLE STRENGTH
- FUN AND WARM-HEARTED
- SOMETIMES FICKLE
- FRIENDLY

Mr Orange

The man loves his freedom, flirting, flings and anything that makes him feel great. He is flamboyant and travel makes him tick. While he is out and about, he enjoys studying people. He loves nature programmes, animals and kids and he is a bit of all three himself; the kid in him is eternal. He likes strong, organised and disciplined partners. While he can play and party he also performs well in the boardroom.

Mr Orange will always have his finger on the pulse of the latest trend; drive branded cars, wear designer shades and live exciting, albeit unpredictable, lives. These men are not for the faint-hearted!

Ms Orange

'Ms Independent' highly values her own company though she is far from a wallflower in her personal or business life. She will give as good as she gets in the bedroom, workplace, with family or any situation she lands in. She is also flirty, fun and enjoys self-expression.

The orange female is often single but not because she's over-fussy – she needs a strong partner and is intolerant of weakness in love or business. She loves unpredictability so change is good for her, as too much routine will make her feel boxed in and zap her energies.

Young Orange

The orange child loves to play, perform and especially adores an audience. It is important that they are given plenty of stimulation and activity – send them to drama or music class and they'll love it. They enjoy being seen as individuals and like to talk; they spend quite a bit of time on the phone! As they are eager to rise to a challenge they will be good with any creative project. Orange children are usually the ones in class on the social club organizing the next event. As they dash around a bit, they can be prone to having accidents so a little caution should be encouraged whilst out and about.

The Orange Parent

The orange parent is born to party and born to parent. In both situations they give it their all and love to have more than one child. They have a very optimistic nature and encourage their children to explore and experiment. These parents foster a healthy curiosity in their children and encourage them to venture along all avenues in life and love talking to friends and colleagues about their little 'stars'. Their children may be enrolled in all types of leisure, sport, music and educational pursuits and certainly never have time to be bored.

The Orange Career

The orange personality brings spontaneity and enthusiasm to any project. They also like to keep things moving, but they'll make sure the project is finished before moving on to bigger and brighter things. They are brilliant team-players, hard-working and get the job done regardless of what's going on around them. Sales, merchandising, promotion and entertainment are all good areas for orange personalities to work in. They can apply their excellent business acumen in any of these areas.

The orange personality loves breaking down barriers and looking to the future. They have plans about becoming bigger and better and look for ways to develop. They have a tremendous capacity to make money and are good at sharing it too! It is important for the orange personality to get recognition for their work – a prize or trophy makes their mind and body tick.

Guide to Wearing Orange

By wearing orange you give off the signal that adventure thrills you. Your appetite will be boosted and you will be more fearless in your life. In summer if you have an even tan, orange nail polish will look funky and fantastic on you. To feel sparkling and glittery, add some shimmer cream to your feet and hands. Go on – have a vivacious and glitzy holiday season. Wear some orange underwear with sweet lace or bows for happy days ahead. An orange scarf in winter will brighten any outfit and will boost your mood and attitude. An orange tie worn on a Tuesday for example, may well be the little pick-me-up your day needed. Buddhist monks wear orange all the time to represent love, happiness and humility.

EXERCISE AND LEISURE ACTIVITIES

AS THE ORANGE PERSONALITY SIMPLY LOVES TO MOVE, IT'S GREAT TO LET THEM DANCE ABOUT. ANY STYLE OF DANCING – SALSA, TANGO, HIP-HOP – WILL DO. THEY WILL ALWAYS HAVE MUSIC PLAYING IN THEIR LIVES.

AS ORANGE PERSONALITIES ARE SO FRIENDLY, PERSONABLE AND SOCIAL, ANY ACTIVITY THAT INVOLVES FIZZY EXUBERANCE AND ZESTY CONNECTION WILL WORK. ORANGE PEOPLE WILL CREATE LIMITLESS OPPORTUNITIES AND POSSIBILITIES.

SHADES OF ORANGE

DARK ORANGE: suits dark-haired people. It seems to wash fairer tones out. It is an ideal colour to wear with jeans, especially deep nectar.

AMBER: the amber stone removes doubt and suspicion and gives confidence. It is a beautiful colour worn on auburn/ brunettes with brown or green eyes.

PEACHES AND CORALS: are delicate shades. They are lovely in spring or summer on warm blondes with blue or green eyes. They are shades that encourage communication and are a terrific colour to use if you do not have a clear direction regarding your future study path or work life.

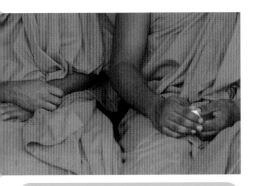

WHEN TO USE ORANGE

When your morale and spirit have taken a bashing wear, eat, drink and be, in orange. It will help you to overcome the shock, strain or whatever has zapped your energy. When you are feeling tired and wrung out, ORANGE WILL HELP YOU REGENERATE AND RESTORE ENERGY. Its great benefit is that, as orange is lighter than red, it helps you to come back to yourself in a more relaxed way.

The International Academy of Colour Science Technologies suggest that orange is a brilliant colour to help release creativity and communicate ideas.

WHEN TO AVOID ORANGE

Stay away from orange if you want to remain neutral in a group. It is also best avoided if you are in a self-indulgent mood because orange can encourage exhibitionist tendencies. So steer clear of orange when you want to present the more serious and reliable side of your nature.

BEST COLOUR PERSONALITY MATCH

The orange personality is best suited to a blue personality. The calm nature, love of routine and organised lifestyle of the blue personality will compliment the flamboyant free-spiritedness of the orange personality beautifully. The orange can help liven up the blue personality.

WORST COLOUR PERSONALITY MATCH

Orange personalities may find the red personality a little too independent and strong-willed. As both colour personalities are extremely energetic and like to get things done, they may have a tendency to go off on their own missions and may need to learn to do things together as a team.

✚ Orange **Health**

BOOSTS THE IMMUNE SYSTEM ✚ STIMULATES THE APPETITE ✚ HELPS THE BODY TO GET RID OF TOXINS ✚ HELPS STIMULATE LUNG FUNCTION ✚ GOOD FOR HEALTHY HAIR ✚ BRILLIANT ENERGISER

Orange is a brilliant colour to wear or have in your environment if you have respiratory challenges. This colour also helps you to focus on breaking your addictive habits and helps support the new lifestyle practices that you have planned for yourself. Whenever I make the decision to do something new, such as joining a new exercise class, cutting out alcohol during week days or getting more organised, this is the colour I bring into my life. It really helps you to ease into the new routine.

Vitamin C

An effective ingredient in many skin care products, Vitamin C promotes an increased production of collagen, as well as diminishing fine lines and wrinkles. It also increases the skin's ability to hold moisture, shield skin from UV light and encourage healthy cell regeneration. Vitamin C also plays a vital role in boosting the immune system as it aids in neutralising pollutants and is required for antibody production. Many people don't realise that smoking depletes the body of Vitamin C.

COLDS IN WINTER

There are nine million colds in Ireland each year. One hundred different but related viruses cause colds. Symptoms include: **runny nose, sneezing, coughing and a sore throat.**

For every person who has the symptoms of a cold, there are another two to three who are carrying the virus at the back of their throat; however it does not always develop into a cold. Influenza is also caused by several related viruses and its symptoms are similar but more severe, including: **fever, aching muscles, sore throats, headaches and weakness.**

It is estimated that if you live to be 75 years old you will have experienced at least 200 colds. According to Professor Eccles, Director of the Common Cold Centre at Cardiff University, that equates to three years of runny noses and hacking throats. Adults average two to five colds a year, whilst children usually have between seven and ten colds in a year. This is because adults have built up immunity to certain strains of cold viruses because they have already experienced them.

NUTRITION AND LIFESTYLE TIPS TO HELP YOU AVOID GETTING A COLD AND FLU THIS WINTER

Winter is the cold and flu season – so you need to optimize your nutrition and lifestyle to minimise the chances of getting a cold or flu in the winter months. Using common sense will help protect you. Stay warm and avoid the cold. Wear warm clothing and put a hat on when walking. It also helps to be aware of the colour orange as it will boost your immune system and keep the lymphatic system primed for action.

If you do get a cold, stay home and take to your bed. Turning up for work because you are 'so invaluable' is silly. If your energy is low and your concentration levels are strained, the virus is clearly spreading rapidly and will infect those around you. Use tissues and cough into them; cover your nose and mouth to help minimize the spread of germs. Wash your hands frequently and dispose of used tissues.

Rest yourself and ensure that you get plenty of sleep each night. Tiredness and stress are two major contributing factors to getting a cold. Boosting your immune system is essential to help ensure a full recovery; otherwise you are at risk of slipping in and out of the cold trap all winter. Vitamin C will be your trusted friend. Maximize your intake of fruit and vegetables such as carrots and dark leafy green vegetables, as these are rich sources of Vitamins A and C (powerful anti-oxidants that will help boost the immune system). Eat garlic and onion daily. Eat a daily serving of freshly ground seeds. For more details turn to The Colour Gold chapter and you may even start to sprout your own! Avoid alcohol.

Get into making fresh homemade soup. Eat soup daily but vary the type or you could end up over-doing the 'soup thing'. Soup is easy to digest and helps break up mucus in the throat and nose.

Take a ginseng supplement which is available at most local pharmacies. Ginseng is used throughout the Far East as a general tonic to combat weakness and give extra energy. Ginseng is beneficial for fatigue because it spares glycogen – the form of glucose stored in the liver and muscle cells by increasing the use of fatty acids as an energy source. Ginseng is used to enhance athletic performance, to rejuvenate, increase longevity and detox and normalise the entire system. There are many varieties available so always check which one is best suited to your needs and be clear about the dosage required. A Canadian study has shown that taking ginseng supplements can lessen the likelihood of getting a cold. The study followed 323 people over four winter months. Only 10% of those who took daily ginseng capsules suffered two or more colds. It is thought that the ingredients in ginseng boost the immune system by stimulating proteins that act as antibodies.

All of the above will help you recover quickly so that you can return to your normal life.

MENSTRUAL PROBLEMS

Orange is the colour that governs the reproductive area of the body. For many women and their partners this time of the month is often dreaded.

Do you experience mood swings around the time of ovulation or as your period approaches?

Do you feel emotional or tired?

Do your eating patterns change or are you aware of lifestyle habits that change around this time?

If you are one of the many women who has painful periods every month it may help you if you understand your body and listen to the signals it gives. We are often busy and life does not offer the considerations that were offered to women in the past. In some aboriginal communities, women would be excused from their regular duties for the two or three days that they were menstruating. At this time they took up artistic hobbies and they were allowed to rest, 'hang out' so to speak. In our modern environment such a notion would be looked upon as insane or a cop out. It is worth remembering, however that this is a very special and unique time for your body. I have spoken to thousands of adolescents and women while presenting seminars and presentations. I always ask the question: 'Hands up who here in the room love when they have their period?' To date I have not yet seen one single hand raised. I have made them all laugh and it always strikes up conversation. Sometimes, an understanding of what is going on with you on the days of your cycle may help a little.

Below is an activity outline of the 28 days.

DAYS 1–5: MENSTRUATION

- Progesterone (the "mothering" hormone) is at its lowest ebb during this stage of the cycle. A study by Tufts University, Massachusetts, indicated that women eat 12% less per day at this point in their cycle than during the last half, when appetite increases so that the body can better sustain a healthy pregnancy.
- The brain's creative talents are at their peak at the beginning of the menstrual cycle, particularly writing skills.
- The glucose content in saliva increases as much as nine-fold early in your cycle. This increases the concentration of bacteria in the mouth that can cause tooth and gum decay so it is advisable to brush your teeth more often during this period. There is a low level of oestrogen at this time. You don't want to end up going to the dentist now, as low oestrogen levels mean a low pain threshold (the highest pain threshold is during days 12–14).
- Breathe easy. If you suffer from asthma – be especially careful now. A report published in the British Medical Journal found a four-fold increase in asthma related admissions to Accident & Emergency Departments in America and this is thought to have been caused by changes in oestrogen levels.

DAYS 6–13: OESTROGEN AND TESTOSTERONE RISING

- Give up smoking. If you are trying to quit, now is the best time. Increasing oestrogen levels mean you will have fewer withdrawal symptoms. Day 13 – when oestrogen peaks – is the easiest day to stop.
- Apply for a new job. High levels of oestrogen and testosterone have been connected to high confidence. Women with peaking oestrogen levels are competent in their abilities, unusually quick to come up with the answers to problem-solving tests and show a reluctance to depend on others for help.
- Day 13 is when libido is at an all-time high thanks to a combination of rocketing oestrogen and testosterone.

DAY 14: OVULATION

- You are at your most attractive time during ovulation. Leave your make-up bag at home today – you're officially irresistible, but only if you show the world your "real" face!
- Don't go speed-dating. High oestrogen levels mean your judgment could be impaired. When a woman is ovulating, she is more likely to prefer men with masculine features, including large chins and low, bushy eyebrows; during less fertile times, she will choose someone more feminine looking, with a smaller chin and thinner eyebrows.
- This is a bad day for running a marathon. During ovulation, women are three times more likely to hurt themselves as high oestrogen levels create "laxity" in the knee ligaments, which increases the risk of injury.

DAYS 15–22: PROGESTERONE RISING

- Exercise feels easier and you can burn up to 30% more fat until day 26.
- Ovulation releases progesterone; causing a delay in word recall and verbal responses so cancel the pub-quiz night!
- Migraine alert. A 50% drop in oestrogen is thought to increase the likelihood of migraines.
- Leave the credit cards at home! Marketing gurus are getting wise to the impact progesterone has on women's shopping habits; any advert featuring puppies, pink fluffy blankets and babies is banking on the fact that progesterone-filled female shoppers are easy targets.

DAYS 23–27: ALL HORMONE LEVELS FALLING

- Hide the alarm clock! Declining oestrogen levels can trigger the production of noradrenalin; a hormone that can promote wakefulness.
- Avoid the deli counter – progesterone is known to boost cravings for salty, sugary and fatty food. Food cravings are more intense now than at other times during menstruation.
- Stay away from caffeine as it exacerbates premenstrual syndrome (PMS). In one study published in Australasian Science Magazine the author, Stephen Luntz, said that women who drank just one cup of coffee per day increased their risk of developing PMS by 30%.

DAY 28: HORMONES AT THEIR LOWEST

- Steer clear of karaoke. The University of Sheffield has studied the influence of sex hormones on the female singing voice. They claim that no matter how brilliant you think you are, today is not the day to sing in public. Inability to reach high notes, loss of vocal flexibility and temporary hoarseness were all found to affect female singers from day 26 until the first day of menstruation. Fluid retention leads to a swelling of the vocal cords, which causes the problems. In the past, in some European opera houses, women were given "respect days" to excuse them from singing during premenstrual and menstrual periods.
- Enjoy your cycle.

TINA'S BEAUTY TIP

Blend together 1 tbsp oats with 3 tbsp water and grate a medium sized carrot.

Mix and apply to face. Leave for 5 minutes and gently clean away. (NB If it tingles, remove immediately as the ingredients are in an active state; the benefits will be natural and results immediate).

Carrots are a mega anti-ageing food. Always choose organic carrots as these root vegetables are the most susceptible to absorbing pesticides and herbicides.

A SELECTION OF ORANGE FOODS AND DRINKS

ACORN SQUASH

APRICOTS

CANTALOUPE

CARROTS

MANGOES

ORANGES

SWEET POTATOES

VEGETABLE MARROW

ORANGE PEPPERS

PUMPKINS

EAT ORANGE FOODS

Orange coloured foods are so due to plant pigments that come from a large family of natural plant compounds called terpens and the best known member of this family are carotenoids.

Carotenoid-rich fruit and vegetables are powerful disease preventing agents. Carotenoids come in several chemical forms that determine their biological activity and, though their biological actions are being increasingly understood, there is still much to learn about how they function.

Oranges

ORANGES are rich in beta-carotene, which boosts eye and skin health and may decrease the risk of developing certain cancers. Studies published in *The American Journal of Medicine* outline the benefits of phytonutrients such as hesperidin. The flavanone hesperidin is an important phytonutrient. Eat oranges fresh to maximise flavone, Vitamin C and folate benefits.

Oranges boost the immune system. They are known to strengthen lungs, pancreas and spleen. They also contain pectin which removes unwanted metals and toxins from the body. It also slows the absorption of food after meals so oranges are good for people with diabetes.

Nutrition
- Vitamin C and B
- Calcium, manganese
- Phosphorus, potassium
- Zinc
- Good source of pectin
- Fibre

Good For
- Helping make collagen – vital for good skin
- Boosting immune system
- Stimulating appetite
- Diuretic and laxative properties

How Much To Eat
- One medium orange per day or 150 ml orange juice

Phytonutrients
- Beta-carotene
- Bioflavonoids
- Hesperidin

Carrots

CARROTS are an ancient root vegetable and there are over 100 varieties. Now they also come in yellow and purple. Women taking the pill may benefit from a regular beta-carotene intake. Like all carotenoids, beta-carotene is best absorbed by the body when eaten with a little oil.

Nutrition
- Anti-oxidants
- Vitamin A, C, E
- Fibre

Good For
- Healthy skin
- Boosting immune system
- Boosting energy levels

How Much To Eat
- Medium carrot – 80g
- Eat them raw, grated in salad, juiced, roasted or stir-fried
- A single carrot provides a whole day's dose of Vitamin A

Phytonutrients
- Beta-carotene

did you know?

ORANGES ARE BEST STORED IN THE FRIDGE.

MIGRAINE SUFFERERS MAY NEED TO AVOID ORANGES AS THEY MAY TRIGGER AN ATTACK.

Sweet Potatoes

SWEET POTATOES are an excellent food for smokers and ex-smokers as they are brimming with beta-carotene. High levels of beta-carotene is said to reduce the skin's sensitivity to sunlight as the beta-carotene acts as an anti-oxidant (NB However this is not a substitute for sunscreen lotions and sun protective).

Nutrition
- Starch
- Vitamin C, E

Good For
- Healthy muscles
- Healthy skin
- Boosting energy
- The lungs (the carotenoids work as an anti-oxidant and mop up potentially damaging free radicals produced by pollutants such as smoke)

How Much To Eat
- Portion size – 130g
- Bake, mash, purée or wedge

Phytonutrient
- Carotenoids
- Beta-carotene

did you know?

Sprouting or green potatoes should not be eaten as they may contain harmful levels of glycoalkaloids – a phytonutrient. A high intake of glycoalkaloids can become toxic in the body and cause severe vomiting and diarrhoea.

Apricots

Often preserved with sulphur dioxide APRICOTS can trigger asthma attacks, so rinse them well before eating.

Nutrition
- Vitamin A, B, C
- Magnesium
- Manganese
- Phosphorus
- Potassium
- Iron

Good For
- Respiratory conditions
- Healthy bones
- Healthy skin

How Much To Eat
- 100g–188g (3–6 oz) dried apricots
- 100g (3 1/2 oz) fresh apricots are best

Phytonutrients
- Beta-carotene

did you know?

DRIED APRICOTS ARE A TERRIFIC REMEDY FOR CONSTIPATION DUE TO THEIR HIGH FIBRE CONTENT. REMEMBER, THEY ARE ALSO HIGH IN SUGAR SO DIABETICS SHOULD TREAT THEM WITH CAUTION.

Carrot and Strawberry Salad

SERVES 4

3 TBSP OLIVE OIL

JUICE OF 1 LIME

500G (1LB 2 OZ) CARROTS – PEELED AND
GRATED

300G (10 ½ OZ) STRAWBERRIES – CHOPPED

Combine, chill, and eat.

did you know?

EATING CARROTS REGULARLY
MAY BE LINKED TO A REDUCED
RISK OF LUNG CANCER. DATA
AND RESEARCH IS REGULARLY
FEATURED ON THE AMERICAN
INSTITUTE FOR CANCER
RESEARCH'S WEBSITE
(WWW.AICR.ORG).

Carrot and Coriander Soup

SERVES 4

1 TBSP OLIVE OIL

2 ONIONS – CHOPPED

700G (1LB 9 OZ) CARROTS
– SLICED

850 ML (1LB 12 OZ)
VEGETABLE STOCK

SEA SALT & BLACK PEPPER

FRESHLY GROUND BLACK
PEPPER

2–3 TBSP FRESH CORIANDER
– CHOPPED

FRESH CORIANDER – TO
GARNISH

Heat the oil in a large saucepan. Add the onions and cook gently for 5 minutes; until softened. Add the carrots, stock and seasoning and cover. Bring to the boil, then reduce the heat and simmer for 25 minutes, stirring occasionally, until the carrots are tender. Remove the pan from the heat and cool slightly.

Purée the soup in a food processor. Return the soup to the rinsed-out saucepan. Stir in the chopped coriander.

Re-heat gently until piping hot, stirring occasionally. Ladle into warmed soup bowls and garnish with the coriander.

Serve with warm wholemeal bread rolls, oatcakes or crisp bread.

Carrot and Almond Jacket Potatoes

SERVES 4

4 LARGE BAKING POTATOES

2 TBSP EXTRA VIRGIN OLIVE OIL

4 LARGE JULIENNE CARROTS

75G (2 ¹/₂ OZ) CHOPPED ALMONDS

1 TSP ORANGE ZEST

1 TSP HONEY

PEPPER TO TASTE

Wash and dry the potatoes and rub in a little olive oil. Pierce them a few times with a fork and bake in a preheated oven at 200°C (390°F) or gas mark 6 for approximately 1 hour; until flesh is soft.

Put the rest of the olive oil in a frying pan. Add the julienned carrots and sauté gently for a few minutes. Add the almonds and cook for another 2 minutes. Add the orange zest, honey and pepper to taste. Turn the heat down as low as possible and simmer until the carrots soften.

When the potatoes are cooked, remove them from the oven and cut a deep cross in the top of each one. Gently open out the potatoes by pressing on the four slits of the cross and add some of the carrot and almond mixture.

Roasted Pepper Salad

SERVES 2

1 ORANGE PEPPER

1 YELLOW PEPPER

50G (2 OZ) SUN-DRIED TOMATOES

50G (2 OZ) GOOD QUALITY BLACK OLIVES

1 GARLIC CLOVE

2 TBSP BALSAMIC VINEGAR

5 TBSP OLIVE OIL

20 FRESH BASIL LEAVES

SALT AND GROUND BLACK PEPPER

Preheat oven to 200°C (390°F) or gas mark 6.

Lightly oil a foil-lined baking sheet and place peppers on the foil. Bake for 45 minutes until beginning to char. Remove from heat and set aside to cool.

Finely slice the sun-dried tomatoes and garlic. Tear half of the basil leaves by hand and add to the tomatoes.

Peel the roasted pepper by hand, remove the stalks and seeds and slice into 2 cm long strips. Add the tomatoes and olives to the peppers and toss until evenly mixed.

Make a dressing by putting the balsamic vinegar into a bowl and gradually whisking in the olive oil. Pour over the salad and serve with toasted slices of spelt bread.

Sweet Potato Wedges with Sesame Seeds

SERVES 2

1 SWEET POTATO – WASHED AND PEELED

2 CLOVES GARLIC

50G (2 OZ) SESAME SEEDS

3 TBSP OLIVE OIL

Cut the sweet potato lengthways and cut into wedges.

Place on baking sheet and drizzle with olive oil.

Add sesame seeds and loosely chopped garlic.

Bake in oven for 30–40 mins until golden brown at 180°C (350°F) or gas mark 4.

Serve with guacamole or coriander salsa, both recipes can be found in The Colour

Green chapter.

Orange Salad

SERVES 6

2 ORANGES – PEELED

2 CARROTS – GRATED

HALF A RED ONION – FINELY CHOPPED

100G (3 ½ OZ) RAISINS

2 TBSP CORIANDER

2 TBSP FRESHLY SQUEEZED ORANGE JUICE

3 TBSP OLIVE OIL

This dish is brilliant for lunch as it will re-energize you.

Segment the oranges and place in a bowl with the grated carrots. Mix in the red onion, raisins, and coriander.

Drizzle the olive oil and orange juice over the salad and mix well.

Apricot and Date Crumble

SERVES 2

200G (7 OZ) DRIED APRICOTS – SOAKED OVERNIGHT AND CHOPPED

100G (3 ½ OZ) OATS

50G (2 OZ) HAZELNUTS – CRUSHED

50 ML (2 FL OZ) ORANGE JUICE

Divide the apricots between two ceramic bowls. Mix the oats and hazelnuts together. Sprinkle over the apricots. Divide the orange juice between the two bowls.

Bake in the oven for 15 mins at 180°C (350°F) or gas mark 4.

Serve hot or cold. Spoon some yoghurt over and drizzle some runny honey.

Makes a great breakfast!

Apricot and Pineapple Crumble

SERVES 2

75G (2 ½ OZ) GROUND ALMONDS

75G (2 ½ OZ) NUTS – CHOPPED

1 RIPE PINEAPPLE – CUT INTO BITE SIZE CUBES

4 FRESH APRICOTS

1 TBSP MIXED SPICE

GRATED RIND OF 1 LIME

SESAME SEEDS TO GARNISH

Preheat the oven to 180°C (350°F) or gas mark 4. Stir the ground almonds and nuts together. Wash and cut the apricots in half. Remove the stone and cut the fruit into bite size cubes. Put the apricot and pineapple chunks into a bowl and add the lime rind and mixed spice to the fruit.

Spoon the crumble over and bake for 40 minutes.

Serve with organic natural yoghurt and sprinkle with sesame seeds.

Carrot Cake

SERVES 8

100G (3 ½ OZ) BUTTER

100G (3 ½ OZ) BROWN SUGAR

200G (7 OZ) CARROT (2 MEDIUM CARROTS)

2 EGGS

125G (4 ½ OZ) SELF-RAISING FLOUR

125G (4 ½ OZ) WHOLE MEAL FLOUR

2 TSP MIXED SPICE

50G (2 OZ) SULTANAS

25G (1 OZ) WALNUTS

FOR EXTRA FRUITINESS ADD SOME CHOPPED
    PINEAPPLE CUBES (2 TBSP).

Preheat oven to 180°C (350°F) or gas mark 4.
Grease tin if not non-stick. Mix flour, spice,
sultanas and walnuts in a bowl. Wash and
grate carrots.

Melt butter and remove from heat. Stir in sugar,
carrots and finally eggs.

Add carrot mixture to flour mix to make a soft
dough. If the mixture is too stiff, add 1–2 tbsps
water. Turn mixture into greased tin.

Bake in oven for 35–45 minutes until nicely
browned.

Cool for 5–10 minutes in the tin. Turn onto
wire rack.

Cream Cheese Icing (Lemon, Orange or Cinnamon)

100G (3 ½ OZ) CREAM CHEESE

25G (1 OZ) ICING SUGAR

ZEST AND JUICE OF ½ LEMON

OR

ZEST AND JUICE OF ½ ORANGE

OR

2–3 DROPS VANILLA ESSENCE

1 TSP CINNAMON

Sieve the icing sugar into a bowl.
Add the cream cheese and zest or
vanilla and cinnamon. Beat well until
smooth. Add enough lemon, orange
or water to give a good flavour but do
not allow icing to become too soft.
Spread over the cold cake and score
with a fork.

Dust with a little more icing sugar or
cinnamon or a little reserved zest.

Orange Cranberry Fruit Loaf

MAKES 1 LOAF

200G (7 OZ) FRESH
  CRANBERRIES

350G (12 OZ)
  SELF-RAISING FLOUR

1 LARGE ORANGE

2 LARGE EGGS

1/2 TSP SALT

100G (3 1/2 OZ) CASTER
  SUGAR

50G (2 OZ) BUTTER –
  MELTED

50G (2 OZ) WALNUTS
  – CHOPPED

Preheat oven to 180°C (350°F) or gas mark 4.

Grease tin. Line bottom if not non-stick. Melt butter in cup in oven. Wash, zest and juice orange. Wash and chop fruit finely.

Sieve flour and salt, and then add sugar, zest, cranberries and walnuts. Mix thoroughly.

Add eggs, 6 tbsp of the orange juice and melted butter. Mix well.

Turn into tin: wet the top, smooth with wet knuckles. Bake on centre shelf for 1–1 1/2 hours.

Remove from tin, cool on wire tray. This is best left for 24 hours before cutting.

Serve with butter or spread.

Macerated Fruit

SERVES 1

20G (3/4 OZ) DRIED APPLE

35G (1 1/4 OZ) DRIED APRICOTS

125 ML (4 FL OZ) FRESH APPLE JUICE

2 TSP FRESH LEMON JUICE

Combine all the ingredients in a bowl and refrigerate overnight. Always select sulphur-free dried fruit mix.

Citrus Breakfast Muffins

MAKES 12

250G (9 OZ) SELF-RAISING FLOUR

25G (1 OZ) GROUND ALMONDS

1 TSP BAKING POWDER

1/2 TSP BREAD SODA

75G (2 1/2 OZ) BUTTER

75G (2 1/2 OZ) CASTER SUGAR

1 ORANGE OR LEMON

100 ML (3 FL OZ) MILK

1 EGG

Preheat oven to 200°C (390°F) or gas mark 6.

Melt butter (microwave for 40 seconds or place in heating oven) and set aside. Grease tins.

Sieve flour, baking powder and bread soda. Add almonds and sugar. Wash, zest and juice the orange or lemon. Measure 100 ml of the juice.

Beat with the zest, milk, egg and melted butter. Pour into the dry ingredients and mix with fork. The batter will be lumpy. Do not over-beat.

Spoon into tins and bake for 20 minutes.

Serve hot with butter and jam.

Yoghurt Muffins

MAKES 12 MUFFINS

125 ML (4 FL OZ) PLAIN YOGHURT

125 ML (4 FL OZ) VEGETABLE OIL

175G (6 OZ) SELF-RAISING FLOUR

175G (6 OZ) CASTER SUGAR

3 EGGS

1 LEMON

4 DROPS VANILLA ESSENCE

PINCH SALT

Preheat oven to 170°C (325°F) or gas mark 3/4.

Grease tins. Wash and zest lemon using the small or medium holes on grater. Brush zest from grater with pastry brush. Stir all ingredients together with wooden spoon.

Fill muffin tins 2/3 full or spoon mixture into cake tin. Bake muffins for 15 minutes until just brown, a cake for 50–55 minutes.

When cooked, they should spring back when pressed in the centre.

Serve warm or cold.

VARIATION:

Lemon Drizzle Muffins or Cake: Do not add the lemon juice to mixture but boil it with 1 tbsp sugar for 1 minute and drizzle over the warm cooked cake or muffins.

Carrot Buns

MAKES 12

250G (9 OZ) PLAIN FLOUR

100G (3 ½ OZ) MARGARINE AT
    ROOM TEMPERATURE

100G (3 ½ OZ) DARK BROWN SUGAR

1 EGG

1 TBSP WATER

225G (8 OZ) GRATED CARROT

1 TSP BAKING POWDER

1 TSP GROUND CINNAMON

½ TSP NUTMEG

2 RINGS PINEAPPLE – CHOPPED FINELY

Preheat oven to 180°C (350°F) or gas mark 4. Grease a 12 cup bun tin.

Cream the margarine and sugar together until light and fluffy. Beat in the egg and water. Sift in the flour and the remaining ingredients.

Combine well and spoon into the tins. Make sure each tin has equal amounts. Place into the oven and bake for 35 minutes.

Let them stand in the tin for about 10 minutes before you take them out.

Sweet Potato and Dried Fruit Bread

MAKES 1 LOAF

275G (10 OZ) PLAIN FLOUR

2 TSP BAKING POWDER

½ TSP SALT

1 TSP CINNAMON

½ TSP MIXED SPICE

450G (1 LB) SWEET POTATO – MASHED

75G (2 ½ OZ) BROWN SUGAR

100G (3 ½ OZ) MARGARINE – MELTED

3 EGGS – BEATEN

100G (3 ½ OZ) MIXED FRUIT –
    APRICOTS, RAISINS, FIGS, DATES,
    PRUNES – CHOPPED

Preheat oven to 180°C (350°F) or gas mark 4.

Grease one loaf tin. Sift flour and baking powder into a bowl. Add the salt, spices and set aside. Using an electric whisk, beat the sweet potatoes, melted margarine and sugar together.

Add the eggs gradually. Stir this mixture into the flour mixture and combine well. Add the mixed fruit.

Transfer into the loaf tin and bake for 1–1 ½ hours. Cool in the tin and then turn out on to a wire tray.

THE yellow COLOUR

YELLOW IS A VIBRANT AND POWERFUL COLOUR. IT RESONATES WITH LIGHT-HEARTED HAPPINESS AND CAREFREE WAYS. LOVERS OF THIS COLOUR ARE GENERALLY SOCIABLE, FUN-LOVING, RADIATE OPTIMISM AND MAKE RELIABLE FRIENDS. THEY ALSO TEND TO BE CONFIDENT AND BRIM WITH HIGH SELF-ESTEEM. THEY LOVE CHALLENGES.

Lovers of yellow can be highly imaginative, idealistic and creative. They seek out a multiplicity of activities and need a wide social network for stimulation.

THE COLOUR YELLOW IS MOST SIGNIFICANTLY ASSOCIATED WITH THE MIND AND HAS AN AFFINITY WITH KNOWLEDGE AND RATIONAL THINKING. Yellow is fundamentally non-violent and in situations where conflicts arise, yellow personalities would rather use dialogue to over-come difficulties as opposed to physical prowess.

People who dislike yellow are not overly excited by experimentation and prefer the tried and tested method of doing things. They are practical, often critical of others who are not, thrive on deadlines and details and need a signature on the dotted line before making any final decision. They will leave the design/creative side of things to others.

WHAT IS YOUR COLOUR PERSONALITY? TO FIND OUT TURN TO PAGE 2.

THE YELLOW COLOUR PERSONALITY

- INTELLIGENT
- OPTIMISTIC
- HAS A KNACK AT PINPOINTING THE ISSUES
- RESPONDS WELL TO PRESSURE
- BRILLIANT IN THE HOSPITALITY BUSINESS AND PR
- THINKS BIG WHEN IT COMES TO MONEY
- LIKES TO KEEP TRIM
- SELF-CONFIDENT
- LOVES EXPANSION
- CHATTERBOX

Mr Yellow

The yellow male is a happy, fun-loving person who likes to talk and is never short of words. He loves to spar intellectually with you and it is challenging to win an argument with him as his mind is very agile and witty. He loves fast cars, fine wines, trendy restaurants and packs a lot into his busy day.

Mr Yellow becomes restless easily and, as he is influenced by trends and fashion, changes his mind and hobbies regularly. He has a healthy curiosity so enjoys experimenting with new activities, exploring new territory and travelling. Yellow males are classic workaholics. They like independent partners and cannot resist romantic intrigues and the excitement of 'the chase'. His mood changes quickly at times but he is always fun to be with!

Ms Yellow

The yellow female is happy, self-confident and possesses high self-esteem. She broadcasts a feeling of well-being; she is rarely sick and likes to keep trim. She loves to experiment with colour and her image will always have a dramatic twist; she doesn't mind if she looks bizarre sometimes! Ms Yellow is fabulous fun to be with; a vivacious lady, who is always looking forward. She is the busy girl with a quicksilver temperament. She may appear dizzy-headed or butterfly-minded but do not be fooled – she is very intelligent and a master at multi-tasking. Ms Yellow is not too fond of heavy-laden dramas or intense romantic links and can take a while to win over. But when she finally commits, you can be sure that you are one very special person indeed.

Young Yellow

The yellow child brings fun and laughter into your life. As soon as they can talk they are the family chatterbox and seem to talk before they can walk. While they are quick students and enjoy the challenges that learning presents, they need some guidance doing projects and homework as they have the inclination to skip from one thing to the other. They are extremely creative, have boundless energy and love to play. Yellow children take on each day with enthusiastic gusto and can display daredevil tendencies. They adore exploring and don't like limits – so let them go!

The Yellow Parent

Forever young at heart themselves, the yellow parent loves the activity, fun and magic that the young bundle has to bring. In fact, the yellow parent will be fascinated with the new baby. Yellow parents are the most suited to combining parenthood with a career as both yellow mum and dad can balance the two responsibilities extremely well. They are rather relaxed in the discipline department, creating an opportunity for 'spoilt streak syndrome'. Yellow parents are focused on education and the house will be filled with books, toys and games to stretch junior's imagination. They also encourage physical exercise and healthy eating. Meal-times can be quick though as there is always somewhere wonderful to get to. One thing is certain, the household buzzes with laughter, fun and games.

The Yellow Career

As the yellow personality loves networking and likes to be well known, they are brilliant in the hospitality business and great at PR. They are also drawn to media, publishing and journalism as they pay great attention to detail, can extract information from a stone and have a knack at pinpointing the relevant issues. They are flexible and adaptable with magnificent communication skills. They are smart and information seems part of their daily diet as they always have a big desire to learn. They have no hesitation in doing things – deciding and acting quickly in all matters – and respond well to pressure. They think big when it comes to money but keeping it may be more difficult. They have the Midas touch – turning everything they touch to gold. Many a deal will be clinched over a drink or on the golf course!

Guide To Wearing Yellow

As it is one of the brightest colours, yellow is a perfect colour to wear on a drab winter's day, as it will help to lift the spirits. Wearing this colour can give you a positive outlook, even if you are not in brilliant form. When studying, this is the colour to wear as it stimulates the mind and aids clear thinking. It is a colour often used in public relations and marketing environments as it helps stimulate creative thinking and suggests friendliness and openness.

Yellow will suit you if your complexion is pale, pink or olive and your hair is brown or silver grey. Stay away from dark yellows and mustard at all costs, as these colours will encourage negative thinking, causing you to complain and think the worst.

EXERCISE AND LEISURE ACTIVITIES

The yellow personality enjoys group sport activities where they can network and chatter; netball, volley ball, basketball, five-a-side football are all good activity choices. They like to keep in shape and naturally enjoy exercising. They also like to be well-groomed, so visiting a health spa or beauty therapist will rank highly on their list of priorities. As yellow personalities are high energy operators, chill down time is essential and recovery time will help to reduce the risk of burnout and work over-load.

THOUGHT FOR THE DAY
My whole body is filled with joy and confidence.

A YELLOW DAY PLAN

EXERCISE – DO A BELLY DANCE TO YOUR FAVOURITE MUSIC AND HAVE A GREAT LAUGH WHILE YOU ARE AT IT. IT STRENGTHENS CORE MUSCLES, SO YOUR TUMMY WILL BECOME MORE TONED.

CLOTHES – WEAR SOMETHING FUN TODAY – A PAIR OF EARRINGS WITH CARTOON SHAPES; A FURRY JUMPER; A FRILLY SKIRT.

FOOD – EAT YELLOW FOODS AT BREAKFAST, LUNCH AND DINNER. CHECK LIST AND RECIPES FOR IDEAS.

PERSONALITY – YOU ARE MISS CONFIDENT. "TODAY I AM SMART AND WILL STUDY WELL. I LOVE INFORMATION AND LEARNING. I AM THE CONFIDENT EXPLORER." BE BRIGHT AND GLOW WITH WELL-BEING.

SHADES OF YELLOW

LEMON YELLOW:

This colour helps cut through red tape and it says what has to be said. Be careful not to use too much of this colour as overuse tends to make one over-critical.

CITRON YELLOW:

The positive attribute of this colour is fairness, overuse can put those in its hue under pressure and their characters may become abrasive.

PRIMROSE YELLOW:

This colour can help stretch the mind, promoting a healthy curiosity. Overuse may prompt unreliability.

WHEN TO WEAR YELLOW

If you are feeling confident – use yellow, as it will help you maintain that feeling. Wear it when you need to communicate ideas as yellow will help keep your train of thought clear. Yellow also prompts us to stand back and view the information in a logical way. It is beneficial when we need to create a fresh perspective.

If you are feeling anxious or nervous wear yellow as it has a calming effect on the nervous system.

WHEN TO AVOID WEARING YELLOW

If you are over-critical of yourself or others, try to avoid yellow/green or acid yellow as these will accelerate the condition. It is best to use lavender and purples to help yourself relax. If you are involved in gossiping or find yourself chattering too much, avoid darker shades of yellow and choose sunny yellows; these colours will help you to feel more centred. If you are prone to nagging over silly things, the deeper shades of yellow will cause you to become caustic.

BEST COLOUR PERSONALITY MATCH

Yellow personalities get on really well with purple personalities. Both personalities are imaginative and will share their love for art, music and food. Both personalities are sociable and enjoy travel. The two have a formidable ability to adapt to change and can cope with the whirl-wind of unexpected events that a day can bring.

WORST COLOUR PERSONALITY MATCH

Yellow personalities may be challenged with the blue personality, as blues tend to have a methodically slower approach when dealing with daily activities. The blue personality enjoys time alone and may find it over-powering to socialize to the extent that the yellow personality can do so effortlessly.

✚ Yellow Health

YELLOW IS A STIMULANT FOR THE AREA OF THE BODY KNOWN AS THE SOLAR PLEXUS WHICH IS SITUATED IN THE STOMACH AREA AND GOVERNS THE PANCREAS, LIVER, GALL BLADDER AND SPLEEN. IF YOU HAVE POOR SKIN, NAILS OR HAIR, CHOOSE YELLOW AS IT SUPPORTS THE LIVER – THE POWER HOUSE IN THE BODY THAT ELIMINATES TOXINS. YELLOW CAN HELP LIFT YOUR MOOD. LAUGHTER IS THE BEST YELLOW TONIC AND IT GIVES THE INTERNAL ORGANS AN AEROBIC WORK-OUT.

WHAT DOES YOUR FACE SAY ABOUT YOU?

"Mirror, Mirror on the wall … Who's the fairest of them all?" Does this bring back some childhood memories from storybooks of old?

"Physiognomy" or face reading has been used by practitioners of Chinese medicine for centuries. Your own mother has probably said to you at least once in your lifetime: "I can read your face like a book". Think of how you can look at someone you know well and with a glance you know how they are feeling. Do they look fresh, well-rested, happy, washed out, worried or anxious? It is often easy to tell from the face when someone is depressed or simply angry; they may have a permanent scowl, their smile may be forced or they may express surprise falsely. You see, if we look carefully enough, the face can tell us so much.

The shape of your face can tell you about your own personality and can be indicative of illness. What does your face reveal about you? You can begin by taking a look in the mirror. Look closely at the area around the hair line. This reflects the activity and health of the bladder. If you find that you have any type of congestion in this area (such as black or white heads) it may be indicative that the bladder could be strengthened.

The forehead represents the large and small intestines. Have you any congestion or mega lines? Congestion here may indicate weak assimilation and elimination. The lines running along the forehead are indicative of how you have dealt with life issues. Long straight lines show that you have made good transitions through your life and dealt with challenges as you were faced by them. Broken and uneven lines are indicative that you have had some upset or trauma in your earlier life that has caused emotional upset.

The area between the two eyes represents the liver. Plenty of fresh colourful food, as well as plenty of water and exercise, will help to maintain balanced liver function.

The top of the nose indicates the pancreas and if it shows any signs of redness it may be useful to keep an account of the sugar contribution in your diet.

How is the chin area? This area represents the stomach. If there are signs of congestion (i.e. spots, pimples, dead skin or lack lustre) it would be beneficial to eat a diet rich in colourful fresh foods. Many facial treatments now include a face map outline and your therapist will be able to recommend cleansing and lifestyle practices and techniques, so that you can help your face remain vibrant and fresh.

SUNLIGHT

Sunlight provides us with our main source of Vitamin D, which promotes calcium absorption, maintains a healthy nervous system and boosts the immune system. Ten minutes of exposure each day will supply us with all the Vitamin D we need. The sun can actually alter moods chemically and prevent depression. The onset of spring gives thousands of people relief from Seasonal Affective Disorder or SAD. This condition is experienced by many people during the winter months. (See The Colour Black chapter for more details.)

ALCOHOL AND YOUR BODY

There is an old Japanese proverb that states: "First the man takes the drink: then the drink takes the man." As the liver can only cope with breaking down one unit of alcohol per hour, the rest builds up in your system, making you drunk. A unit of alcohol is a small glass of sherry, a standard glass of wine, $1/2$ pint of beer, $1/3$ glass of cider or a single measure of aperitif or spirit. Alcohol as we know impairs behaviour, judgement, memory and co-ordination. In large amounts, alcohol acts like an anaesthetic inducing sleepiness and slowing down your breathing.

A hangover is a sign of alcohol poisoning. As alcohol gets broken down in the liver into smaller substances, which are poisonous to the cells in the body, these substances cause the kidneys to produce more urine and you become dehydrated – which gives you the hangover headache.

ALCOHOL GUIDELINES

Remember to drink sensibly.

One alcoholic beverage per hour is recommended.

Drink plenty of water in between this to prevent dehydration and reduce the 'hangover' feeling the next day.

Drink plenty of vegetable juice and fresh fruit for breakfast such as berries or citrus fruits, as these contain Vitamin C – a powerful anti-oxidant that will help to remove the free radicals. Apples are especially beneficial as they contain the flavonol quercetin – one of the most potent of all the anti-oxidants.

Fresh air and exercise will work wonders so get up and get out walking! I don't recommend setting yourself up with a big fry-up as overloading on carbohydrates will promote sluggishness and exacerbate the 'hungover' feeling.

If you have an event or party to go to, ensure that you give yourself a 24-hour reprieve as this will allow your body and liver to rejuvenate.

Whilst hosting; always use spirit measures as it's far more responsible and your guests will be able to gauge their consumption. If you don't do this the measures can be all over the place and you and your guests most probably will also!

ALCOHOL'S EFFECTS ON ...

LIVER Drinking alcohol in large quantities (that is more than 14 units per week for women and 21 for men) causes the cells in your liver to become swollen and filled with fat. This is known as "fatty liver" and can cause liver failure. It is reversible if you stop drinking. You will know your liver is over-worked and under-hydrated when you see symptoms such as: itchy skin, yellowish colour in the whites of the eyes, bruising easily and fluid retention in the face, hands and legs.

STOMACH Alcohol irritates the lining of the stomach and causes gastritis which affects the mucus membrane leading to the development of peptic ulcers in the stomach and the first part of the bowel. A peptic ulcer is where the tissue becomes eroded. The pain may vary from mild to severe and symptoms will include; nausea, vomiting, stomach pain, loss of appetite and sweating.

HEART Alcohol weakens the heart muscle causing cardiomyopathy (an irregular heartbeat) and can lead to heart failure. Alcohol can speed up the heart beat and this can be fatal.

IMMUNE SYSTEM Drinking large amounts of alcohol will weaken your immune system and rob your body cells of nutrients. It will slow down breathing, not to mention accelerate the ageing process as it causes dehydration.

FOODS TO AID

TOMATOES

They are great anti-oxidants, containing beta-carotene and lycopene that can prevent the generation of damaging free radicals.

CARROTS

They contain beta-carotene and Vitamin A which are vital for skin health.

SWEET POTATOES

They contain Vitamin A, C, beta-carotene and a huge amount of carotene. Vitamin C is an anti-oxidant and helps build collagen; a substance vital for healthy skin.

SWEDES

They give us a significant quantity of Vitamin C – 100g (3 ¹/₂ oz) of swede provide 75% RDA (Recommended Daily Allowance).

SKIN DEEP

SKIN IS THE LARGEST ORGAN IN THE BODY AND IT ACCOUNTS FOR APPROXIMATELY 16% OF YOUR TOTAL BODY WEIGHT. SKIN PERFORMS A NUMBER OF FUNCTIONS. IT PROTECTS ALL THE DELICATE ORGANS OF THE BODY INCLUDING THE LIVER, SPLEEN AND PANCREAS. IT HELPS REGULATE BODY TEMPERATURE BY INCREASING PERSPIRATION WHEN YOU ARE TOO WARM. IT IS A MAJOR ORGAN FOR THE ELIMINATION OF WASTE AND WORKS WITH THE COLON AND LUNGS TO HELP ELIMINATE TOXIC WASTE FROM THE BODY.

MANY FACTORS CAN INTERFERE WITH THE NATURAL BEAUTY OF THE SKIN, SUCH AS: STRESS, DEHYDRATION, POOR DIET, MIXED WITH IRREGULAR EXERCISE. ACNE IS ONE

AVOCADO

They contain Vitamin E. This is vital for skin health as it is a powerful anti-oxidant and it neutralises free radicals that can damage the skin.

PEPPERS

They contain carotenoids, lutein and zeaxanthin – all vital phytonutrients that have anti-oxidative properties and help protect the skin from degeneration.

COURGETTES

A slice of courgette gently rubbed over blackheads will combat stubborn spots by drying out the skin.

BROCCOLI

It is rich in carotenoids – the pigment that gives yellow and orange fruit and vegetables their characteristic colour and acts as an anti-inflammatory.

CABBAGE

It contains Vitamin C.

HEALTHY SKIN

SKIN COMPLAINT AND CAN BE CAUSED BY A HORMONE IMBALANCE OR IT MAY BE A POOR DIET. IF THE SEBACEOUS GLANDS UNDER THE SKIN PRODUCE TOO MUCH OIL, THE PORES OF THE SKIN GET BLOCKED AND THE TRACES OF SEBUM THAT CAUSE THE PORES TO BE BLOCKED CAN ATTRACT BACTERIA RESULTING IN BLEMISHES AND INFLAMMATION. TO ENSURE THAT SKIN IS FRESH AND VIBRANT, A REGULAR SKIN CARE PROGRAMME OF CLEANSING, TONING AND MOISTURISING IS IMPORTANT. IT IS VITAL THAT YOU USE THE PRODUCTS BEST SUITED TO YOUR SKIN TYPE AND IT IS ADVISABLE TO SEEK PROFESSIONAL ADVICE FROM YOUR SKIN THERAPIST TO DETERMINE YOUR SKIN TYPE. EATING A DIET RICH IN THE FRESH COLOURFUL FOODS FEATURED HERE WILL HELP.

GRAPES
They are uniquely nourishing, strengthening, cleansing and regenerating.

PAPAYAS
They contain beta-carotene and Vitamin C.

KIWI
They have twice as much Vitamin C as oranges.

HERBS
Borage contains large amounts of gamma linoleic acid (GLA). It makes an excellent remedy for eczema.

HONEY
Used after an operation as honey can reduce scarring.

PULSES
French beans contain Vitamin A and C.

BRUSSEL
Sprouts
They contain beta-carotene.

OLIVES
They have a reasonable amount of Vitamin E.

CUCUMBERS
They make an excellent astringent facial cleanser for oily skin as they help remove excess oil.

APRICOTS
They contain beta-carotene – a phytonutrient that protects the skin from damage from free radicals.

LEMONS
Lemon juice applied neat with a cotton bud to pus-filled spots is a powerful bactericide and particularly useful for acne.

BLACKBERRIES
They are rich in Vitamin C – a powerful anti-oxidant.

HEALTHY NAILS

Beautifully manicured, strong, healthy nails can work wonders for your confidence and can also be good for your health. The nail is composed mainly of a fibrous protein called keratin. **NAILS ARE ONE OF THE BODY'S STRONGEST TISSUES.** They grow at a rate of around 1 mm (0.04 in) a week. It is not uncommon for nails to stop growing at a time of medical trauma (such as an accident) and when they start to grow again, there is often a little ridge to mark this point, which eventually grows out. It takes around three to four months for a nail to renew itself from base to tip and six or seven months for the rest of the nail to grow. As a result, nails can provide important clues to underlying deficiencies, health disorders, food intolerance's and nutritional imbalances. With this in mind, nails should be viewed as one of the best windows on the body's internal workings. An important clue to look for is any change of colour in the nail. Healthy nail beds are pink in colour due to the rich blood supply underneath them.

The following are things to look out for on your nails and can be helpful in pinpointing exactly how your health needs improving.

- Look out for pitting, which makes nails look as though they've been shot with an airgun as they will have a small pin mark. This can indicate a skin condition called 'psoriasis' which is often a hereditary condition, linked to rapid growth of cells in the nail's outer layer. These growths never mature. Psoriasis is not contagious and, although you might expect it to cause skin problems, sometimes it only causes joint inflammation. The nails can give an important clue as to whether this has developed or not.
- Splinter haemorrhages in the nails – which look like tiny red splinters – can be a sign of infection in the heart or blood.
- Clubbing is where the nail loses its angle at the base and bends in at the top. This can be a sign of a lack of oxygen in the blood, caused by lung or heart disease.
- There is an on-going debate regarding the little white flecks that appear on the fingernails. Some say it is due to a poor diet and deficiencies in calcium and zinc. Others claim that they are minute air pockets, and they will generally disappear over time. I would tend to agree with the latter.
- Certain nail irregularities may signal a serious medical disorder: a blueish tint under the nail could be indicative of asthma. Red/purple nails may indicate an upset digestive system caused by over-consumption of sugars, fruit juices or pharmaceutical drugs. Dark red nails could mean a high content of fatty acids and cholesterol due to too much dairy, sugar and salt in the diet.

NAILS: SOME PROBLEMS, SOLUTIONS AND SUGGESTIONS ON EATING

PROBLEM	SOLUTION	FOODS TO USE
WHITE BANDS	Protein	Organic lean red beef
		Eggs
		Pulse vegetables
		Tofu
	Folic Acid	Dark green leafy vegetables
		Nuts
		Wholegrains
	Vitamin C	Blackcurrents
		Green peppers
		Oranges
		Kiwis
		Raw red cabbage
DRYNESS	Vitamin A	Carrots
		Spinach
		Broccoli
	Calcium	Nuts
		Fruit
		Yoghurt
		Beans
BRITTLENESS	Vitamin A	Carrots
		Spinach
		Broccoli
SPLITTING	Calcium	Nuts
		Fruit
		Yoghurt
		Beans
VERTICAL RIDGES	Vitamin B group	Dark green leafy vegetables
		Fish
		Nuts
		Avocado
		Oatmeal

NAILS: SOME PROBLEMS, SOLUTIONS AND SUGGESTIONS ON EATING

PROBLEM	SOLUTION	FOODS TO USE
ROUND, CURVED AND DARKENED NAILS	Vitamin B12	Dark green leafy vegetables
		Wholegrain cereals
		Nuts
	Iron	Peas
		Raisins
		Dates
		Lentils
		Oily fish
		Edible seaweed
WHITE SPOTS	Zinc	Oats
		Sardines
		Pumpkin seeds
		Almonds

Good nutrition is the key to nail vitality. Good growth depends on a healthy diet which helps to nourish new cells of the nail that are developing from the base. For healthier nails – eat protein-rich foods including: eggs, grains, legumes, oatmeal, nuts and seeds. Eat foods rich in sulphur and silicon such as: broccoli, fish, onions and sea vegetables like nori and dulse (refer to The Colour Silver chapter). I also suggest you eat foods such as: wholegrain cereals, grains, citrus fruit, berries, yellow and orange coloured fruit and vegetables as well as fish. Essential nutrients for healthy nails gained from these foods include: Vitamin A, B2 and Vitamin C, biotin (a vitamin that aids in cell growth), calcium, zinc, garlic, Omega-3 oils and acidophilus (which fights fungal infections that can affect the nail).

Tina's Tip

To strengthen nails – soak in warm olive oil or cider vinegar for 15–20 minutes. Use nail polish removers as little as possible as they contain solvents that leach oils from the nails and make them brittle. Eating yellow foods can help detoxify the system and eliminate waste products, which will in turn, help to strengthen nails.

A SELECTION OF YELLOW FOODS AND DRINKS

YELLOW LENTILS

EGGS

PINEAPPLE

BUTTERNUT SQUASH

PEACHES

SWEETCORN

LEMON

BANANAS

YELLOW PEPPERS

AVOCADO

TINA'S TOP EGG TIP

Eggshell is porous so must be kept away from strong smelling foods such as onions and ripe cheese. Remember that while nutritious, eggs are high in calories so moderate consumption is advised. Refer to The Colour Blue chapter for more details on cholesterol. Note: For cooking, eggs need to be at room temperature. Eggs used straight from the fridge will crack if plunged into boiling water. A cold yolk will not emulsify reliably and cold whites will not whisk well.

Eggs

Always choose organic or free range varieties for optimum health. **EGG** yolk contains a substance called "lecithin", which makes eggs an important brain food; they contribute to memory and concentration as they help to stabilize anti-oxidants. Lecithin is a natural emulsifier and is used as an emulsifier in products that are high in fats and oil. Hens lay up to 250 eggs a year. Other eggs include: Ostrich eggs – one ostrich egg is equal to two hen eggs and are rarely sold in shops. Duck eggs – these are best used in custards, mousses and other puddings. Goose eggs – rich and make excellent omelettes, custards and mousses. Quail eggs – make a good first course served hard-boiled or with celery salt.

Nutrition
- Protein
- Zinc, Potassium
- Vitamins A, D, E, B12

Good For
- Muscle support
- Healthy skin and nails (due to the high biological protein)

How Much To Eat
It has been advised that people with regular cholesterol levels can eat up to seven eggs a week. For those on a cholesterol lowering programme it is recommended to eat much less if any at all. Your health therapist can advise you best.

Phytonutrients
- None

Pineapple

PINEAPPLES are great for any problems with digestion as it contains the enzyme 'bromelain' which aids the digestion of protein.

Nutrition
- Vitamin C
- Fibre
- Potassium
- Magnesium
- Enzyme – bromelain

Good For
- Sore throats
- Sinusitis (due to the bromelain)
- Easing joint pain

How Much To Eat
Thick slice is about 80g (3 oz) (eat as part of your five to nine servings a day)

Phytonutrients
- Phenolic acids

Did You Know?

EGGS PROBABLY STARTED LIFE IN PERU. THEY ARE A GOOD SOURCE OF POTASSIUM; A MINERAL THAT HELPS BOOST MOOD AND LIFT DEPRESSION. THEY ARE GREAT FOR COMBATING STRESS AND ARE EVEN SAID TO BOOST THE SEX DRIVE TOO!

Sweetcorn

SWEETCORN is famous for containing the plant enzyme "bromelain". Bromelain breaks down protein and is found mostly in the stem rather than the fruit of the plant.

Nutrition
- Protein
- Fibre
- Vitamin A, E

Good For
- Energy (due to the carbohydrate content)
- Eye health (due to the zeaxanthin contribution)

How Much To Eat
Portion weighs 85g (3 oz) (eat as part of your five to nine servings per day)

Phytonutrients
Zeaxanthin (a type of carotenoid)

did you know?

BROMELAIN IS USED AS A COMMERCIAL TENDERIZER FOR MEAT. IT IS PRESENT IN THE SEEDS OF THE PAW-PAW FRUIT. YOU CAN DRY THESE SEEDS AND PLACE IN A GRINDER, THEN SPRINKLE OVER MEATS AND MARINADE OVERNIGHT. THE TENDERIZING ACTIVITY WILL HELP DISSOLVE THE MEAT FIBRES MAKING THE MEAT TENDERER.

Lemon

LEMONS are a good source of limonoid phytonutrients and a related phytonutrient called limonene. Laboratory studies show that citrus limonoids have cholesterol lowering properties. Limonoid and limonene are found in the fruit, pith, peel and juice – so make sure you use the whole lemon.

Nutrition
- Vitamin C
- Small amounts Vitamin B, E
- Magnesium
- Calcium
- Phosphorus
- Fibre
- Potassium

Good For
- Helping the body absorb iron (due to the Vitamin C content)
- Boosting immune system
- Digestive challenges (due to the fibre and Vitamin B content)
- Boosting liver activity (as Vitamin A and E act as powerful antioxidants)
- Lowering cholesterol

How Much To Eat
- 100g (3 $^{1}/_{2}$ oz) provides more than one day's dose of Vitamin C. Juice from a medium lemon weighs 20g ($^{3}/_{4}$ oz).
- Use in dressings, sauces and drinks.

Phytonutrients
- Bioflavonoids – limonene
- Flavonoids
- Phenolic Acids

Yellow Peppers

PEPPERS are extremely versatile and work well sliced in salads, stir-fries, in Mexican dishes or stuffed and baked. They are a good food to eat as part of your five to nine servings a day. The yellow pepper is native to tropical America and the West Indies. The green sweet pepper is the unripe yellow pepper. The yellow pepper is mild in flavour and can be eaten raw or cooked.

Nutrition
- Vitamin C
- Vitamin A
- Vitamin E
- Folic acid
- Fibre
- Potassium
- Folate

Good For
- Skin problems (due to the Vitamin E and C contribution)
- Boosting immune system

How Much To Eat
- Half a yellow pepper weighs 80g (3 oz).
- 100g (3 $^{1}/_{2}$ oz) peppers provides almost all RDA Vitamin A.

Phytonutrients
- Lutein
- Beta-cryptoxanthin
- Beta-carotene
- Carotenoids

Avocado

Avocados are a natural source of monosaturated fat which makes them an ideal self-contained heart food. The oil from avocados has been used as a skin treatment and it is known that chemicals in avocados stimulate the production of collagen.

Nutrition
- Vitamin B6
- Vitamin C
- Vitamin E
- Potassium
- Magnesium
- Fibre

Good For
- Healthy heart
- Skin/anti-ageing
- Lowering LDL (as it is a natural source of monounsaturated fats)
- Reducing cholesterol levels
- Stress relieving

How Much To Eat
- Half a medium sized avocado weighs 65g (2 oz).
- Eat as part of your five to nine servings a day.
- Serve with sliced fruit, guacamole or in salads.

Phytonutrients
- Phenolic acids
- Alpha-carotene (can help reduce arthrosclerosis – stiffening of the joints)
- Lutein
- Carotenoids
- Biogenic Amines

TINA'S TIP

Mash half an avocado and butter a slice of wholegrain brown bread with it. Add a slice of fresh turkey breast and find calm and freedom again so you can move on to the next activity in your life. The widely held view that avocados are high in fat is in fact, a myth! Many people think that they are to be avoided because they are fattening. This is not true. The fat in avocado is monosaturated fat. Monosaturated fat is burned more efficiently than saturated fat. They are so good to eat as they contain Omega-3 fatty acids that facilitate heart health. They are cholesterol free, sodium free and low in saturated fat.

I find you either love or hate avocados. Trust your own body. If they disagree with you choose another food that your body enjoys. If you enjoy them: eat them!

Did You Know?

ALTHOUGH MANY PEOPLE THINK AVOCADO IS A VEGETABLE, IN FACT, IT IS A FRUIT.

TINA'S BEAUTY TIP

Half lemon juice and half water diluted makes a brilliant facial wash.

Did You Know?

LEMONS ARE NATURAL DISINFECTANTS DUE TO THEIR HIGH ANTI-BACTERIAL ACTIVITY. THEY MAKE A GOOD GARGLE FOR SORE THROATS AND CAN BE A REFRESHING MOUTH WASH.

Eggs Benedict

SERVES 4

4 EGGS

4 SLICES SPELT BREAD

55G (2 OZ) BUTTER

1 TSP OLIVE OIL

4 SLICES OF HAM

HOLLANDAISE SAUCE

Heat the grill.

Trim the crusts off the slices of bread and fry them in a mixture of oil and butter until crisp and golden brown.

Lay a piece of ham on each piece of toast.

Lightly poach the eggs. Drain well and lay on the toast and ham.

Generously spoon the Hollandaise sauce over each piece of toast, eggs and ham.

This makes an ideal choice for a brunch dish. A spelt or rye muffin may be used instead of the toast. Smoked salmon makes a tasty alternative to the ham.

Paprika Herb Omelette

SERVES 1

3 FRESH FREE RANGE EGGS

LARGE PINCH PAPRIKA

SMALL KNOB BUTTER

SMALL HANDFUL MIXED FRESH HERBS SUCH AS PARSLEY, CHIVES AND BASIL – CHOPPED

SEA SALT AND BLACK PEPPER

Put the eggs and paprika into a bowl and lightly whisk to combine. Season with some sea salt and black pepper.

Put the butter in a 20 cm (8 in) non-stick frying pan over a medium/high heat.

When the butter starts to foam, add the egg mixture. As the base begins to cook, use a fork to draw it aside and allow the uncooked egg to run beneath.

Continue doing this until the omelette is set but still soft. Scatter the herbs on top. Use a palette knife to fold over half the omelette, and then carefully slide onto a serving plate.

Serve with bread and a dressed green salad.

Hot Lemon Water

MAKES 1 LITRE

875 ML (29 FL OZ) BOILING WATER

125 ML (4 FL OZ) FRESH LEMON JUICE

Combine the two liquids. You can make hot grapefruit water by switching the fruits.

Pineapple and Cucumber Salad

SERVES 2

300G (10 ½ OZ) FRESH PINEAPPLE – PEELED, CORED AND CUBED

300G (10 ½ OZ) CUCUMBER – PEELED AND CUBED

2 TBSP LIVE PRO-BIOTIC NATURAL YOGHURT

2 TSP LIME JUICE

2 TBSP FRESH MINT – CHOPPED

2 TBSP SUNFLOWER SEEDS

Chill the chopped and cubed pineapple and cucumber in a bowl in the fridge for a while.

Mix the yoghurt, lime juice, mint and seeds together.

Toss into the pineapple and cucumber.

Serve chilled with grilled chicken or fish cakes.

Roasted Yellow Pepper Mayonnaise

MAKES 1 JAR/10 SERVINGS

2 YELLOW PEPPERS – QUARTERED AND DE-SEEDED

OIL FOR BRUSHING

1 SMALL RED ONION – FINELY CHOPPED

100G (3 ½ OZ) FLAKED ALMONDS

2 CLOVES GARLIC – CRUSHED

50G (2 OZ) GRATED PARMESAN CHEESE

2 TSP LIME JUICE

4 TBSP OLIVE OIL

Preheat oven to 180°C (350°F) or gas mark 4.

Place the pepper skins side up on a baking sheet.

Brush well with oil. Roast in the oven until the skins have blackened.

Then remove from the oven and place in a plastic bag. Seal and leave for 10 minutes.

Peel back the skins. Place the peppers in a blender and whisk until smooth.

Now mix in the other ingredients.

This is a gorgeous alternative to store-bought mayonnaise on a wrap or blend with pasta.

Egg Fried Rice

SERVES 4-6

3 EGGS

SALT AND PEPPER TO SEASON

2 SPRING ONIONS – CHOPPED FINELY

3 TBSP OLIVE OIL

400G (12 OZ) COOKED BROWN RICE

120G (4 1/2 OZ) PEAS

FLAT LEAF PARSLEY – TO GARNISH

Lightly beat the eggs and season.

Heat the oil in a wok.

Add the eggs and stir until they have slightly scrambled.

Add the brown rice, peas and spring onion.

Serve in a large bowl and garnish with parsley.

Sunflower Pâté

SERVES 4

100G (3 1/2 OZ) SUNFLOWER SEEDS

1 TBSP SOY SAUCE

2 TBSP EXTRA-VIRGIN OLIVE OIL

1 SHALLOT – FINELY CHOPPED

200G (7OZ) COOKED GREEN LENTILS

1–2 TBSP LEMON JUICE

1 TSP GROUND CORIANDER

1–2 TSP BLACK PEPPER

Toast the sunflower seeds in a dry frying pan. When they begin to pop and brown, turn off the heat and add the soy sauce. Stir well, then put in a mortar or food processor and grind to a coarse powder.

Put the oil in the frying pan, add the chopped shallot. Soften for a few minutes over a low heat. Put the ground sunflower seeds and cooled shallot in a food processor with the other ingredients and blend to a smooth consistency.

This makes a tasty alternative to hummus.

Mellow Yellow Cake

SERVES 8

375G (13 OZ) SOFTENED UNSALTED BUTTER,
PLUS EXTRA TO GREASE

375G (13 OZ) GOLDEN CASTER SUGAR

FINELY GRATED ZEST OF 2 ORANGES

375G (13 OZ) GROUND ALMONDS

1 TSP GROUND MIXED SPICE

5 LARGE ORGANIC EGGS

200G (7 OZ) HAZELNUTS – TOASTED AND
FINELY CHOPPED

100G (3 1/2 OZ) PLAIN FLOUR

1/2 TSP BAKING POWDER

8 TBSP FRANGELICO (HAZELNUT LIQUEUR)

300G (10 1/2 OZ) GOOD QUALITY WHITE
CHOCOLATE

50G (2 OZ) UNSALTED BUTTER

250G (9 OZ) WHITE MARZIPAN

ICING SUGAR – FOR DUSTING

MINI CHOCOLATE EGGS – TO DECORATE

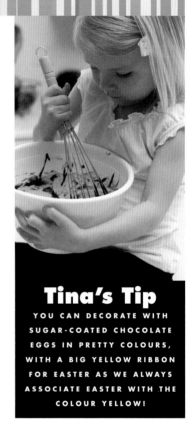

Tina's Tip

YOU CAN DECORATE WITH SUGAR-COATED CHOCOLATE EGGS IN PRETTY COLOURS, WITH A BIG YELLOW RIBBON FOR EASTER AS WE ALWAYS ASSOCIATE EASTER WITH THE COLOUR YELLOW!

Preheat the oven to 160°C (315°F) or gas mark 3. Grease and line a 23 cm (9 in) round cake tin with non-stick baking paper.

In a large bowl, beat the butter, sugar and orange zest together until light and fluffy.

Stir in the ground almonds and mixed spice.

Beat in the eggs one at a time.

Fold in the hazelnuts, flour, baking powder and the hazelnut liqueur until smooth.

Spoon into the prepared tin and bake for 1 hour, then cover with foil and bake for a further 50 minutes or until a metal skewer inserted into the centre comes out clean.

Leave to cool for 10 minutes in the tin, then turn out onto a wire rack to cool completely.

Next melt the chocolate and butter in a bowl set over a pan of simmering water. Stir until just smooth, but don't over-beat. Spread all over the top and sides of the cake with a palette knife and leave to set.

Lightly dust a flat surface with icing sugar large enough to cover the whole cake – roll out the marzipan. Roll up on rolling pin, then unroll over the cake and press lightly into the sides and trim neatly.

Place mini chocolate eggs on top.

Meringues with Mango and Coconut

MAKES 20

MERINGUE CASES	FILLING
OIL – FOR GREASING	275 ML (10 ½ OZ) WHIPPED CREAM
3 EGGS WHITES – AT ROOM TEMPERATURE	1 RIPE MANGO – CHILLED AND
175G (6 OZ) CASTER SUGAR	CHOPPED FINELY
1 TSP CORNFLOUR	2 TSP COCONUT
1 TSP LEMON JUICE	COINTREAU OR BAILEYS – OPTIONAL

Preheat oven to 110°C (230°F) or gas mark 4.

Prepare two baking sheets by lining each tin with grease-proof paper and brushing the paper with oil also. Set aside. Place the egg whites into a bowl and whisk until the mixture stands in peaks. Gradually add in half the sugar – a tablespoon at a time. Whisk until the mixture becomes stiff and has a good gloss. Then add the remaining sugar, fold in the cornflour and lemon juice. Spoon into 20 small bundles on the sheet. Bake for 25–35 minutes. Allow to cool completely. Put the cream into a bowl and whisk until stiff.

Mix the mango, coconut and cream together and decorate the meringue cases.

To make the whipped cream a little special, fold 1–2 tbsp of Cointreau or Baileys into it.

Upside-Down Pineapple Sponge Pudding

SERVES 6

	SPONGE
SYRUP MIX	100G (3 ½ OZ) BUTTER
25G (1 OZ) BUTTER	100G (3 ½ OZ) CASTER SUGAR
25G (1 OZ) SOFT DARK BROWN SUGAR	2 EGGS
TOPPING	100G (3 ½ OZ) SELF-RAISING FLOUR
4 SLICES PINEAPPLE	WHIPPED CREAM OR CRÈME FRAICHE

MAKING THE SYRUP: Melt the butter and brown sugar in a dish on high for 1 minute. Swirl the melted butter around dish to coat. Arrange the pineapple slices on the syrup in the tin.

MAKING THE SPONGE: Beat the butter and sugar until light and fluffy. Then beat in the eggs, sieve flour and fold into the mixture. Spread gently over the topping.

Then cook at 190°C (375°F) or gas mark 5, for 45 minutes. Test with a knife or skewers as it will look uncooked on top but will be done on the inside. Leave the pudding to stand for 8–10 minutes. Loosen the edges with a knife. Turn onto a plate.

Serve with whipped cream or crème fraiche.

Lemon Sorbet

Tina's Tip

THIS MAY BE SERVED
AS A LIGHT DESSERT
OR BETWEEN
STARTER AND MAIN
COURSE. IT WILL
HELP YOUR GUESTS
DIGEST AND CLEAR
THE PALATE. LIME
OR ORANGE MAY BE
USED INSTEAD OF
THE LEMONS IF
DESIRED.

SERVES 3

3 LEMONS

175G (6OZ) CASTOR SUGAR

600 ML (20 FL OZ) WATER

10 CUBES ICE

Wash lemons. Grate the zest into a saucepan.

Add the water and sugar. Place the saucepan on the heat and bring to the boil. Then simmer gently until the sugar is totally dissolved. Stir continuously for 10 minutes. Allow to cool completely.

Cut the lemons in half and using a squeezer – extract the juice. Be really careful so that you keep the lemon shell intact. Remove the pith from the lemon shells and place in the fridge.

Add the lemon juice to the zesty potion. Pour into a plastic container and put into the freezer for 2 hours.

Then remove the lemon shells from the fridge, crush the ice and add to the sorbet.

Spoon the sorbet into the lemon shells. Serve with a fresh mint leaf.

Lemon Tart

SERVES 8

200G (7 OZ) PLAIN FLOUR

50G (2 OZ) GROUND ALMONDS

1/2 TSP SALT

2 TBSP ICING SUGAR,
    PLUS EXTRA TO DUST

125G (4 1/2 OZ) CHILLED
    BUTTER – DICED

2 MEDIUM EGG YOLKS

1 EGG WHITE BEATEN

FOR THE FILLING

200G (7OZ) GOLDEN CASTER SUGAR

4 MEDIUM EGGS

142 ML (4 FL OZ) CARTON DOUBLE
    CREAM

GRATED ZEST AND JUICE OF
    2 UNWAXED LEMONS

Tina's Tip

USE DRIED BEANS – KIDNEY OR
BLACK-EYED PEAS – TO HELP KEEP
THE PASTRY IN SHAPE AND FLAT. BE
CAREFUL REMOVING THEM AS THEY'LL
BE VERY HOT.

Put the flour, ground almonds, salt, icing sugar and butter into a food processor and process to make fine crumbs. Add the yolks and 2–3 tbsp of cold water and pulse until the mixture comes together to make a firm but moist dough.

Lightly shape the pastry into a ball, then roll out on a floured surface and use to line a 20 cm (8 in) fluted flan tin. Chill for 30 minutes.

Preheat the oven to 190°C (375°F) or gas mark 5.

Place greaseproof paper on top of the pastry and cover with your baking beans. Bake for 10 minutes. Then remove the paper and beans and return the pastry to the over for 5 minutes, until it's dry.

Brush the pastry case with egg white and return to the oven for 5 minutes until the egg white has dried and the pastry is shiny. This will prevent the pastry going soggy once the filling is poured in. Now lower the oven temperature to 150°C (300°F) or gas mark 2.

FOR THE FILLING: Whisk the caster sugar and eggs until foamy. Beat in the cream, then the lemon zest and juice. Pour into the tart case and return to the oven for 40–50 minutes until just set. Don't worry if it's wobbly in the centre as it will set as it cools.

Leave it to cool, slip out of the tin, then dust with extra icing sugar.

THE COLOUR
green

GREEN IS THE COLOUR OF NATURE, WHERE WE GO TO REFRESH OURSELVES AND RECHARGE OUR BATTERIES AFTER A BUSY DAY OR WEEK. GREEN IS THE MIDDLE COLOUR OF THE COLOUR SPECTRUM AND HOLDS THE BALANCE BETWEEN THE COLD BLUES AND WARM YELLOWS. YELLOW IS THE LAST COLOUR OF THE MAGNETIC SIDE OF THE SPECTRUM AND BLUE THE FIRST OF THE ELECTRIC SIDE SO, IF YOU ARE FEELING OFF-BALANCE, GREEN IS THE COLOUR THAT WILL HELP BRING YOU BACK TO CENTRE. THIS SENSE OF BALANCE MAKES GREEN ONE OF THE SAFEST COLOURS, AS IT RESTORES STABILITY. THIS MAY EXPLAIN WHY MANY MEDICAL AND THERAPEUTIC ENVIRONMENTS ARE GREEN. NOTE THE SYMBOL OF A GREEN CROSS OUTSIDE A PHARMACY.

Those who love the colour green are often seeking balance and harmony. Their perception and awareness in relationships is good and they are kind and generous. They are great at joining clubs and enjoy being out and about. They often have big appetites for both food and gossip. People who like green are brilliant organisers as they are meticulous and truly have an enviable ability to recognise the essentials of any situation.

People who love green can often be quite conventional and enjoy a steady routine. They dislike sudden surprises and are less inclined to take risks. People who dislike the colour may tend to be resistant to the established way of seeing or doing things.

WHAT IS YOUR COLOUR PERSONALITY? TO FIND OUT TURN TO PAGE 2.

THE GREEN COLOUR PERSONALITY

- BALANCED
- ENVIRONMENTALLY AWARE
- CAN EXERCISE SELF-CONTROL
- LIKES FINANCES AND MATERIAL WEALTH
- LOVES PROPERTY AND REAL ESTATE
- LOVES OPEN SPACES AND NEEDS ROOM TO MOVE AROUND IN
- LOVES HOME LIFE AND GOOD FOOD
- EXTREMELY ROMANTIC AND FEMININE
- LOVES PARTNERSHIP – LOVES TO HAVE CLOSE FRIENDS
- TWO FEET FIRMLY PLACED ON THE GROUND
- LIKES GOING PLACES

Mr Green

Mr Green loves food and will be a terrific dinner party host or BBQ man but what Mr Green is really all about are relationships. He enjoys the art of dating and the ceremony that goes with it. After a reasonable amount of time he will move the relationship along. He won't waste your time as he's either into it or not. If you're in, you can expect to go to fabulous restaurants, holiday resorts and receive beautiful perfumes. Mr Green will be the king in your castle as he loves taking the lead. If he likes you, he will be the one who will ask you out. Do not rush this man and always remember that he likes to be in control of the relationship. He is very affectionate and passionate, with sensitivity in abundance. Work that goddess magic around him and you have a best friend for life.

Ms Green

She is Ms Adaptable – exerting genius skill in flexibility management. She adores nature and it is extremely therapeutic for her to spend time out in the hills and green fields. She loves dressing up – hair, make-up and fashion magazines are all passions that fill her days. She also loves sensuality and luxury and potters around her home endlessly embellishing. She's good at de-cluttering and does not like to hang on to things for too long; contents in the fridge will get the heave-ho daily. Companionship, such as a cat, is vital to Ms Green. She will be seen out at exhibitions, art galleries, wine merchants and any other fun social gatherings.

Young Green

These children are sensitive and display tenderness with hugs and kisses. They are also loveable and playful. In fact, it is advantageous for them to have a pet of their own to play with. They are calm and can play for hours happily imitating and exploring. A cookery course or an art class is beneficial as these activities helps nurture their creative side. Music is also good for them to be around as food, art and music awakens and stimulates the senses – taste, touch, smell, vision and hearing. The younger ones explore their sensitivity in a creative way. They are well-behaved and attentive in school and will thrive when the environment allows them the space to be the star they are; too much discipline or an authoritarian environment will impede their growth.

The Green Parent

The green mum and dad are devoted to their roles. They are fair and work diligently to ensure that their child does not miss out. They encourage their child to get involved and develop skills from an early age. They like discipline and can be strict with their children, though they must watch this tendency so as not to impede their child's growth too much.

The Green Career

The green personality is a money-making machine. Green is the colour of finance so they do well in any related area. They also excel in real estate, industry and make brilliant entrepreneurs. Due to their finance skills, they rarely go bankrupt. They are loyal to co-workers and bosses and the idea of job and financial security is important to them. They will keep their head down until the job is done and have a clever and uncanny ability to bring calmness to a chaotic atmosphere – restoring balance and rhythm.

A GREEN DAY PLAN

EXERCISE – I WILL GO FOR A WALK IN A GREEN OR WOODED AREA AND BREATHE THE FRESH AIR.

CLOTHES – I WILL WEAR SOMETHING GREEN TODAY AND KNOW THAT I HAVE MY OWN SPACE.

PERSONALITY – I AM A LOVING PERSON.

Guide To Wearing Green

When you wear green you ooze freshness and show the world that you have a big heart that is kind and generous. This makes green a great colour to wear if you are starting a new relationship or on a new date with someone you really fancy, as it encourages balanced judgement. There are over 40 shades to choose from, so experiment and you are sure to find one that suits you. For example, dark greens can indicate that you are unreliable or have a belief system that everything revolves around you; this can be dangerous if you are out on a first date. Emerald green unlocks your heart and shows that you are generous. It can work magic, making us feel brilliant when we're out and about. Olive green looks great on brunette/auburn toned hair as it brings an earthiness to your look and is very feminine. Fresh springtime greens are gorgeous – showing the world you feel alive and open to a fresh start.

Green is a brilliant colour to wear when starting a new project, either personal or work-related, as it brings with it a sense of freshness and symbolises a new beginning. It also helps give a sense of space and supports the new ground you hope to tread. Eye make-up is an area for experimentation. Green eyeshadow looks especially good on brown or hazel eyes.

GREEN EXERCISE AND LEISURE ACTIVITIES

Hill-walking or any activity that involves being in the 'outdoors' are enjoyed by the green personality. Safari's makes an ideal trip for holiday time. Scuba-diving, theatre outings, restaurants and dining activities would all be enjoyed by Mr or Ms Green alike.

DIARY

In Columbia I met people who worked in the infamous emerald mines. The rich green emeralds are among the finest in the world and are believed to enhance the clairvoyance of the wearer. They are the birth stone for May and the traditional gift for the 55th wedding anniversary.

WHEN TO USE GREEN

If you find yourself at a crossroads in life and are unsure of the direction to go – surround yourself with green as it will help you make decisions and foster your imagination. When you are feeling hemmed in, green will help you to create a personal space to operate in. It is a useful colour for people who are claustrophobic and is a great colour to help you open up if you are feeling heavy-hearted or closed off.

GREEN has a calming effect on the blood, as its balancing properties realign the body's energies, so it heals nervous tension. The calming quality of green can be used success-fully to calm hyperactivity in children as it gives reassurance. Use green when you are meeting new people as it will help you to remain balanced and true to your own personality. As green is also associated with kindness you will come across as sensitive and sympathetic.

WHEN TO AVOID GREEN

Avoid green when you are feeling jealous, 'green with envy', or in any way depressed as it can exacerbate the negative emotions and further drain emotional energy. The hypochondriac often has an over-abundant dose of green energy, so avoid green if you are constantly talking about your health and other ailments.

THOUGHT FOR THE DAY

This is a great day to start something new.

BEST COLOUR PERSONALITY MATCH

A red personality is best suited to a green personality. The green tends to have the ability to calm the energetic forces and nature of the red personality. Both like exuberant and luxurious belongings and the mix of raw and sensuous passion ignites the lights between the pairing.

WORST COLOUR PERSONALITY MATCH

Green and blue personalities may have some communication problems. The blue personality enjoys being in control and this may hinder the green personality's progress as they like to have their space and work at their own pace. Both can be very relaxed and so it works best if there is a vibrant and energetic colour mix to keep things moving along.

⊕ Green **Health**

What Is Your Tongue Saying About You?

Most of our 10,000 taste buds are on the tongue. Problems with taste are the result of such things as smoking, colds, zinc deficiency, ageing, high blood pressure, diabetes and certain medications. An unpleasant taste could be due to dry tongue, dental problems, certain drugs like Captopril, a drug commonly used to treat high blood pressure, zinc supplements or throat lozenges which can trigger a metallic taste.

The tongue is an important indicator of health. When you enter a doctor's surgery or acupuncture clinic one of the first things your medical therapist will do is look at your tongue. What they see can tell a lot about your state of physical and emotional health.

A good healthy tongue will be smooth, supple and slightly moist, pale red in colour, with a very thin white film. Certain foods and drinks discolour the tongue. A white patch could indicate friction from dentures for example or infection such as candida, which is a single-celled fungus that is always present in the genital and intestinal tract. If it is present in disproportionate quantities it can cause infection. When candida fungus infects the mouth it is called thrush and white sores form on the tongue, gums and inside the cheeks.

What Is Your Tongue Saying About You?

A midline crack not reaching the tip indicates that the stomach is weak and digestion may be poor. If this is the case you may feel bloated or have energy slumps after lunch. Your body may be nutrient deficient and so it would be advisable for you to focus on eating warm soups and stews as they are easily digested. Eating millet porridge would also help. Avoid fizzy drinks and drink lots of warm or tepid water.

If you have a sore tongue it indicates that you are nutrient deficient, often iron and Vitamin B6 or Niacin (B3), which are needed for proper circulation and healthy skin. These nutrients also aid in the functioning of the nervous system, in the metabolism of carbohydrates, fats and proteins and in the production of hydrochloric acid for the digestive system. Take a liquid mineral supplement and drink nettle tea to help combat this.

If you look at your tongue and the tip is red it indicates emotional upset or emotional stress. Emotional stress upsets the normal energy balance and will cause the inner energy to stagnate, leaving you feeling tired and irritated. It will interfere with the hormone balance and will cause illness if the body has to sustain this imbalance for a period of time. Ginseng is recommended for helping the body to deal with stress and to help you restore your natural balance. (See The Colour Orange chapter.)

Have you got a horizontal crack in your tongue (often referred to as a 'geographic tongue')? **Cracking on the tongue is a sign of a malabsorption of nutrients, especially Vitamin B, and is often accompanied by energy slumps.** If you have small cracks, grooves or a horizontal crack it will have taken some time for this to develop and it is recommended that you take a Vitamin B supplement daily. Aloe Vera juice or an echinacea tincture may help the body to move lymph and eliminate toxins that are impeding nutrient absorption.

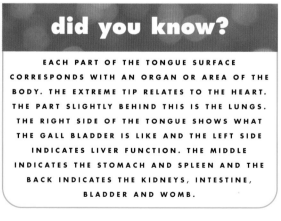

did you know?

EACH PART OF THE TONGUE SURFACE CORRESPONDS WITH AN ORGAN OR AREA OF THE BODY. THE EXTREME TIP RELATES TO THE HEART. THE PART SLIGHTLY BEHIND THIS IS THE LUNGS. THE RIGHT SIDE OF THE TONGUE SHOWS WHAT THE GALL BLADDER IS LIKE AND THE LEFT SIDE INDICATES LIVER FUNCTION. THE MIDDLE INDICATES THE STOMACH AND SPLEEN AND THE BACK INDICATES THE KIDNEYS, INTESTINE, BLADDER AND WOMB.

A little girl showing off her tongue on the island of Amantani, Lake Titicacca, South America.

A SELECTION OF GREEN FOODS

BROCCOLI

BRUSSEL SPROUTS

CABBAGE

CAULIFLOWER

CHINESE LEAF

KALE

SPROUTING

BROCCOLI

SWISS CHARD

KIWI

PEAS

SPINACH

These foods are rich in detoxifying sulforaphane, isothiocyanates and indoles. These all-powerful phytonutrients play a key role in stimulating cancer fighting liver enzymes. In 1992, cancer researchers at John Hopkins University, USA tested a range of vegetable extracts in their laboratories. They found that the phytonutrient sulphoraphane seemed to be the chemical that prevented the cancerous tumours from forming. Research is still on-going in this area.

Sulphoraphane is a sulphur-containing compound that is not only responsible for giving broccoli its characteristic bitter smell and taste but acts as a built-in pesticide, designed to repel anything that tries to invade it.

A SELECTION OF YELLOW/GREEN FOODS

AVOCADO

COLLARD GREENS

COURGETTES

CUCUMBERS

GREEN BEANS

GREEN PEPPERS

YELLOW PEPPERS

HONEYDEW MELONS

KIWI

MUSTARD GREENS

PEAS

ROMAINE OR COS LETTUCE

SPINACH

SWEETCORN

These foods are good sources of eye-friendly lutein and xezanthin. These phytonutrients have attracted universal scientific interest in recent years as research has shown that they could contain properties that help in fighting cataracts and macular degeneration. Green/yellow foods act on the nervous system, stimulate the intellect, help the liver with the elimination of toxins, aid indigestion and help to combat skin problems.

Green and green/yellow foods also have a calming effect on the blood. Many are high in sugars such as sucrose and fructose, which means they provide quick energy to satisfy hunger. The high levels of sugar could have a negative, pro-inflammatory influence on the blood, if it wasn't for the fact that many of these foods are high in fibre, which slows down the absorption of the sugars into the blood stream. To maximize your intake of these phytonutrients, eat the whole fruit including pith, flesh and peel where applicable, as many of the beneficial nutrients are concentrated in the most colourful parts.

A SELECTION WHITE/GREEN FOODS

ARTICHOKES

ASPARAGUS

CELERY

CHIVES

ENDIVES

GARLIC

LEEKS

MUSHROOMS

ONIONS

SHALLOTS

White/green foods offer multiple health benefits. Garlic and onions are a rich source of tumour fighting allicin – a compound that inhibits the production of enzymes responsible for creating inflammatory prostaglandins and thromboxanes. (These are two types of autocrine hormones known as eicosanoids that produce inflammation in the body.) Mushrooms contain other disease-battling chemicals and the rest contain powerful cell-protecting flavonoids.

TINA'S BEAUTY TIP

Blend 1 tbsp fresh cream with 1 tbsp cucumber, melon and pumpkin seeds in a blender. Apply to face for 30 minutes and rinse off with water.

A SELECTION OF HERBS

BASIL

CORIANDER

ROSEMARY

THYME

OREGANO

MINT

Culinary herbs provide exceptional anti-oxidant and anti-inflammatory protection. We consume them in smaller quantities to other foods but they can be used liberally in many dishes. Try seasoning fish, vegetables and fruit a little more as nothing in the plant world can rival the many medicinal properties of herbs and spices.

Kiwi

An American study ranked KIWIFRUIT as the most nutritious of 27 popular fruits. It has a high Vitamin C content and its juice can also block the formation of nitrosamine, a potential cancer causing agent.

Kiwifruit is particularly high in potassium – a mineral that is essential to make sure all body cells are functioning properly. It also contains an enzyme called actinidin which is an efficient aid to digestion and has fibre and a particular type of mucilage which makes it an excellent yet gentle laxative.

Nutrition
- Vitamin C
- Potassium
- Fibre

Good For
- Skin – due to high potassium
- Digestive challenges
- Boosting the immune system

How Much To Eat
- 1 kiwi a day

Phytonutrients
- Chlorophyll
- Beta-carotene

Cucumber

CUCUMBER works great in juices as it is a terrific beauty food. It also helps to relieve tired or puffy eyes as cucumber is high in organic sodium.

Nutrition
- Water 96.4%
- Tiny amount Vitamin A
- Minute amount iodine

Good For
- A natural diuretic
- Skin health

How Much To Eat
- Low in calories, high in water
- Eat regularly

Phytonutrients
- Chlorophyll (See Glossary for more details)

Cabbage

The majority of the nutrients in CABBAGE are found in the dark outer leaves, so make sure you do not get rid of them. Cooked cabbage may be indigestible so steam or boil it in its own juices. When cooking cabbage, make sure it is only cooked briefly to conserve the required Vitamin C.

Nutrition
- Rich in sulphur compounds
- Iron
- Folate
- Vitamin C

Good For
- Skin
- Anaemia
- Easing stress

How Much To Eat
- 2 tbsp portion size (100g) – five to nine a day

Phytonutrients
- Beta-carotene
- Glucosinolates
- Lutein

did you know?

DESPITE ITS NAME, KIWIFRUIT ORIGINALLY CAME FROM CHINA AND WAS CALLED 'CHINESE GOOSEBERRY' BUT NEW ZEALAND GROWERS HAVE POPULARIZED IT WORLDWIDE.

IN JULY 1940 A COMPREHENSIVE REPORT ON CHLOROPHYLL, WRITTEN BY DR BENJAMIN GURSKIN, THE DIRECTOR OF EXPERIMENTAL PATHOLOGY AT TEMPLE UNIVERSITY, WAS PUBLISHED IN THE AMERICAN JOURNAL OF SURGERY. THE REPORT FOCUSED ON 1,200 PATIENTS WHO WERE TREATED WITH CHLOROPHYLL. THE REPORT STATED THAT ALL PATIENTS HAD MADE SIGNIFICANT IMPROVEMENTS IN AFTER SURGERY CARE.

GLUCOSINOLATES ARE THE PHYTONUTRIENTS FOUND IN CRUCIFEROUS VEGETABLES SUCH AS CABBAGE, BROCCOLI AND TURNIP. VERY HIGH INTAKES OF THESE FOODS, ESPECIALLY RAW CABBAGE, MAY CAUSE A CONDITION KNOWN AS GOITRE. THIS IS A SWELLING OF THE THYROID GLAND THAT IS LOCATED IN THE NECK AND IF IODINE LEVELS IN THE BLOOD ARE LOW IT IS DIFFICULT TO MAKE THYROID HORMONES.

Broccoli

BROCCOLI is an excellent source of sulforaphane – a type of isothio-cyanate which can inhibit the action of cancer causing agents. Researchers from the Institute of Food Research in the UK have recently bred a super-broccoli which is a cultivated broccoli crossed with a wild relative that has much higher levels of sulforaphane. A team of scientists in the US actually patented this cultivation technique and these broccoli sprouts are now selling in shops and health food stores.

Nutrition
- Vitamin E, A, C
- Iron
- Folate
- Calcium

Good For
- Healthy eyes and skin
- Combating stress
- Boosting immune system
- Easing fatigue

How Much To Eat
- 100g broccoli provides ⅓ of the daily Vitamin E requirement

Phytonutrients
- Carotenoids • Sulforaphane
- Glucosinolates • Lutein

Courgettes

COURGETTES are baby marrows. They are usually green in colour but there are light green and yellow varieties as well. They belong to the same family as melons, pumpkins and cucumbers.

Buy and eat them quickly as storing in the fridge makes the texture deteriorate.

Nutrition
- Folic acid – 100g portion will supply more than a quarter daily need of folic acid
- Rich source of potassium

Good For
- Healthy skin
- Low calorie diets

How Much To Eat
- 100g serving contains only 18 kcal

Phytonutrients
- Beta-carotene

Spinach

One of the great virtues of SPINACH is its ability to protect against eye disease – namely ARMD (Age-Related Macular Degeneration). Scientists suggest that this is not due to its beta-carotene content but to two other compounds, lutein and zeaxanthin, which are phytonutrients that are part of the carotenoid family. A study in the US found that people who ate spinach or green leafy vegetables (five or more portions a week) had 43% lower risk of developing ARMD. Eating spinach regularly may also improve vision for some ARMD sufferers.

Nutrition
- Folate
- Vitamin E

Good For
- Healthy eyes
- Healthy colon

How Much To Eat
- Average portion 90g or 2 tbsp
- Eat 5 portions of lutein-rich (green and leafy) foods a week

Phytonutrients
- Beta-carotene • Indoles
- Sulforaphane • Lutein
- Zeaxanthin

did you know?

BROCCOLI MEANS "LITTLE ARMS" IN ITALIAN. BROCCOLI IS PART OF THE CRUCIFEROUS CLAN. IT IS A RELATION OF CAULIFLOWER, CABBAGE, BRUSSEL SPROUTS AND SPINACH. YOU CAN BUY LIME GREEN, WHITE AND PURPLE BROCCOLI TOO.

FOR A QUICK VITAMIN A FIX – LIGHTLY COOK SOME BUCKWHEAT PASTA, ADD TWO GRATED COURGETTES, DRIZZLE A TBSP OLIVE OIL AND SOME CHEESE SHAVINGS.

SPINACH WAS FIRST CULTIVATED IN ANCIENT PERSIA; NOW CALLED IRAN. IN THE 1930S IT WAS HAILED THE "WONDER FOOD", DUE TO ITS HIGH IRON CONTENT.

GREEN HERBS

Peas

Don't make **PEAS** the only greens you eat as they contain phytate (phytic acid), which can stop iron, calcium and zinc absorption.

Nutrition
- Vitamin A, C
- Protein
- Folic acid
- Thiamine

Good For
- Relieving stress
- Boosting digestion
- Boosting energy
- A healthy heart

How Much To Eat
- 150g supplies more than the required daily intake of Thiamine B1 (its main function is the conversion of carbohydrates into energy).

Phytonutrients
- Lutein

ROSEMARY

Good For
- Promoting perspiration
- Natural diuretic

Did You Know?
Rosemary is a strong anti-oxidant and the flavonoids that it contains aid the elimination of uric acid, the end product of the metabolism. If uric acid accumulates in the blood and tissues it can cause a type of arthritis called gout.

BASIL

Good For
- Acting as a tonic for the nervous system (due to the volatile oils and tannins it contains)
- Easing mental fatigue (Try eating it when studying for exams)

Did You Know?
There are many types of basil – all of which have different flavours. Sweet basil or Genoa has a spicy smell and is used extensively in Italian cooking. Opal basil has purple leaves and Greek basil has smaller leaves with a pungent flavour. Basil should be torn, not chopped, as you risk losing some of the flavour.

MINT

Good For
- Stimulating the nervous system
- Promoting restful sleep
- Asthma and bronchitis challenges

Did You Know?
3% of the total population suffers from asthma. Most sufferers are children and twice as many more boys than girls have asthma.

TINA'S TIP

Lutein, the phytonutrient in peas, is absorbed more efficiently with a little oil. Mediterraneans are famous for drizzling oil over their vegetables. It is recommended that you eat the following as part of your 5 a day to get the lutein you need: Broccoli – 350g or one small bunch; Peas – 7 tablespoons; Cabbage – 1 large tablespoon.

TINA'S TIP

Burn rosemary oil if you are feeling emotional or restless as it is very soothing. It is also good for muscle cramp. If you get muscular cramp, the following are also helpful in soothing the pain: bananas, avocados, nuts, seeds, tonic water, olive oil and buckwheat.

Courgette and Broccoli Stir-Fry

SERVES 2

2 TBSP OLIVE OIL

2 CARROTS CUT INTO MATCHSTICK (JULIENNE) STRIPS

225G (8 OZ) SMALL BROCCOLI FLORETS – HALVES

1 COURGETTE – SLICED

1 LARGE CLOVE GARLIC – FINELY CHOPPED

2 ½ CM (1 IN) PIECE OF FRESH ROOT GINGER – PEELED AND FINELY CHOPPED OR
    GRATED

115G (3 OZ) BEAN SPROUTS

1 TBSP FRESH LEMON JUICE

1 TBSP LIGHT SOY SAUCE

FRESHLY GROUND BLACK PEPPER

250G SPELT PASTA

Heat the oil in a non-stick wok or large frying pan. Add the carrots, courgettes, broccoli, garlic and ginger. Stir-fry over a high heat for 4–5 minutes.

Add the bean sprouts, lemon juice and soy sauce, and stir-fry for a further 1–2 minutes; until the vegetables are just cooked.

Season to taste with ground black pepper. Serve with spelt pasta.

Broccoli and Potatoes with Tahini Dressing

SERVES 4

BROCCOLI AND POTATOES

800G (27 OZ) POTATOES – QUARTERED

250G (9 OZ) BROCCOLI – CUT INTO SMALL FLORETS

CHIVES – FINELY CHOPPED

TAHINI DRESSING

3 TBSP TAHINI

3 TBSP LEMON JUICE

3 TBSP COLD WATER

1 CLOVE GARLIC – CRUSHED

1/2 TSP SALT

Boil the potatoes in lightly salted water and cool under cold running water.

Steam the broccoli until tender and cool under cold running water.

Put the potatoes and broccoli into a serving bowl.

Combine the ingredients for the tahini dressing and mix gently with the vegetables.

Garnish with chives. Serve with a salad such as: baby spinach and watercress salad (recipe below).

Baby Spinach and Watercress Salad

SERVES 4

1 TBSP SESAME SEEDS

200G (7 OZ) WASHED BABY SPINACH LEAVES

2 BUNCHES WATERCRESS – COARSELY CHOPPED (DISCARD THE THICK ENDS OF THE STALKS)

1 STICK OF CELERY – FINELY CHOPPED

20 FRESH RASPBERRIES

Toast the sesame seeds in a dry frying pan.

Place the baby spinach and watercress in a salad bowl with the celery and raspberries on top.

Garnish with the toasted sesame seeds.

Drizzle with dressing (See The Colour Gold chapter for Five of the Best Dressings).

Mixed Club Chargrilled Vegetables

SERVES 4

2 FENNEL BULBS

1 BUNCH OF ASPARAGUS

2 COURGETTES – SLICED

2 SWEETCORN COBS

1 AUBERGINE

1 RED PEPPER

1 ORANGE PEPPER

SALT AND GROUND PEPPER

CITRUS DRESSING

LEMON JUICE

FLAT LEAF PARSLEY

CLOVE OF GARLIC

3 TBSP OLIVE OIL

Slice the fennel bulbs into quarters lengthways. Cut diagonal slices. Cut the peppers into quarters and de-seed and finally cut the aubergine in 1 cm slices lengthways.

Once you have prepared all the vegetables you can just simply brush them with olive oil, season with salt and pepper and put onto the grill in the correct cooking order. The corn, fennel and aubergine will take the longest, so they go on first. Then add the peppers and courgettes and finally the asparagus.

Allow 30 minutes grilling for the first lot. The asparagus will only need 10 minutes. Mix all dressing ingredients together.

Serve the citrus dressing with the chargrilled vegetables.

Zingy Stir-Fry

SERVES 2 GENEROUSLY

2 TBSP VEGETABLE OIL

2 CLOVES GARLIC – CHOPPED

1 RED CHILLI – SEEDED AND
   CHOPPED

1 LEVEL TSP GINGER – FRESH
   CHOPPED

1 KILO (2 LB) BROCCOLI –
   TRIMMED

1 RED ONION – FINELY SLICED

JUICE OF 1 LIME AND HALF ITS
   GRATED ZEST

2 LEVEL TBSP SOY SAUCE

1 TSP RUNNY HONEY

Heat the oil in a wok. When hot; add the garlic, chilli and ginger.

Fry; stirring for about 30 seconds before adding the broccoli and the red onion.

Stir and fry for another 30 seconds before adding the lime juice and zest.

A minute or so later add the soy sauce and the honey. Now taste a piece of broccoli. I like mine crunchy, but keep going another minute or so if you don't feel it is done.

This stir-fry is fantastic with seafood – a few scallops or prawns, or a couple of squid, cut into rings, would make great partners. Alternatively (and this would be much easier on your pocket) – pop it on a plate next to a whole grilled mackerel for a very virtuous supper.

Cauliflower Steamed in Olive Oil and Garlic

SERVES 2 GENEROUSLY

3 TBSP OLIVE OIL

2 TBSP MINCED FRESH GARLIC

1 MEDIUM HEAD CAULIFLOWER
   – CLEANED AND CUT INTO
   FLORETS

2 TBSP DRIED OREGANO

SALT AND PEPPER TO TASTE

WATER AS NEEDED

Heat the olive oil in a large pot over medium/high heat. Add the garlic. Sauté.

Add the cauliflower.

Season with oregano, salt and pepper.

Add just enough water to cover the bottom of the pan. Cover; reduce heat to medium/low on the hob, and cook until very tender for about 30 minutes. Stir occasionally and add a little more water as needed.

TINA'S TIP

Drizzle a little oil over the cooked vegetables before serving.

Creamy Guacamole

SERVES 2

1 RIPE AVOCADO

1 GARLIC CLOVE – CRUSHED

1–2 TBSP LIME OR LEMON
 JUICE – FRESHLY SQUEEZED

1 TBSP OF EXTRA-VIRGIN OLIVE
 OIL

1 TBSP OF CORIANDER –
 FRESHLY CHOPPED

SEA SALT AND FRESHLY GROUND PEPPER

Scoop out the avocado flesh. Mash with a fork.

Add the garlic, lime or lemon juice, oil and coriander.

Now add salt and pepper to taste.

Cover with cling film immediately, as fresh guacamole discolours quickly.

Ideal with potato chips, bread or crackers.

Coriander Salsa

SERVES 2

10 CAPERS – CHOPPED FINELY

1 TBSP DIJON MUSTARD

HANDFUL OF MIXED FRESH HERBS – BASIL, MINT AND CORIANDER

3 ANCHOVY FILLETS – FINELY CHOPPED

25 ML (1 OZ) WHITE WINE VINEGAR

50 ML (2 OZ) OLIVE OIL

SALT AND PEPPER

Combine the above ingredients either by hand or in a blender and serve with fresh sea bass or
a fish of your own choice.

Vegetable Crumble

SERVES 4

200G (7 OZ) FLOUR

2 TBSP FLAKED ALMONDS

125G (4 ½ OZ) VEGETABLE MARGARINE

1 RED ONION – SLICED

2 MEDIUM CARROTS – SLICED

2 STICKS CELERY – SLICED

A QUARTER HEAD OF MEDIUM SIZED
   CABBAGE – SHREDDED

125G (4 ½ OZ) HAZEL NUTS – CHOPPED

1 TBSP YEAST EXTRACT DISSOLVED IN
   175 ML (6 FL OZ) BOILING WATER

225G (8 OZ) TOMATOES – SKINNED
   AND CHOPPED

SEA SALT AND PEPPER TO TASTE

FLAKED ALMONDS TO GARNISH

Blend the flour with the almonds and half the margarine, keeping a tablespoon of flour aside.
Melt the rest of the margarine in a large pan and gently sauté the onions, carrots, celery and
cabbage until soft.

Add the hazelnuts and heat through. Stir in the remaining flour.

Pour in the yeast extract mixture and stir until it thickens.

Add the tomatoes, season with the salt and pepper, and pour into a greased casserole dish.

Then sprinkle the crumble mixture on top, garnish with flaked almonds and cook in the oven
for approximately 1 hour at 180°C (350°F) or gas mark 4 until golden brown. Serve with
steamed french beans and sweetcorn.

Basil Pesto

SERVES 2

110G (4 OZ) FRESH BASIL LEAVES

150 ML (5 ½ OZ) EXTRA-VIRGIN OLIVE OIL

2 CLOVES OF GARLIC

25G (1 OZ) PINE KERNELS

50G (2 OZ) PARMESAN – FRESHLY GRATED

PINCH OF SALT

Put the basil, olive oil, pine kernels, garlic, salt and
parmesan into a food processor.

Process until the ingredients are blended but not puréed.

Serve with wholemeal pasta of your choice or
as a spread on spelt bread or with turkey.

A great lunchtime treat!

Spinach and Rasher Bread

MAKES 1 LOAF

8-10 PORTIONS

225 ML (7 ½ FL OZ) WARM WATER

1 TSP DRIED YEAST

1 TSP SUGAR

1 TSP FULL VEGETABLE OIL

1 RED ONION – FINELY CHOPPED

100G (3 ½ OZ) RINDLESS SMOKED
   RASHERS – CHOPPED

150G (5 ½ OZ) BABY SPINACH LEAVES

340G (12 OZ) STRONG FLOUR

1 TSP NUTMEG

50G (2 OZ) PARMESAN CHEESE –
   GRATED

Put the warm water into a bowl and sprinkle the dried yeast over it and add the sugar. Leave for 10 minutes.

Grease the tin. Heat the oil in a pan and fry the rashers and onions until golden brown.

Add the spinach leaves and allow them to wilt. Set aside.

In a bowl sift the flour and nutmeg, make a well in the centre and add the yeast mixture. Then add the rashers, onion and spinach mixture. Turn out onto a floured board and knead for 5 minutes.

Return to a clean bowl and place a damp dish cloth over it and place in a warm spot for 2 hours, until it has doubled in size.

Place on a floured board and knead again.

Place into the loaf tin and place the grated parmesan cheese on top.

Bake for one hour at 200°C (390°F) or gas mark 6.

Delicious with a slice of Brie and cranberry chutney.

Raita

SERVES 2

A QUARTER MEDIUM SIZED CUCUMBER

150 ML (4 FL OZ) NATURAL YOGHURT

½ TSP OF WHOLE CUMIN SEEDS

1 TBSP OF CORIANDER – FRESHLY
   CHOPPED

Chop the cucumber up into small dices.

Roast the cumin seeds in the oven for about 3 minutes.

Mix the cumin, yoghurt, cucumber and coriander in a bowl.

This is gorgeous with vegetable or lamb curry.

Mint and Raisin Spread

SERVES 2

250G (9 OZ) RAISINS

A HANDFUL OF FRESH MINT LEAVES

HOT WATER

Put the raisins and the mint in a blender; adding a little hot water at a time until the mixture blends to form a smooth paste. Serve spread on freshly toasted Four Seed Bread (See Gold Chapter for Four Seed Bread recipe).

Courgette Tea Buns

MAKES 12 BUNS

50G (2 OZ) BUTTER

3 EGGS

250 ML (8 FL OZ) VEGETABLE OIL

300G (10 ½ OZ) SUGAR

2 COURGETTES – GRATED

280G (10 OZ) PLAIN FLOUR

2 TSP BICARBONATE SODA

1 TSP BAKING POWDER

1 TSP SALT

1 TSP MIXED SPICE

1 TSP CINNAMON

100G (3 ½ OZ) CHOPPED ALMONDS

Preheat oven to 180°C (350°F) or gas mark 4. Grease the bun tin. Melt the butter over a low heat. Set aside.

Using an electric mixer beat the eggs and oil together until thick. Beat in the sugar. Add the melted butter, salt, mixed spice, cinnamon and grated courgettes. Set aside.

In another bowl sift the flour, bicarbonate of soda and baking powder together. Then add the courgette mixture and stir in the chopped almonds.

Spoon the mixture into the bun tins and bake for 1 hour.

Leave to set in the tin for about 10 minutes before turning out.

Delicious with soup.

THE COLOUR
blue

BLUE IS UNIVERSALLY THE MOST POPULAR COLOUR. IT IS THE COLOUR OF THE SKY ON A CLEAR DAY AND WHEN WE THINK OF THE COLOUR BLUE, WATER USUALLY COMES TO MIND. THE BLUE OF THE SEA OFFERS, TO MANY, A TRANQUIL PLACE TO CONTEMPLATE LIFE IN A REJUVENATING SETTING.

Blue is associated with intelligence and the ability to conciliate or use words to create a sense of peace. Blue is peace with a purpose. **HONESTY AND INTEGRITY ARE BLUE QUALITIES.** When we describe someone as a "true blue" we mean we can count on them, as they are loyal and trustworthy. Blue people prove to be very persuasive; they can cajole you into doing what they want almost without you realising it.

Although they seem cool and confident, blue lovers can sometimes be vulnerable and sensitive. They have a great need to trust and a tendency to form strong attachments. Betrayal is the worst way to hurt a blue personality. The blue personality can have perfectionist tendencies which can make them unrealistic and demanding in their relationships with others.

A dislike of the colour may mean restlessness and a desire for stimulation and excitement. People who dislike blue often have a longing for the good things in life and wish they did not have to work so hard to get them. To these people, blue represents sadness and the colour may induce melancholy.

WHAT IS YOUR COLOUR PERSONALITY? TO FIND OUT TURN TO PAGE 2.

THE BLUE COLOUR PERSONALITY

- PATIENT
- PHILOSOPHICAL IN NATURE
- EXCELLENT HEALERS
- THEY MAKE LOYAL FRIENDS AND ASSOCIATES
- INTEGRITY IS VITAL FOR THEM TO WORK AND LIVE IN BALANCE
- THEY ENJOY QUIET TIME TO CONTEMPLATE
- EMOTIONAL AND UNRELIABLE WHEN OUT OF BALANCE
- SUPERSTITIOUS
- THEY CAN FIND IT HARD TO FORGIVE IF YOU CROSS THEM

Mr Blue

The blue male is calm, cool and organised. He is wildly romantic and believes in love at first sight. If he has his sights on you, expect to be showered with treats and flowers. His charm will make you feel so respected and he will express his emotional needs well. He loves to speak the truth – it's really important to him. He is the cosmic philosopher who enjoys exploring the hidden secrets that the universe may hold. He likes his own space and adores his independence; you make a foolish mistake to interfere with his chill down time.

Ms Blue

The blue female loves male company and is the kittenish temptress. Her only demands from you are love and romance and if the attracted partner delivers, he will surely have a great time. Although she is dreamy, soft and uncompetitive, the blue female is no pushover; she will defend herself and may well have a boxing glove under that gentle exterior. She will always remain loyal. She is always immaculately groomed with exquisite taste. Ms Blue is feminine, dreamy and delightful company.

Young Blue

The blue child seems docile and charming, but their parents need to be prepared for the antics and changeable moods of this little bundle. This child is constantly on the move and strives to achieve a lot daily. Strong-willed, blue children do what they want to; they certainly keep you busy. They leave a trail of overturned objects in their path. They love to go walk about; to explore what is around the next corner. They absolutely adore the beach environment or any space that houses creepy crawlies and small animals, rocks, seashells and weeds. They love creative pursuits and are extremely artistic. Keep them busy drawing, painting and always have a good supply of materials. School can challenge them as their concentration span is short. They can be high achievers if they desire it and often get involved in humanitarian causes.

The Blue Parent

More than any other colour, the blue parent takes the responsibility of parenting seriously and protects their child forever. They can find it challenging to see their children grow up and move into adulthood. Blue parents have very generous hearts. For the blue mother, motherhood is a vocation and she listens attentively to her child. She can live out her own childhood dreams through them. Discipline is lax with the blue mother but she will push her children to achieve. The blue father is very laid back but places a strong emphasis on education.

The Blue Career

Brilliant with numbers – the blue personality can apply itself to auditing and accounting. They are good at science also as they are highly inventive not only in the science arena but also in the arts. The blue personality keeps their cards close to their chests in business; valuing integrity, they work with a discreet and tactful manner. They will complete any project they take on as they are very conscientious and never give up. The blue careerists love to have things in order and routines are vital to their success.

A BLUE DAY PLAN

EXERCISE – GO FOR A SWIM OR DO AN AQUA AEROBICS CLASS IN A POOL OR IN THE OCEAN.

CLOTHES – WEAR SOMETHING BLUE TODAY (PERHAPS A SCARF NEAR YOUR NECK AS THE THROAT AREA IS GOVERNED BY THE COLOUR BLUE).

FOOD – DRINK PLENTY OF WATER TODAY. IT HELPS THE BODY ELIMINATE TOXINS THAT CAN CAUSE POOR SKIN AND DELICATE HEALTH. YOU WILL LOOK BRILLIANT AND AGE WELL TOO!

PERSONALITY – I AM MS/MR LOYAL – I CAN COMMUNICATE WELL WITH WORDS AND WILL USE THIS POWER TODAY.

SHADES OF BLUE

There are so many shades of blue to choose from, you will surely find one that suits you.

ROYAL BLUE: wearing royal blue or navy demonstrates that you are reliable and productive; this is a colour you might wear to a job interview or as part of a work uniform.

SKY BLUE: this will help you keep calm and has a romantic appeal to it.

POWDER BLUE OR PALE BLUE: these tones can help bring something positive to a harsh environment and looks wonderful on fair-haired people. Pastel blue suits a complexion that has fair, translucent or rose undertones.

TURQUOISE: this is truly a brilliant colour and it makes people feel magical. This colour is good if your complexion is peachy, golden, beige or ivory with brown, chestnut or red hair. Try using turquoise mascara to bring out the whites in your eyes and totally refresh a tired face.

BLUE EXERCISE AND LEISURE ACTIVITIES

The blue personality enjoys any type of water sports like sailing, canoeing, surfing, even swimming. These sports suit Mr and Ms Blue far more than gym activities, as there is an element of freedom involved. They are great performers so joining a drama company or rock band will allow them to be wild. They need an avenue to express creativity and originality.

THOUGHT FOR THE DAY

I am an organised person. I am in complete control.

GUIDE TO
WEARING BLUE

Blue is the colour that cools and calms you so it is a terrific colour to wear in stressful moments, as it relaxes the parasympathetic nervous system. In the 1940s, a Russian Scientist SV Krakov established that the colour red stimulates the sympathetic part of the autonomic nervous system, the part that arouses activity, while blue stimulates the parasympathetic part, the part that encourages tranquillity. These findings were later confirmed in 1958 by Robert Gerard from the USA.

Red has a very positive influence on energising the body when the body is relaxed and healthy to start with but, if the nervous system is tired or stressed at all, red will only exacerbate the irritable tension in the body. So next time you have a hangover or have had a late night watch to see if you automatically select something red to wear. Your body is flagging in energy and you unconsciously know that red will energise you, so the selection is made. In this instance, however, you should pick a blue article of clothing to wear as it will help you go about your daily business, with a sense of tranquillity and calm.

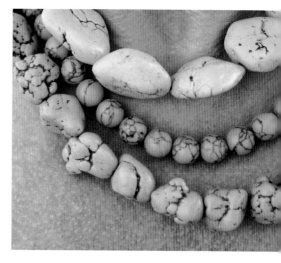

WHEN TO WEAR BLUE

Blue is the colour that governs the throat so if you find it difficult to speak out or cannot find your voice, treat yourself to blue as it is the colour for communication. It will help support your voice and vocal expression and is the colour recommended if you have throat problems. Wear something blue around your neck – a tie, necklace or scarf – when you have to give a presentation. Also always wear blue when you need to express your feelings as it will encourage you to speak the truth.

WHEN TO AVOID WEARING BLUE

Avoid wearing blue if you are feeling cold or stiff as it will add to the uncomfortable feeling. If you are feeling depressed, isolated or lonely, wearing blue will help accelerate these feelings.

did you know?

IN 1990, SCIENTISTS REPORTED AT THE ANNUAL CONFERENCE OF THE AMERICAN ASSOCIATION OF THE ADVANCEMENT OF SCIENCE ON THE SUCCESS IN USING BLUE LIGHT TO TREAT A WIDE VARIETY OF PSYCHOLOGICAL PROBLEMS, INCLUDING ADDICTIONS.

BEST COLOUR PERSONALITY MATCH

Blue personalities get on really well with orange personalities. The blue personality is drawn to the bright and outgoing personality of orange. Orange personalities value their independence; the two personalities share this lifestyle requirement. This means they can respect each other's need for independence and freedom. Orange personalities are good at breaking down barriers in business. This characteristic can be intriguing and challenging for the blue personality and so offers a platform for convivial business relations.

WORST COLOUR PERSONALITY MATCH

Blue and green personalities can clash at times as the green personality can be a little too possessive of the blue personality's time. The green personality may smother the blue in a relationship and restrict blue's independence and freedom. The green personality has a tendency to be demanding; at a party, for example, the green personality will expect all eyes to be on them.

WATER

Water and beauty make perfect companions, as many spa resorts around the world will testify.

Our bodies are composed of 65–70% water; each of the 100 billion cells of the body is made up of mostly water. These cells need constant replenishment to maintain health so the body has to build its own water regulatory system which works automatically day and night.

Drinking water is better than any facial. Skin needs water for elasticity and the lack of it causes dehydration with the result that the skin looks tired, dried out and delicate. If you have dark circles under your eyes it may be indicative that you need hydration; they are a sign that the skin is thin and bruised as the fluid has been drained away.

Water is essential to fat metabolism, as fat is metabolised, water helps flush waste from the body. It also helps combat the sagging skin that can follow fat loss as water plumps up the shrinking cells and leaves the skin clear, healthy and resilient.

It is a powerful detoxification substance as it helps the body flush out poisons from pollutants, junk food and additives. If you are dehydrated, the toxins of the body hang around your liver making you feel tired and sluggish. Water will help flush these toxins away. It will prevent and remedy fluid retention, signs of which include puffy fingers and ankles. If you get headaches, water is the best cure of all.

DID YOU KNOW?

Experts suggest that we should drink at least eight glasses of water (about 2 litres) per day. In 2002, a study from the Dartmouth Medical School in New Hampshire, USA highlighted the probable source of this recommendation. The research showed that information from a study in 1945 was misinterpreted. The report by the US Food and Nutrition Board explained that the body needs one millilitre of water to process each calorie consumed. The average diet is comprised of 2,000 calories, which suggest a 2 litre intake of water. The report did mention a significant fact, however, that most of this water is contained in prepared foods, something that the modern view on water intake overlooks. The debate is on-going.

✚ Blue Health

AS MENTIONED EARLIER IN THIS CHAPTER, THE COLOURS FROM THE BLUE SPECTRUM CAN HELP CALM THE PARASYMPATHETIC NERVOUS SYSTEM, WHICH GOVERNS OUR ABILITY TO RELAX. ALTHOUGH OUR INTENTION IS GENERALLY TO REMAIN CALM, SERENE AND DE-STRESSED, OFTEN LIFE CAN BE DEMANDING AND WE MAY NOT ALWAYS FEEL THAT WE HAVE SUCCESSFULLY DEVELOPED A WORK/LIFE BALANCE. HERE IS AN OPPORTUNITY TO SEE HOW YOUR OWN STRESS LEVELS FAIR. ANSWER THE QUESTIONS BELOW HONESTLY AND THEN READ YOUR SCORE.

Live More – Stress Less Test

This self-evaluating questionnaire will give you an indication of your current stress levels. The more questions you say yes to, the greater your stress level.

Answer: YES   NO

1. Are you stressed?

2. Do you suffer from fatigue?

3. Do you feel you have too much work to do?

4. Are you ever short of breath?

5. Do you feel guilty about taking time off to relax?

6. Does your hand tremble for no reason?

7. Do you feel rushed?

8. Do you have difficulties getting to sleep or staying asleep?

9. Do you have a feeling of tension in the back of your neck or around your stomach?

10. Do you smoke, drink alcohol or eat more than you need?

11. Have you experienced hair loss?

Body Score Guide

0–4: Your stress levels are low. **Comment:** Your lifestyle pattern obviously suits your rhythm.

4–7: Moderately stressed. **Comment:** Take a few hours off and have a little down time. It will help you recharge the batteries and you will have more energy and improved focus when you return to do your next task.

7–10: Your stress levels are high. **Comment:** Obviously this is a busy time in your life. It would be helpful to book a massage, go out for a walk and look at the foods you are eating. Start delegating and ask for some help.

STRESS

Stress is the manifestation of how we handle our life episodes. Some people are innately and genetically good at dealing with stress. The right food choices can radically assist the body in handling stress in a more constructive manner. The more you control your reactions to life situations, the more control you will exercise over your stress levels. When you are under pressure with deadlines, completion dates and targets to attain, it is vital that you control and manage your life in a good way, making healthy food choices and topping up on extra supplements if required. Stress tends to deplete the body of vital nutrients and anyone under long-term pressure needs to be extra careful to incorporate plenty of these into the diet with the right foods, such as fresh fruit, fresh vegetables and pulse vegetables. Vitamin B complex is a great stress buster. However, always check with your health therapist before taking any supplements.

Relaxation, meditation and open-air exercise, combined with small dietary changes can alleviate many symptoms that may cause the body to feel agitated, nervous or irritable.

It is important to remember, however, that a little stress in your life is good as it initiates productivity and motivates us to positive action.

STEPS FOR DEALING WITH STRESS

Eat a nutrient dense whole food diet – wholegrain, pulses, seeds, nuts, oily fish, lean meat and a wide range of colourful fresh fruit and vegetables. Add ground flaxseed or wheat germ to your cereals for extra Vitamin B, as this will support nerve functioning. Vitamin C is a great help in times of stress as it will help strengthen the immune system so that your energy levels can be boosted. Avoid alcohol and excessive amounts of caffeine as these are stimulants and may exacerbate your anxiety levels. Exercise, deep breathing and relaxation are all helpful ways to de-stress. Book yourself a massage or take a siesta to slow down the mind and calm the nervous system. Yawning helps relieve stress and it is a really healthy action for the body as it indicates that the system has received the message that it is time to relax. When the eyes water, it is a further sign that the parasympathetic nervous system is chilling down.

THE COLOUR
indigo

INDIGO S THE COLOUR OF THE MYSTERIOUS SKY AT NIGHT. INDIGO CONTINUES THE ACTION OF BLUE, HAVING COOLING AND CALMING EFFECTS. IT, HOWEVER, GOES A LITTLE FURTHER AS THIS COLOUR HAS A SEDATIVE EFFECT. INDIGO HELPS TO TAKE US AWAY FROM THE MUNDANE WORLD AND BRING US OFF TO SPIRITUAL DIMENSIONS.

Indigo is made up of dark blue and dark violet. It is the colour that supports the mind as it causes us to reflect and ponder the deeper meaning of life. **INDIGO REPRESENTS THE REALM OF MYSTERY AND CAN LEAD US INTO PSYCHIC DIMENSIONS.** Someone with the ability to tap into indigo has a reputation as a spiritual teacher and healer. Going to a seminar or session with such a person can help you deal with issues that you have hidden, sometimes from childhood and often fears in your life like death.

People who like indigo will defend people's rights as they like law and order and support the establishment to the end. However, indigo personalities can also be blinkered or deluded in their visions. This can develop into fanaticism about things they believe in and cause them to disregard other people's point of view.

WHAT IS YOUR COLOUR PERSONALITY? TO FIND OUT TURN TO PAGE 2.

THE INDIGO COLOUR PERSONALITY

- IDEALISTIC
- PERCEPTIVE
- HIGHLY DISCIPLINED
- THEY LIKE TO HAVE STRUCTURE IN THEIR LIVES
- TEND TO ENJOY RITUALS AND TRADITIONS
- CAN COME ACROSS AS ALOOF OR SELF-RIGHTEOUS
- EXTREMELY CONSCIENTIOUS
- ENJOYS WORKING HARD TO ATTAIN RESULTS
- WHEN OUT OF BALANCE CAN BECOME ADDICTIVE AND FANATICAL

Mr Indigo

This male likes to get his own way. He values his independence and has made his own decisions well before a partner comes along. This male has slight 'commitment phobia'; he checks out many people before committing and even then he cannot be sure that he will stay with just one partner. Time keeping is not a big issue on his agenda and if he's not enjoying a place, party or vibe he won't hang around for pleasantries or to display a degree of decorum. Indigo person-alities can be moody and self-centred. However all of the above may just rock your world.

Ms Indigo

Ms Indigo is quite chic; she has great taste and so always dresses impeccably. She has a loyal heart, loves drama and enjoys playing the temptress. She can change mood suddenly from fabulous form to bad form.

This Miss knows what she likes and makes her mark in whatever she does. She'll have her cake and eat it! As a doer, she is conscious of moving up the ladder. She loves to study and getting qualifications are a paramount indicator of success to her. Her addiction to qualifications can be a give away.

Ms Indigo gives it her all and gets quite consumed by the job at hand. She needs to watch, however, that she doesn't become too fanatical about things.

Young Indigo

The Indigo child is calm and quiet; they like lazing around. At school they can go unnoticed, but once they are noticed the teacher will be bowled over with their genius. Young Indigos like to get their own way so they are always in plan mode and are cute enough not to give the whole plan away so they can hold a little back for another day. They always have a trick up their sleeves. Teen years excite them and they adore 'the flirt and find' time; they are eager to explore the potential opportunities in the dating arena, as Young Indigo exudes charm and magnetic energy.

THE INDIGO PARENT

Indigo mothers and fathers make dedicated parents. The indigo mother will take the role very seriously indeed, and will work very diligently to have a steady, sure routine and their child will certainly know who rules the roost. The indigo father is laid back; he supports free speech and has a huge interest in education. He enjoys the friendship part of parenting and will prefer to leave the mundane duties to someone else. While the indigo dad may not be over the moon with fatherhood at the start, he will get into it quite passionately as his child grows up.

THE INDIGO CAREER

The indigo career is one that has authority, routine, structure and rules. To work well, there needs to be a balance between this sense of order, inspiration and creativity. Those inclined towards an indigo career enjoy working in a team and on a good day can charm anyone or turn any situation so that the deal goes their way. The indigo personalities have a knack of bringing solutions to the table. They are good at hiring the right people for the job, so they make superb recruitment specialists or developers.

AN **INDIGO** PLAN

EXERCISE – TODAY I WILL GET INVOLVED IN A TEAM SPORT

CLOTHES – I WILL WEAR INDIGO SOCKS

FOOD – I WILL EAT FRESH FOODS

PERSONALITY – I WILL KEEP MY LIFE SIMPLE TODAY

Guide To Wearing Indigo

Indigo supports you when dealing with painful memories. It helps you regain direction if you have been emotionally shattered, as it can help people see things that are normally difficult to see. Indigo helps you to look at the structure of your life and identify positive steps forward. It is the universal colour for work clothing as it symbolises structure and integrity.

Indigo encourages us to shed what we no longer require and helps us to off-load the unnecessary baggage that we all carry around with us. If we don't get rid of this it might hold us back and divert us from a new path of travel. Indigo symbolizes the strength that we need to break free and conquer weakness.

THOUGHT FOR THE DAY

Today I will co-operate joyfully with the purpose of my life.

INDIGO EXERCISE AND LEISURE ACTIVITIES

Astrology and the subject of the unknown interest the indigo personality. They enjoy reading biographies about famous people who died through drugs, sex and rock 'n' roll or crime programmes which appeal to their enquiring mind. They enjoy activities such as chess, board games and crosswords. As the indigo personality loves law and order, established routines and structure, they enjoy participating and organising any event. You will find the indigo personality on the committee or management team in any club.

WHEN TO WEAR INDIGO

Indigo can be worn by people who have ivory and fair complexions. French navy is best accented with peach, coral, powder blue and golden yellow. British navy is best accented with rose, pastel blue and lavender.

Indigo governs the pituitary gland and as the eyes and nose fall under its dominion, indigo aids sinus challenges. Indigo is seen as the strongest painkiller in the colour spectrum.

WHEN TO AVOID WEARING INDIGO

If your colouring is best described as warm and dark, golden beige or golden black, it would be better to avoid wearing indigo on the top portion of your body.

Avoid indigo if you have an addictive personality, as all addictions are related to indigo and negativity connected with indigo can combine to show a disturbing lack of purpose. If you are feeling down it is best to avoid indigo as overuse of this colour can exacerbate depression or the 'feeling blue' syndrome; it may encourage you to over-think your situation and pull you deeper into the fear zone.

BEST COLOUR PERSONALITY MATCH

Yellow or gold personalities make a great match for the indigo personality. The indigo personality can see right through people so they enjoy the gold personality's frankness and wisdom. The mood swings that indigo personalities can demonstrate are gently and sensitively nurtured by the gold personality. Both personalities enjoy a little drama – but just the kind that keeps life interesting. Silver personalities are also a good match.

WORST COLOUR PERSONALITY MATCH

Red personalities may be a little too abrasive for comfortable relationships to flourish between red and indigo. Red personalities are physically energetic but their explosive behaviour can cause distress to the sensitive and spiritual nature of the indigo personality. The red personality may find it difficult to understand or appreciate the language, ideals and spiritual beliefs of the indigo personality.

✚ Indigo Health

WHAT IS CHOLESTEROL?

Cholesterol is one of the body's fats or lipids. It is important in producing hormones and helps maintain healthy body cells. Too much cholesterol in the body is not a disease in itself, but can cause hardening and narrowing of blood vessels. This, in turn, increases the risk of problems such as heart attacks and strokes. In many cases a high cholesterol level is due to a poor diet, but in other cases the person will have inherited the tendency regardless of dietary factors.

Cholesterol is measured by a blood test conducted after a 12 hour fasting period. Generally, the average cholesterol level is just under six mill moles per litre (mmol/l) of blood. It is recommended that a reading of less than five mmol/l is healthy which means that the average person suffers from high cholesterol.

There are two types of cholesterol: low-density lipo-protein (LDL) or bad cholesterol and high-density lipo-protein (HDL) or good cholesterol. HDL is carried in the blood away from arteries and levels should be higher than three mmol/l whereas LDL levels need to be below three mmol/l. A healthy balance between them is desired, as an imbalance can cause heart disease.

WHY GET A CHOLESTEROL TEST?

It is important to get your cholesterol level tested, as not only will you find out what your cholesterol level is, the test can also rule out other conditions such as an under-active thyroid, diabetes, kidney and liver problems. Also, your doctor can determine whether you have familial hypercholesterolemia. This is an inherited condition in which the liver produces too much cholesterol. It is mainly treated with drugs called statins which help to reduce the amount of cholesterol the body makes each day. There is a downside to using these drugs and side effects include muscle inflammation and muscle breakdown. But for the majority of people, high cholesterol levels are largely due to diet.

What To Do When Cholesterol Is High

- Cleanse your larder. Cut out fatty foods such as pastries, puddings, ready made meals, biscuits and cakes and be watchful of some breakfast cereals. Many of these products contain the lethal saturated fats called trans-fats.

- Always remember to read food labels. Try to choose items with less than 3g fat per 100g serving and avoid foods with 5g or more of saturated fats per 100g serving. It is good to eat lots of fresh fruit and vegetables and the top three include: avocados, pomegranates and pears. Avocados contain beta-sitosterol – a super nutrient that blocks cholesterol absorption through the intestine wall. Pomegranates boost levels of the paraoxonase enzyme – which attacks and breaks down cholesterol patches on every artery. Pears are an excellent source of pectin – this soluble fibre is not only a valuable bowel regulator it also helps eliminate cholesterol. Soluble fibre such as oats, apples, peas, beans and kidney beans are also good for combating high cholesterol levels due to their beta-glucan fibre content. (Go to The Colour Gold chapter for more details on oats.)

- Aim to eat at least 3–5 servings of vegetables per day and 2–3 fresh fruits. Eat only lean meat, such as organic lean beef or lamb. Enjoy fresh fish three times a week. Nibble on sunflower and sesame seeds. Drink water every day as this helps the body to maintain proper functioning and helps the body metabolise fat.

- Stay away from foods containing trans-fatty acids/trans-fats/partially hydrogenated fats/hydrogenated fats. Few labels specify the trans-fats content to date but we are likely to see this change soon because from the 1st January 2006 the US Food and Drug Administration have ruled that food labels must list the trans-fatty acid content. In Europe, the EU has yet to reach a decision on labelling foods containing trans-fatty acids, but Denmark have banned oil containing more than 2% industrially produced trans-fatty acid since 2004.

Food market selling different varieties of grains, beans and sugarcane in Vilcabamba – the Valley of Longevity – in Ecuador.

WHAT ARE TRANS-FATS?

Trans-fats are completely artificial fats; they are chemically produced and are created by hydrogenation. The oil is placed into large tanks in the presence of a reactive metal such as cobalt. Hydrogen gas is pumped in to change the nature of the oil. This process makes the vegetable oil more stable, raises its melting point and improves storage, flavour and texture characteristics.

ESSENTIAL FATTY ACIDS

THE BODY CANNOT MAKE ESSENTIAL FATTY ACIDS (EFAS) – SO YOU MUST GET THEM THROUGH THE FOODS YOU EAT.

WHY YOU NEED EFAS:
- **MAINTAINING A HEALTHY WEIGHT**
- **LOWERING CHOLESTEROL**
- **BOOSTING THE IMMUNE SYSTEM**
- **NOURISHING THE REPRODUCTIVE ORGANS**
- **REDUCING PMT**
- **LUBRICATING BODY JOINTS**
- **STRONG HAIR, SKIN AND BONE TISSUE**

NEGATIVE EFFECTS OF TRANS-FATS

Trans-fats make no nutritional contribution to the diet as they contain absolutely no nutrients. They interfere with vitamin and mineral absorption and cause digestive disorders and leaky gut syndrome. They promote fatty liver, poor hair, nails and skin. Trans-fats also cause the body to feel lethargic. They increase LDL (bad cholesterol) and reduce HDL (good cholesterol). Trans-fats cause blocked arteries, strokes, heart attacks and eventually can lead to death.

There is not one piece of research in all the libraries in the entire world that can produce any positive test results about these fats. One of the simplest and most effective ways to reduce a number of health dysfunctions would be to eradicate them completely from your diet. In a recent article in Science Daily, Dana-Farber Cancer Institute researchers have identified a molecular mechanism in the liver that explains, for the first time, how consuming foods rich in saturated fats and trans-fatty acids cause elevated blood levels of cholesterol and triglycerides and increases one's risk of heart disease and certain cancers.

Blue/Indigo Food Matters

While blue is one of the most popular colours, it is one of the least appetising. Blue and indigo foods are rare in nature. Food researchers say that when humans searched for food, they learned to avoid toxic or spoiled objects, which were often blue, black or purple.

Artificial food colourings are used to dye foods blue. There are two main blue food colourings. One is called Brilliant Blue FD & C (sometimes called Blue Number 1) and this gives food a blue shade. The second artificial blue food colouring used is Indigotine (iBlue) – a dark blue shade also referred to as FD & C Blue Number 2. A recent study by experts at Liverpool University identified a possible harmful effect of artificial colours and chemicals on the nervous system. Concerns about Brilliant Blue also include a link to hyperactivity and skin rashes. It is even listed as a cancer risk by the US Environment Protection Agency. iBlue is one of the colours that the Hyperactive Children's Support Group recommends be eliminated from the diet of children and has been prohibited in Austria, Belgium, Denmark, France, Germany, Greece, Italy, Norway, Spain, Sweden and Switzerland.

Brilliant Blue FCF is a bright blue dye that is sometimes used in beverages, dairy products, powders, jellies, icings, syrups, extracts and condiments. Blue Smarties, introduced in 1989 to replace the light-brown variety, are dyed using Brilliant Blue (E133). Nestlé Rowntree has now removed the blue 'Smarties', with their artificial colour casing, as part of a long-term drive 'to improve the nutritional qualities' of its products. For now, the blue 'Smarties' will be replaced with white 'Smarties', at least until a natural blue dye is found. At the moment there is no natural alternative to the blue chemical currently used. The Co-op and Marks & Spencers have already removed artificial colours and additives from their own-label products. Many other retailers have followed their example.

In experiments, when food dyed blue is served to study subjects, they lose their appetite. Green, brown and red are the most popular food colours. Red is often used in restaurant decorating schemes because it is an appetite stimulant.

A SELECTION OF BLUE AND INDIGO FOODS

BLUEBERRIES

BLUE POTATO

Blueberries

When cut, BLUEBERRIES are white or pale green inside and have really small seeds that are hardly noticeable. Blueberries have been growing wild in Asia and North America for thousands of years. Their natural chemicals are antibacterial and have a tonic effect on blood vessels which make them very beneficial in helping to treat cystitis and other urinary infections. They are related to cranberries, which also play an important role in helping with urinary care.

Choose firm, plump berries without any squashed or leaking fruit. Blueberries react with metal so line tins with paper or cling film. They freeze well so you can have them all year round.

Nutrition
- Rich in Vitamin C
- Small amount Vitamin B1
- Potassium

Good For
- Anti-ageing
- Tummy upset – easing diarrhoea
- Treating cystitis and other urinary infections
- Kidneys

How Much To Eat
- 30 berries as part of five to nine portions of fruit and vegetables a day

Phytonutrients
- Flavonoids
- Tannins

Blue Potato

All BLUE POTATOES have a striking colour, wonderful flavour and moist texture. Steam or bake to preserve the colour. They should be kept in a dark, dry, cool area or in a brown paper bag. Blue potatoes rank lower on the glycaemic index than regular white potatoes. (See The Colour Purple chapter for further information on the glycaemic index.)

Nutrition
- A low fat source of Vitamin C
- Carbohydrates
- Protein
- Potassium
- Iron
- Niacin
- Magnesium
(The skin provides calcium, zinc and phosphorus)

Good For
- Weight control as they are in fact a low fat source of nutrients and polyphenols
- Low rating on the glycaemic index

(Watch the butter you put on your potato as this is the fat offender!)

How Much To Eat
- 175g (6 oz) is an average portion

Phytonutrients
- Flavonoids
- Anthocyanins

did you know?

A HALF CUP OF BLUEBERRIES WILL GIVE THE SAME AMOUNT OF ANTI-OXIDANTS AS FIVE SERVINGS OF PEAS, BROCCOLI, CARROTS OR APPLES.

LIKE THE PURPLE POTATO OF PERU, BLUE POTATOES HOLD THEIR SHAPE AFTER COOKING SO ARE PERFECT FOR BLUE POTATO SALAD.

Warm Blue Potato Salad

SERVES 4

400G (12 OZ) SMALL BLUE POTATOES

4 RASHERS

1 SMALL RED ONION

1 TBSP COOKING OIL

1 TBSP HONEY

3 TBSP CIDER VINEGAR

2 TSP CORN FLOUR

3 TBSP WATER

2 TBSP CHOPPED DILL

FRESH DILL – TO GARNISH

Scrub and wash the blue potatoes well. Cut into quarters. Steam the potatoes to help them retain their natural colour, until soft. Drain well.

Grill the rashers and then cut them into small pieces with a pair of scissors.

Peel, chop and dice the onion and then sauté in oil until soft.

Mix the corn flour, vinegar and water and add to the onion mixture. Bring to the boil and cook until thickened. Add the rasher, honey and chopped dill.

Mix the warm potatoes and pile into serving bowl. Decorate with some fresh dill.

Brilliant Blue Potato Cakes

SERVES 2

250G (9 OZ) STEAMED BLUE
   POTATOES – COOKED

50G (2 OZ) SELF-RAISING FLOUR

SALT

75G (2 $^1/_2$ OZ) MARGARINE – MELTED

OIL OR MARGARINE – TO FRY

CHOPPED PARSLEY – TO GARNISH

Mash blue potatoes in bowl; add flour and salt and mix.

Then add melted margarine, mix well.

Turn onto a floured board. Knead lightly and cut into two.

Roll out each piece into a circle about 2 cm (0.7 in) thick. Cut out 4 triangles.

Fry each cake until golden on both sides. Garnish with chopped parsley.

Blue Potato & Bacon Rosti

SERVES 2

4 LARGE BLUE POTATOES

3 TBSP OIL

3 RASHERS

HALF AN ONION

1 CLOVE GARLIC

PEPPER TO TASTE

1 TSP CHOPPED FRESH PARSLEY

TOMATO – TO GARNISH

FRESH PARSLEY – TO GARNISH

Tina's Top Cooking Tip

YOU COULD MIX IN SOME CHOPPED BONELESS FISH TO THE MIXTURE AND TRANSFORM THIS DISH INTO STAR FISH CAKES.

Scrub blue potatoes. Now steam them in boiling water for 5 minutes only.

Peel and dice onion and garlic very finely.

Snip the rashers into very small pieces. Heat 1 tablespoon of oil and sauté the bacon and onion until soft.

Drain, cool, peel and grate potato into a bowl. Mix blue potato with garlic, parsley, pepper, onion and bacon.

Heat the remaining oil in pan. Put spoonfuls of the mixture onto hot pan and flatten a little.

Reduce heat and cook gently for 5–7 minutes, until golden. Turn, and then brown other side.

Drain on kitchen paper. Wash and chop parsley and tomato for garnish.

Blue Potato Tortilla

SERVES 2-4

2 MEDIUM BLUE POTATOES

1 LARGE RED ONION

1 CLOVE GARLIC

5 TBSP PEAS

6 LARGE EGGS

1 LARGE SPRIG PARSLEY

BLACK PEPPER

2 TBSP OLIVE OIL

Wash, peel and slice the blue potatoes, very thinly.

Peel and dice onion very finely. Peel and crush garlic.

Wash and chop parsley. Keep some for garnish.

Heat oil, add potatoes, and fry on medium heat for 10 minutes.

Add onion. Fry until golden and potato is soft.

Beat eggs, garlic, parsley, pepper and onions. Add the blue potatoes to the eggs, mix, return to the pan.

Cook over a low heat for 10 minutes, until the top has just set.

Place a large plate over the pan, turn out the tortilla, and then slide it back onto pan to cook the other side for 5 minutes.

Slide onto a warm serving plate. Cut into wedges.

Blueberry and Apple Loaf

MAKES 1 LOAF OR 8–10 PORTIONS

125G (4 $^1/_2$ OZ) CHILLED BUTTER – DICED, PLUS EXTRA FOR GREASING

225G (8 OZ) SELF-RAISING FLOUR

175G (6 OZ) GOLDEN CASTER SUGAR

2 LARGE EGGS – LIGHTLY BEATEN

2 LARGE EATING APPLES, PEELED, CORED AND THINLY SLICED

125G (4 $^1/_2$ OZ) BLUEBERRIES

2 TBSP APRICOT JAM

SALT AND PEPPER

Preheat the oven to 190°C (375°F) gas mark 5.

Grease a 900g loaf tin, and line with baking paper or a paper loaf tin liner.

Sieve the flour into a food processor with a pinch of salt and add the butter. Process until it resembles breadcrumbs. Add the sugar and eggs and process again to make a smooth mixture.

Spoon half the cake mixture into the loaf tin and then scatter with half the apples and half the blueberries.

Spoon over the remaining cake mixture; then scatter with the remaining fruit.

Bake for 1 hour, or until risen and firm. To test it, insert a skewer into the centre – it should come out clean.

Put the apricot jam into a small bowl and microwave the jam on high for 20 seconds to melt (or melt in a small pan over a low heat). Brush the glaze over the cake as soon as it comes out of the oven.

Cool for 10 minutes in the tin, then turn out onto a wire rack to cool completely.

Why not serve at your next dinner party?

TINA'S TOP COOKING TIP

Often during cooking blue potatoes change colour slightly and they may look purple, so don't worry if this happens.

Blueberry and Spinach Salad

SERVES 2

450G (1LB) FRESH SPINACH LEAVES

3 TBSP HAZELNUTS – CHOPPED

350G (12 $^1/_2$ OZ) FRESH OR FROZEN
    BLUEBERRIES

HALF A MEDIUM RED ONION, THINLY SLICED

200G (7 OZ) CANNED MANDARIN ORANGES
    – (IN NATURAL JUICE) DRAINED

HONEY-SESAME DRESSING

1 TBSP SESAME SEEDS

60 ML (2 FL OZ) CIDER VINEGAR

2 TBSP OLIVE OIL

3 TBSP LIQUID FROM MANDARIN ORANGES

1 TBSP HONEY

$^1/_4$ TSP PAPRIKA

Trim, wash and dry spinach. Tear spinach into bite sized pieces. Place in salad bowl and set aside.

Dressing: Toast sesame seeds in an ungreased skillet; stir over medium heat until browned. Combine toasted sesame seeds, cider vinegar, olive oil, paprika and honey. Mix well.

At serving time, pour dressing over spinach and mix well to coat leaves. Add blueberries, red onion slices, mandarin orange segments and hazelnuts and toss just enough to mix.

Blueberry Ice-cream

SERVES 4

3 EGGS

150G (5 $^1/_2$ OZ)
    ICING SUGAR

1 TSP VANILLA
    ESSENCE

170 ML (6 FL OZ)
    CREAM

300G (10 $^1/_2$ OZ)
    BLUEBERRIES –
    WASHED

1 PLASTIC CONTAINER
    FOR PUTTING THE
    ICE-CREAM IN

Turn freezer temperature to lowest setting. Chill the container for 1 hour if possible beforehand.

Separate egg yolks from whites. Whisk egg whites stiffly. Whisk in sieved icing sugar – 1 tsp at a time. Gently whisk in egg yolks and vanilla essence.

Whip cream. Stir in any flavouring at this point. Fold cream gently into the egg mixture.

Add the blueberries and leave whole. Pour into a large container; cover and freeze for 4–6 hours, until firm. When flavours are added to ice-cream, it should be stirred once after 1 hour during freezing to prevent the blueberries sinking.

To serve: Stand ice-cream at room temperature for 15 minutes before serving or put it into the fridge for 15–20 minutes to soften a little. Storage time: 3 months.

Blueberry Morning Muffins

MAKES 12

250G (9 OZ) SELF-RAISING
    FLOUR
25G (1 OZ) GROUND
    ALMONDS
1 TSP BAKING POWDER
$^1/_2$ TSP BREAD SODA
75G (2 $^1/_2$ OZ) BUTTER
75G (2 $^1/_2$ OZ) CASTER
    SUGAR
100 ML (3 FL OZ) MILK
1 EGG
100G (3 $^1/_2$ OZ) FRESH
    BLUEBERRIES – WASHED

Preheat oven to 200°C (390°F) or gas mark 6. Grease tins.

Melt butter in a saucepan and set aside.

Sieve flour, baking powder, bread soda into a bowl together. Add almonds and sugar.

Beat milk, egg and melted butter together. Pour into the dry ingredients and mix with fork. The batter will be lumpy but that is correct. Do not over-beat.

Add the blueberries.

Spoon mixture into tins and bake for 20 minutes.

Serve hot with butter and jam.

did you know?

THE DEEP BLUE COLOUR OF FRESH BLUEBERRIES IS DUE
TO THE ANTHOCYANIN PIGMENT. THIS IS A POWERFUL
ANTI-OXIDANT THAT FIGHTS FREE RADICALS. THE
POLYPHENOLS IN BLUEBERRIES MEAN THEY ARE A
GREAT ANTI-AGEING FOOD AS THEY HAVE THE HIGHEST
ANTI-OXIDANT LEVELS OF ANY FRUIT.

THE COLOUR
purple

PURPLE IS SULTRY AND SEXY AND AT THE SAME TIME SOPHISTICATED AND GRAND. PURPLE IS OFTEN ASSOCIATED WITH ROYALTY. IN FACT, IN THE MIDDLE AGES PURPLE DYE WAS THE MOST EXPENSIVE, SO IT WAS ONLY USED ON THE ROBES OF ROYALTY AND PRIESTS. THE COLOUR PURPLE EVOKES AN ELEMENT OF MYSTERY AND INTRIGUE. PEOPLE WHO LOVE PURPLE ARE OFTEN ENIGMATIC AND HIGHLY CREATIVE INDIVIDUALS. PURPLE IS THE COLOUR CHOICE OF THE ARTIST AND THOSE INTERESTED IN SPIRITUALITY AND MYSTICISM.

Purples and lilacs evoke a sense of smell more than actual images. **LAVENDER HAS LONG BEEN THOUGHT OF AS A ROMANTIC COLOUR**, yet it is widely used to heal the body and spirit, as well as to woo the heart.

Those who dislike purple approach life with a no holes barred approach – 'a time is money' philosophy. They are usually direct, focused and tell it like it is. These personalities are go-getters who have little tolerance for others who daydream or who are not as dedicated as themselves.

WHAT IS YOUR COLOUR PERSONALITY? TO FIND OUT TURN TO PAGE 2.

THE PURPLE COLOUR PERSONALITY

- HUMANITARIANS
- INVENTIVE AND ENJOY CREATING THINGS
- ARTISTIC AND ADEPT AT THINKING OUTSIDE THE BOX
- PSYCHIC IN NATURE
- ENJOYS THE FINER THINGS IN LIFE
- LOVES TO TRAVEL AND EXPLORE NEW PLACES
- CAN HAVE GRANDIOSE IDEAS
- WHEN OUT OF BALANCE THEY CAN BE ARROGANT AND POMPOUS
- LOVES TO CLIMB THE SOCIAL LADDER – SOCIAL BUTTERFLIES
- ENJOYS MEDITATION AND THIS HELPS KEEP THEM GROUNDED AS THEY ARE SPIRITUALLY ORIENTATED

Mr Purple

The purple male likes to play a leading role in the community. He is curious and dynamic, with a fascination for mystic arts reaching up to the higher planes of consciousness and knowledge. As purple is made up of red and blue, the cool energy of blue will give him an air of stability and the red will show an extreme talent for sexual love. He will not waste time with mediocrity when searching for his partner, friend or lover; at a glance, purple men can tell a quality person. This man likes to savour the challenge of seduction. It will be more like an obstacle course for you, but do not make it easy for him, as he respects a partner who values themselves. Mr Purple is truly a man to die for!

Ms Purple

The purple female is a natural leader so she may initially appear demanding. She has an enquiring mind and is a vibrant individual with an inspirational personality; she is very exciting to be around. She knows her own mind and can be enticing, secretive and even dangerous. She will weave magic and mystery into life on a daily basis. She has an enormous variety of interests and never gets side-tracked from the project at hand. Purple females have an uncanny understanding of the opposite sex and she has amazing seductive powers; she is passionate and has brains also. She will not keep you dangling on a string, as she instantly likes or dislikes you. It is all or nothing with the purple lady and if she has chosen you, your luck has landed!

Young Purple

Young Miss Purple can be quite the tomboy as a child and this is why she is so good with male company in her teens and adult life; she knows exactly what makes boys tick. From an early age she recognises that boys have the edge and that society favours them, so she concludes that if you cannot beat them, join them! Young Mr Purple never seems to act like a child – he possesses a wise head on his young shoulders. He is simply the boss! Both young Mr and Miss Purple are inclined to be moody and need to be encouraged to think beyond themselves. They can be very secretive and are deep thinkers. They love to daydream!

The Purple Parent

The purple parent is a great teacher for their children. They keep their children hard at it by encouraging them to sample an enormous variety of interests; they do not let them waste time. The purple mum gives them constant support while they move through their fears and the children gain confidence just by watching her.

Purple parents put great effort and energy into their parenting and the purple mum feels it is essential for their dad to participate in their upbringing. Mummy purple cannot be left at home alone with the kids for too long, and is best if she has boys, as she cannot be bothered with girlish frills. Daddy purple can appear to be harsh with discipline, but mum will keep an eye on this. The plus about having a purple parent is that come what may, loyalty is the name of the game. You are their child and nothing will stop them from putting your welfare first.

The Purple Career

The purple personality makes an excellent business person, as he or she has the ability to squeeze the best possible deal from any business project. This is due to their excellent attention to detail and amazing ability to cover every angle for negotiating. They also make brilliant artists, designers, humanitarians and mediators. Self-employment suits them well, as they are leaders and capable of great self-rule; they have definite goals in mind and will achieve them. They command respect despite being overbearing and avid social climbers. They can be challenging personalities to work for and can appear harsh at times, but possess a motivational personality and a surprising grasp of universal consciousness.

A PURPLE DAY PLAN

CLOTHES – I WILL WEAR SOMETHING PURPLE TODAY.

EXERCISE AND BEAUTY – TODAY I WILL TAKE A LONG, HOT BUBBLE BATH WITH LAVENDER OIL AND IT WILL BE VERY RELAXING.

PURPLE PERSONALITY – I AM A LEADER. I AM HIGHLY INVENTIVE. I AM CREATIVE AND ARTISTIC.

FOOD – TODAY I WILL EAT SOMETHING PURPLE.

Guide to Wearing Purple

The great thing about purple is that there are so many shades of this romantic colour to choose from, that you are certain to find one which suits you. Purple and lilac are feminine colours. Deep purples can be vampish and gothic and are ideal for creating a sultry evening look. In contrast, soft powdery lilacs give a delicate prettiness that suits flirty clothes and summery daywear.

Purple is rare in nature which makes it an exquisite and sought after treasure. To single yourself out as a rare beauty, use the flower shades of hyacinth, violet, lilac and lavender in your clothing this season.

Purple is often the colour chosen by leaders, by people who naturally move to the beat of their own drum and by people who express individuality and can appear somewhat different.

THOUGHT FOR THE DAY

Purple is rare in nature; I single myself out as a rare beauty and sought after treasure today.

Exercise and Leisure Activities

The purple personality enjoys walking, yoga, pilates, sculpting, painting and designing. Music thrills them so going to gigs and concerts will excite them and playing instruments like the drums or saxophone will suit them.

WHEN TO USE PURPLE

The colour purple is made up of red and blue so it will take on all the cooling energy of blue which will help calm the nervous energy and prevent mental fatigue. On the other hand, red is the colour of action and movement and so can have a positive impact by helping the user to move in their chosen direction. Also it helps the user to move out of the thinking zone and into the action zone.

The gentle, calming energy that purple evokes can help those grieving. It is a colour used in many religious ceremonies to symbolise death and the afterlife.

Bring more purple into your life if you suffer with insomnia or have regular headaches, excessive hunger, are over-anxious or over-excited. If you are over-critical of yourself, feeling stuck or unable to move forward, you should also turn to purple.

WHEN TO AVOID PURPLE

Avoid the colour purple if you are feeling depressed and have challenges with drugs or alcohol as this colour can impact on your mood; it is sometimes thought to be the colour associated with madness. Also avoid this colour if you are feeling lethargic or over-sleeping as it can promote excessive rest. If you are craving sweet foods evade purple as it aids and abets these 'must-have' cravings — look at chocolate bar wrappers.

Purple is not helpful if you are an over-analytical person who tends to over-think situations. It is wise to avoid the colour purple if you find that the situations listed above are familiar to you. Lavender would be more beneficial in such cases and lilac is another good alternative.

BEST COLOUR PERSONALITY MATCH

Purple personalities get on extremely well with yellow personalities. The yellow personality will excite the mind of the purple personality as they are witty, humorous and intelligent. Both are creative in nature and have plenty of surprises for each other that will keep the relationship alive and healthy. This union is certainly not predictable. If you are a purple personality, gold is also a good match.

WORST COLOUR PERSONALITY MATCH

Purple personalities can feel challenged by orange personalities. The purple visionaries are inspired to help people and causes and can view the daring actions of the orange personality as unproductive and time wasting. Both are intelligent and enjoy their independent nature, but disagree with the other's way of going about their purpose in life.

The need to be an individual can get a little lost in our modern world and Jenny Joseph sums this modern reality up well in the lines below from her exuberant poem, 'Warning'.

"When I Am an Old Woman I shall wear
purple
With a red hat which doesn't go, and doesn't
suit me
And I shall spend my pension on brandy and
summer gloves
And satin sandals, and say we've no money
for butter ...
... And make up for the sobriety of my youth.
I shall go out in my slippers in the rain ...
... And learn to spit."

She demonstrates the misconceptions people can have about the colour purple. These are the people who want her to "... *set a good example for the children*".

But why put off wearing or using purple until you are old? Jenny Joseph is so right to ask if she "... *ought to practice a little now? So people who know me are not too shocked and surprised/ When suddenly I am old, and start to wear purple.*"

The world loves the colour purple. Add a little purple to your life now – it will help keep the earth vibrant and alive with creativity and individuality.

did you know?

A POWER WALK WILL HELP CLEAR YOUR MIND AND THE GOOD NEWS IS THAT 30 MINUTES BURNS AS MUCH AS 180 CALORIES!

GIANNI VERSACE LOVED THE COLOUR PURPLE AND MANY CREATIVE PEOPLE WHO HAVE A GENIUS FOR DETAIL WILL SELECT PURPLE AS THEIR FAVOURITE COLOUR.

Lavender

When used in aromatherapy, the spicy smell of lavender in essential oil or floral water induces relaxation, calm and peace. It is a wonderful aid for de-stressing, easing nervous tension and easing insomnia. Lavender oils, hydrosols, and the blossoms can also be used in cooking, to add a subtle flavour to food.

The benefits of lavender have been known since the Middle Ages when the disinfectant powers of the flower were discovered and the petals were added to bathwater. Convinced that epidemics spread through smells, the people of the time burned lavender in the streets and in their houses. Trade in the essence began during the Renaissance. In the traditional medicinal practices of Provence, lavender was used to soothe, disinfect and heal wounds. Today the most advanced scientific laboratories have analysed the herb's powers in detail and have confirmed its therapeutic reputation. It has indeed been proven to aid relaxation, help relieve anxiety and depression, work as an anti-inflammatory, help heal cuts and burns and balance both body and mind.

✚ Purple Health

INSOMNIA

The purple gland is the pineal gland and physically it represents the top of the head, the crown, the brain and the scalp. So as purple is the colour that governs the head, it can promote relaxation and sleep. As your body needs a period of recuperation to maintain itself, sleep is vital for everyone. A lack of sleep or poor quality sleep makes us irritable and prone to mood swings. Serious sleep deprivation can induce uncontrolled behaviour and loss of balance.

The general theory is that we need eight hours sleep a night, but nowadays this has been reduced to as little as six hours for most people, because of their lifestyle. Continuous sleep is not essential and it can be averaged. Three really good nights sleep will compensate for other nights that are restless or wakeful, but whether this will work for you depends on your own unique constitution.

There are so many interesting and informative studies available in which you can read up on sleep, such as Isaac Wolf's study on students' sleep patterns, Mary A Carskadon's study on normal adolescent sleep patterns or Mitler MM and Miller JC's study on the practical considerations of sleep patterns.

You should ask yourself the following questions: How many hours a night do you usually sleep? Has your sleep pattern changed recently? Do you wake up refreshed and ready to take on the day's adventures?

If you feel you are having sleep troubles here are guidelines to help you get a good night's rest.

FACTORS THAT MAY INFLUENCE POOR SLEEP

An uncomfortable or unfamiliar bed
A snoring partner
A bedroom that is too hot or cold
Poor ventilation
Electrical gadgets in the room such as alarm radio or TV
Worries that are challenging to set aside at night
Working late and activating the brain
Watching TV
Eating heavy meals prior to bedtime
Insufficient exercise

DEALING WITH INSOMNIA

There is no universal remedy for sleeplessness or insomnia. The best advice I can offer here is that you are your own best sleep manager. As a general tip – four solid hours of sleep will be far more beneficial than eight broken hours.

- Helpful tips include burning lavender in your room about 30 minutes before bedtime, listening to calming music or a meditation CD and having a blackout blind for morning light.
- It is wise for you to assess your bedroom and sleeping environment. I suggest that you ensure that the room has good ventilation. Try to make sure the walls are thick so that you are in a quiet space but if this is not possible invest in a set of ear plugs to help with sound management. Decorate your room in lavender and soft hues of purple to create a calming environment. A bedroom that is decorated in energy giving colours (such as red) will be a room that will promote more energetic activities rather than restful ones.
- Ensure that you do not drink too many rich or caffeine-filled products after six in the evening as caffeine is a stimulant and will keep the adrenal glands over producing hormones that can increase stress levels so as to keep the body in an over active state. Alcohol interferes with sleep as it stimulates the secretion of adrenaline. That will result in challenges such as nervous tension and irritability.
- Get regular exercise as this will help relaxation and release endorphins which have a calming effect on the body.
- Have a laugh daily to keep the happy hormones in good shape!

APPETITE AND DIETS

It can be so confusing in this world of many diets to know how to satisfy our appetite these days. We are constantly told about new ideas that will lead to weight loss – from food combining, which encourages us to eat protein with protein and carbohydrate with carbohydrate and so on, to various other theories, such as the reduced carbohydrate programme, the high protein and fibre diet and the raw food diet; the list keeps getting longer.

As the colour purple has an impact on the brain-centre that controls appetite, it can also have an impact on these diet issues, particularly on decisions regarding the extremely popular GI diet. The glycaemic index is an index used to measure how long carbohydrate foods take to be absorbed into the bloodstream once they are eaten. Foods that have a low number on the glycaemic index (see on the next page) release their sugars slowly and gradually. They are known as low GI foods and provide long-term energy. These are the foods you want to eat as they are more beneficial than high GI foods such as sugar, sweets, white bread, couscous and pineapples. A successful approach is to combine some of the higher-index foods with lower index foods, to ensure a more sustained release of energy.

THE GLYCAEMIC INDEX COUNTER

In order to balance the high and low GI foods the table on the next page will give you the index count. Carbohydrates are broken down into glucose during digestion. The glucose travels in the bloodstream to the muscles, brain and all other cells. It is then converted into energy and will be used for specific functions, for example to help the lungs to breathe and muscles to move effectively while you are out walking. Food is evaluated according to the rate at which it is broken down and converted into glucose. The slower it is broken down the better, as it will help you to function more effectively. It is advisable to choose foods with a GI rating of less than 50.

LOW GI FOODS

Red	Apples, raspberries, strawberries, rhubarb, tomatoes, peppers
Orange	Oranges, tangerines, peaches, peppers
Yellow	Apples, grapefruit, pears, peppers
Green	Apples, grapes, bean sprouts, broccoli, cabbage, peppers
Blue	Blueberries
Purple	Cherries, grapes
White/Gold	Cannelloni beans, chickpeas, onions, oat bran, porridge, pearl barley, quorn

Golden and White Foods Glycaemic Index

Rainbow of Colours

Cereals

Rice Krispies 82

Porridge oats 49

Rice bran 19

Grains

White bread 95

Rice cakes 82

Brown rice 60

Oat cakes 54

Barley 26

Dairy Products

Plain yoghurt 36

Full-fat milk 34

Skimmed milk 32

Fruits

Raisins 64

Bananas 62

Grapes 45

Oranges 40

Apples 39

Pears 34

Grapefruits 26

Plums 25

Cherries 23

Vegetables

Carrots (cooked) 92

Potatoes (baked) 85

Beetroots 64

Peas 51

Sweet potatoes 51

Tomatoes 38

Snacks and Drinks

Chocolate bar (milk) 68

Apple juice 40

Popcorn 38

Dark chocolate 22

Fruit and vegetables for sale in the market in Ecuador.

HOW MUCH TO EAT

It is important to remember that portion size matters when considering a healthy and balanced diet. Eating a great mix of foods that are fresh, tasty and colourful is the most effective and fun way to go but don't overload on your portions.

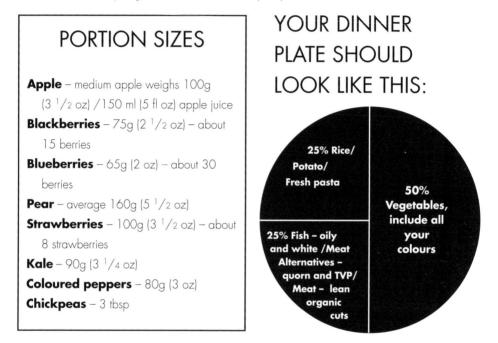

PORTION SIZES

Apple – medium apple weighs 100g (3 ^{1}/$_2$ oz) /150 ml (5 fl oz) apple juice

Blackberries – 75g (2 ^{1}/$_2$ oz) – about 15 berries

Blueberries – 65g (2 oz) – about 30 berries

Pear – average 160g (5 ^{1}/$_2$ oz)

Strawberries – 100g (3 ^{1}/$_2$ oz) – about 8 strawberries

Kale – 90g (3 ^{1}/$_4$ oz)

Coloured peppers – 80g (3 oz)

Chickpeas – 3 tbsp

YOUR DINNER PLATE SHOULD LOOK LIKE THIS:

25% Rice/ Potato/ Fresh pasta

50% Vegetables, include all your colours

25% Fish – oily and white /Meat Alternatives – quorn and TVP/ Meat – lean organic cuts

Brightly coloured fruits and vegetables are so fantastic, friendly-looking, sociable and freedom loving that they deserve a special spot on your plate daily. All the fruits and vegetables mentioned in this book should be readily available, can be purchased organically and score high on the ORAC scale also.

THE ORAC SCALE

The ORAC (Oxygen Radical Absorbance Capacity) scale is a scientific measurement that allows us to see the anti-oxidant value of each fruit and vegetable. Colourful vegetables such as carrots, broccoli, spinach and tomatoes are packed with very high-quality anti-oxidants, protective phytonutrients and friendly fibre. This fibre will help you stay full for longer and also help maintain balanced blood sugar levels.

With so many free radicals raging ahead to attack body cells and cause premature ageing, fatigue, brain deterioration and eye challenges – anti-oxidants and phytonutrients are the way forward for a healthy and carefree future.

THE COLOUR PURPLE 127

A SELECTION OF **PURPLE** FOODS

GRAPES

PLUMS

RAISINS

PRUNES

AUBERGINES

BEETROOT

EAT PURPLE FOODS

Foods such as aubergines, blackberries, purple grapes, beetroot and plums contain powerful anti-oxidants known as anthocyanins. Research has shown that anthocyanins can significantly reduce the risk of heart disease and stroke by inhibiting clot formation due to potent anti-oxidant and anti-inflammatory agents. They can also reduce the amount of bad cholesterol in the blood (See The Colour Blue chapter).

Grapes

GRAPES are nourishing and a regenerative food. They are excellent for boosting energy and useful for anaemia and arthritis. Dried grapes are called raisins.

Grapes ferment quickly in the stomach so it is advised to eat them on their own before a meal.

Nutrition
• Rich aromatic compounds

Good For
• Skin problems
• Losing weight
• Anaemia, fatigue and joint problems

How Much To Eat
• 8 grapes per serving (about 60 kcal)

Phytonutrients
• Flavones • Geraniol
• Nerol • Linalol

Plums

In oriental medicine **PLUMS** are used to treat digestive disorders.

Nutrition
• Good source of potassium
• Small amounts of Vitamin A

Good For
• Heart circulation
• Fluid retention

How Much To Eat
• Three small plums or 90g (3 oz) is a portion

Phytonutrients
• Hydroxycinnamic acids called ferulic acid (these are in the phenolic acid group)
• Carotenoids and flavonoids

did you know?

GRAPES CONTAIN AN ENORMOUS NUMBER OF AROMATIC COMPOUNDS, FAR MORE THAN ANY OTHER FRUIT. THE ASTRINGENT TANNINS, FLAVONES, RED ANTHOCYANINS, GERANIOL AND NEROL ALL CONTRIBUTE TO HELP MAKE THE GRAPE A CANCER PROTECTIVE GEM.

THE JAPANESE PLUM WAS INTRODUCED TO THE USA AS FAR BACK AS THE 17TH CENTURY BUT PLUMS ORIGINATED IN EUROPE.

Prunes

PRUNES are more concentrated in nutrients than plums; especially in iron and potassium. As prunes are dried, they rank high on the ORAC scale.

Nutrition
- Potassium
- Iron

Good For
- Fluid retention
- Healthy heart
- Healthy colon
- Natural laxative

How Much To Eat
- 3 small prunes, standard portion (20 kcal) as part of the five to nine a day

Phytonutrients
- Flavones
- Condensed tannins
- Carotenoids

did you know?

AUBERGINES ARE ALSO CALLED EGGPLANT, BRINJAL, GUINEA SQUASH AND GARDEN EGG.

Aubergines

AUBERGINES are originally from India and parts of South East Asia and are part of the Solanaceae family of plants, which includes potatoes and tomatoes. You can buy aubergines in various colours: green, white, yellow and purple. They can be slim, with glossy purple or almost black skins, or plump, ivory-white ovals. The ivory-white versions go by their American name "eggplant" instead of the French aubergine, but they all have the same slightly acrid taste.

Aubergines taste really fabulous with basil, coriander, cumin, garlic, ginger, mint and/or yoghurt and are best eaten cooked. Plump aubergines are marginally juicier and are ideal to use when making moussaka. The long, slim ones are best for frying, as they are drier.

Nutrition
- Vitamin A, B, C
- Calcium
- Copper
- Magnesium
- Manganese
- Phosphorous
- Potassium
- Zinc

Good For
- Stimulating liver function
- Healthy cells
- A happy heart

How Much To Eat
- Low in fat; eat 150g (5 1/2 oz) – half an aubergine – as part of your five to nine fruit and vegetables a day

Phytonutrients
- Anthocyanins

Beetroot

BEETROOT increases the cellular uptake of oxygen. It contains betaine which regulates gastric PH and so aids digestion. Specific anti-carcinogens are bound to the red colouring matter in beetroot.

Nutrition
- Folate
- Vitamin A, C
- Iron
- Magnesium
- Manganese
- Potassium
- Zinc
- Betaine

Good For
- Digestion
- Anaemia
- Chronic fatigue – boosts energy
- Reducing stress
- Healthy liver function

How Much To Eat
- 100g (3 1/2 oz) portion as part of your five to nine fruit and vegetables a day

Phytonutrients
- Beta-carotene

Purple Beetroot Herb Salad with Tarragon Dressing

SERVES 4

1 SMALL HEAD OF RED LETTUCE – SHREDDED

6–8 SORREL – CHOPPED

HANDFUL OF BEETROOT LEAVES – CHOPPED

BUNCH OF CORIANDER LEAVES – CHOPPED

6–9 DANDELION LEAVES (OR CHICORY) – CHOPPED

Mix all the ingredients together in a salad bowl and serve with tarragon dressing.

TARRAGON DRESSING

FOR ONE SALAD BOWL

3 TBSP LEMON JUICE

1 STALK FRESH TARRAGON

$^1/_4$ TSP SALT

1 CLOVE GARLIC

100 ML (3 FL OZ) SAFFLOWER OIL

EXTRA-VIRGIN OLIVE OIL TO TASTE

PINCH OF PEPPER

Put all the ingredients (except for the olive oil) in a blender and blend for 30 seconds. Add the olive oil to taste.

Spice Aubergine with Mint Yoghurt

SERVES 4

2 AUBERGINES – SLICED THICKLY

3 TBSP OLIVE OIL

1 TSP CUMIN

HANDFUL FRESH CORIANDER

$^1/_2$ TSP CHILLI PEPPER

150 ML (5 FL OZ) GREEK YOGHURT

Heat the oil in a pan and gently sauté the aubergine for 3–5 minutes. Add the cumin and allow to cook until tender.

In another bowl blend the fresh coriander, fresh chilli and yoghurt together.

When the aubergine is cooked allow to cool and add the yoghurt dressing. Serve chilled.

Ratatouille au Gratin

SERVES 4

6 TBSP OLIVE OIL

1 AUBERGINE – SLICED

2 GARLIC CLOVES

1 COURGETTE – SLICED

1 RED PEPPER – CORED, SEEDED AND
   SLICED

1 TIN TOMATOES – CHOPPED

10 FRESH BASIL LEAVES

225G (8 OZ) MOZZARELLA CHEESE –
   THINLY SLICED

Heat half the olive oil in a pan and add the aubergine and fry on both sides until just beginning to brown. Add more oil if required.

Remove and drain on kitchen paper. Set aside.

Add the remaining oil to the pan and sauté the garlic, courgette and pepper for 8–10 minutes. Add the tomatoes, basil, and aubergine and season well, simmering for 10 minutes. Transfer into an ovenproof dish and arrange the cheese on top.

Place under the grill until the cheese has melted. Serve immediately with steamed fish or chicken breast.

Mushroom Stuffed Aubergines

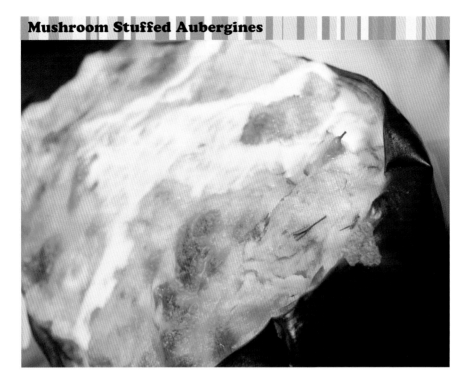

SERVES 4

2 AUBERGINES

2 SMALL ONIONS – FINELY CHOPPED

2 TBSP OLIVE OIL

3 CLOVES GARLIC – FINELY CHOPPED

200G (7 OZ) MUSHROOMS – MIXED VARIETIES OF YOUR CHOICE

100 ML (3 FL OZ) FRESH CREAM

SALT AND FRESHLY GROUND CHILLI PEPPER

BUNCH FRESH PARSLEY – CHOPPED

75G (2 $^1/_2$ OZ) FRESHLY GRATED PARMESAN CHEESE

Halve the aubergines lengthways and remove the flesh. Reserve the skins. Chop the flesh finely.

Heat the oil in a pan, sauté the onions and add the garlic and mushrooms until soft.

Add the aubergine flesh and cook until golden brown. Season well and add the parsley.

Stuff the aubergine skins with the flesh.

Drizzle the fresh cream evenly over the dish. Sprinkle with the cheese and place under the grill for 5 minutes or until the cheese has melted.

Serve immediately with ground chilli peppers.

Ratatouille with Polenta Cakes

SERVES 4

RATATOUILLE

2 ONIONS – SLICED

5 TBSP EXTRA-VIRGIN OLIVE
   OIL

2 SMALL AUBERGINES
   (EGGPLANTS) – CHOPPED

2 SMALL COURGETTES
   (ZUCCHINI) – SLICED

1 RED PEPPER – SLICED

1 GREEN PEPPER – SLICED

2 CLOVES GARLIC – CRUSHED

450G (1 LB) RIPE TOMATOES –
   SKINNED AND CHOPPED

HANDFUL OF BASIL

WATER

SEA SALT AND PEPPER

TOMATO PASTE

POLENTA CAKES

300G (10 $^1/_2$ OZ) PRE-COOKED POLENTA

2 TSP HERBES DE PROVENCE

$^1/_2$ TSP SEA SALT

PINCH BLACK PEPPER

275 ML (9 FL OZ) BOILING WATER

GRAPESEED OIL

Sauté the onions in the olive oil and add the other vegetables one at a time in the order given above.

Stir in the basil (keeping a few leaves to garnish the dish) and cook for 2 more minutes, adding extra water if required.

Season with salt and pepper, turn down the heat, cover and simmer gently for approximately 20 minutes.

Remove the lid and simmer for a further 5 minutes, thickening with a little tomato paste.

Garnish with fresh basil.

Put the polenta in a bowl. Add the herbs, salt, pepper and mix well.

Gradually add in the boiling water and stir to form a thick dough. Leave for 5 minutes, and then knead to an even consistency.

Break off handfuls of the dough and mould them into small round cakes, 5 cm (2 in) in diameter by 1 $^1/_2$ cm ($^1/_2$ in) thick.

Shallow-fry the cakes in a little grapeseed oil until golden brown, turning frequently.

Serve with the ratatouille and thick slices of fresh, country bread.

Prune and Peel Muffins

SERVES 12

1 EGG

250 ML (8 FL OZ) MILK

125 ML (4 FL OZ) VEGETABLE OIL

50G (2 OZ) CASTER SUGAR

30G (1 OZ) BROWN SUGAR

285G (10 OZ) PLAIN FLOUR

2 TSP BAKING POWDER

$^1/_2$ TSP GRATED NUTMEG

100G (3 $^1/_2$ OZ) PRUNES – CHOPPED

RIND OF ONE LIME

Preheat oven to 200°C (390°F) or gas mark 6.

Break the egg into a bowl and whisk with a fork. Beat in the milk and oil. Sift in the flour, baking powder, sugars and nutmeg in another bowl.

Make a well in the centre of the bowl and add the egg mixture. Stir well until the mixture is moistened but not overdone. Fold in the prunes and the lime peel.

Fill the prepared muffin cup until 2/3 full.

Bake for 20 minutes until golden brown and serve warm.

THE COLOUR pink

PINK IS ASSOCIATED WITH SWEETNESS AND ROMANCE. MANY PEOPLE CONNECT IT WITH DELICACY AND TENDERNESS. THE COLOUR IS ALSO ASSOCIATED WITH PRINCESS POWER AND IS VERY COMMONLY USED AS GEM STONES IN COSTUME JEWELLERY. PINK IS NOW A VERY POPULAR COLOUR, PROBABLY BECAUSE OF YOUNG CELEBRITIES IN THE USA, COVERING THEMSELVES AND THEIR PETS IN IT!

Those who like pink are generally interested in the world around them and have a desire for living peacefully and creating a harmonious environment to both live and work in. Those who dislike the colour pink are generally adventurous and go-getting and pink may be a little too timid for their liking. They may find it difficult to connect with the innocence and naivety that pink evokes.

But it is worth remembering that pink is red mixed with white, so it will respond to a lot of the same messages and signals as red. Pink, like red, is an extremely dynamic colour. **DETERMINATION AND FORCEFUL TRAITS ARE GIVEN ADDED STRENGTH WITH THIS COLOUR.** So do not be fooled by the fluffy, sweet and feminine appearance of pink.

WHAT IS YOUR COLOUR PERSONALITY? TO FIND OUT TURN TO PAGE 2.

THE PINK COLOUR PERSONALITY

- DETERMINED
- ENERGETIC
- HARMONIOUS
- DILIGENT
- TENDER/AFFECTIONATE
- ROMANTIC
- SENSITIVE
- CREATIVE
- ADVENTUROUS

This is a determined and wilful individual who will work diligently to achieve his goals. He can be very much the romantic partner with the right match, enjoying romantic jaunts in far flung destinations. He has exquisite taste and his partner reflects this, as does his home and work space. Mr Pink is an ideas man and really enjoys creating; his work and living space will be atmospheres of beauty, with exuberant textiles and finishing. He has a large network of associates so there is no limits when it comes to getting what he wants; he can get a lot done in a short time. Both charismatic and stimulating, being around him is fun and exciting. He likes to be involved in the action, so expect to be kept on the move when he is in his groove!

The Pink female is the femme fatale of all the colours. Ms pink knows what she likes and usually has no problem acquiring any object of her affections. She loves to be active and is very dynamic in the pursuit of her own happiness. She is articulate and can express her feelings and emotions without hesitation.
    Ms Pink is adept in household management but while she is superb at getting things done, she may not do all the work herself. She will spend some of her free time at the beauty therapist or hair salon as she enjoys looking and feeling well. Shopping, lunching and generally enjoying the niceties in life will excite this girl's passion.

The pink child is into everything – they love to know what's going on in your house, next door and down the road at friends' houses. Young pink can often be found in their garden enjoying the attention and activities that the household has to offer. Young pinks are very sociable and have a wicked sense of humour. They have an uncanny way of viewing things so it is never boring to be in their company.
They are very affectionate, so hugs and cuddles will be part of their daily ritual as 'youngsters' but this may become less obvious as they move into teen life. They love to shop and accessories galore will make them happy.
    As the sensitive pink child has tremendous creative flair, they enjoy writing a play or performing a short improvisation for everyone to see. Art, music and food are all worthwhile activities to get them involved in and these activities can also help nurture their confidence and self-esteem. If you have a young pink girl in the house who is a tomboy, move out of the way. They are boisterous, energetic and need room to explore. It is all go!

THE PINK PARENT

Pink parents are very attentive and spend a lot of time with their children encouraging all types of activities. They have great ideas for their children's development and enjoy surfing the net looking for school projects and courses. Their child does many such courses and is encouraged to be an all-rounder. Pink parents help in any way possible to advance their child's potential.

THE PINK CAREER

Pink personalities are best suited to self-employment or semi self-employment as they are so creative and dynamic they may be hindered by a more routine based job. They make excellent graphic designers, property developers, managers or financial advisors as they enjoy business deals and money making. Pink personalities love being kept on their toes; they enjoy completing a project they control from A-Z and then are ready for the next one that comes in line. Their business acumen is spectacular and they are adept at making solid and well thought out plans. Do not be fooled into thinking that the pink personality is a walkover as you will be proven wrong!

Guide To Wearing Pink

This colour is now a popular choice for both men and women as it is no longer regarded as a weak colour for the alpha male. It keeps cropping up as a favourite everywhere and is fast becoming a corporate colour of choice. Traditionally, however, the colour pink represented girl power and it is still associated with this. It is little wonder that it is the colour chosen to represent the breast cancer awareness campaign.

Pastel pink will add a warm hint to pale skins, whereas bright hotter pinks will compliment darker skins. Dark pinks and cranberry can look romantic and suit pale, olive and oriental complexions. The softer tones suit fair and delicate complexions, particularly if your hair colour is blonde, caramel or light brown.

WHEN TO USE PINK

Use pink when creating a romantic atmosphere as it relaxes and brings calmness. The colour pink has been found to have a tranquilising effect on people and suppresses hostile and anxious behaviour. A shade of pink known as Baker-Miller pink is widely used in police cells and psychiatric wards. Research has shown that exposure to pink reduces muscular strength within 2.7 seconds.

It is a positive, tranquil colour to wear in sticky and tense situations. **Pink is also a very magnetic colour;** it draws people towards the wearer as it is soft, smooth and rarely intimidates. If you wish to get in touch with your artistic or musical side you should also turn to pink for inspiration.

During the teenage years wear bright cerise shades – salmon pink and orchid pink. Around ovulation and menstruation time, pink will help ease the discomfort. Also during the early menopause years, the colour pink can calm and sooth. Rose pink, in particular, is very beneficial for women in the transition to menopause as it symbolises maturity.

WHEN TO AVOID PINK

Avoid wearing too much pink or making it your signature colour as it can give off the air of a self-obsessed individual. Also, be careful of wearing too much pink in a romantic relationship, as it may zap your partner's desire.

A PINK DAY PLAN

EXERCISE – GET OUT INTO THE FRESH AIR AND HAVE A GOOD WALK OR SOAK IN A HOT BUBBLE BATH FILLED WITH YOUR FAVOURITE SCENTED OILS. LOVE IT!

CLOTHES – THINK PINK TODAY. WEAR SOMETHING PINK AND YOU WILL FEEL PRETTY AND FEMININE ALL DAY.

PERSONALITY – I AM A ROMANTIC, AFFECTIONATE AND KIND PERSON. TODAY MY PERSONALITY WILL DRAW PEOPLE TOWARDS ME. I WILL SHOW PEOPLE I CARE ABOUT THEM.

BEST COLOUR PERSONALITY MATCH

Pink personalities suit green personalities. Green personalities enjoy the finer things in life and so they appreciate good food, fragrance and nature. The green personality can help the energetic and controlling pink personality to unwind, relax and recharge. The pink personality is generally grounded and this is a quality that the green personality appreciates. Both can be extremely passionate and so they can enjoy the adventurous and intimate activities of their relationship.

Pink personalities also do well with most of the other colour personalities, especially gold. Pink and gold personalities are electric together in romance. There is a link between these two that is inexplicable to all around; perhaps it is because they are on the same mental wavelength. The pink personality enjoys the mental challenge that gold offers to start with and this will lead to a more physical union that will leave the heart pounding!

WORST COLOUR PERSONALITY MATCH

Pink and red personalities may clash slightly, mainly because they are similar. They are both energetic, dynamic and enjoy getting attention, so their competition to be the centre of attention may cause conflict. As these two personalities are vibrant and competitive by nature, once paired in a relationship they make little time for relaxing and taking time out. They are more likely to spend a lot of time getting things done, achieving goals and building empires together – in business terms they can attain a great deal. But in romantic relationships the hot passion can fade quickly but afterwards they'll often maintain a terrific friendship.

⊕ Pink Health

PINK IS A VERY NURTURING COLOUR AND CAN HELP SOFTEN THE ROUGH EDGES THAT MOST PEOPLE DEVELOP IN AN ATTEMPT TO PROTECT THEMSELVES FROM THE WORLD. BURN ROSE OIL AND SPRAY ROSE WATER OVER BED LINEN TO HELP RELAX THE BODY AND PERHAPS GET YOU IN THE MOOD FOR LOVING.

PINK IS ASSOCIATED WITH THE FEMALE REPRODUCTIVE SYSTEM. SOMETIMES INFERTILITY CAN INTERFERE WITH A RELATIONSHIP AS IT MAY BECOME THE SOLE CONCERN AND TOPIC OF DISCUSSION. PINK MAY HELP THE INDIVIDUAL TO BE GENTLER WITH HIM/HERSELF AND PROMOTE A POLICY OF SELF-LOVE.

INFERTILITY

INFERTILITY is usually defined as the failure to conceive after a year or more of regular sexual activity during the time of ovulation. It may also refer to the inability to carry a pregnancy to term. Ovulation, fertilisation, and the journey of the fertilised ovum through the fallopian tube and finally into the uterus are highly intricate processes. Many events must work together perfectly for pregnancy to occur.

In 40% of infertile couples, problems affecting the male partner are either partially or wholly the cause of infertility. For men, infertility is most often the result of a low sperm count or an anatomical abnormality. A variety of factors can result in a low sperm count, including alcohol consumption, endocrine disorders, exposure to toxins, radiation, excessive heat, recent acute illness or prolonged fever, testicular injury and very rarely, mumps-induced wasting of the testicles. Varicoceles – abnormal enlargement of veins that drain the testicle – can cause infertility in men because the veins of the testes no longer moderate the temperature of the testicles correctly, so can negatively affect sperm.

INFERTILITY

For women, the most common causes of infertility include ovulatory failure or blocked fallopian tubes, endometriosis, which is the abnormal growth of cells that form in the lining of the uterus, and uterine fibroids which are benign growths that can form on the interior muscular wall as well as the exterior of the uterus. Some women develop antibodies to their partner's sperm, in effect becoming allergic to them. Chlamydia, a sexually transmitted disease can cause many cases of infertility. Psychological issues, such as stress or fear of parenthood, may contribute to infertility as well, although stress is usually the result of infertility, not the cause of it. Often more than one cause for infertility is found, although in approximately 20% of cases, nothing that seems to inhibit conception can be found.

THE FOLLOWING ARE THE MOST COMMON REASONS COUPLES ARE UNABLE TO CONCEIVE:

- THE WOMAN HAS ENDOMETRIOSIS.
- THE MAN HAS ABNORMAL SPERM, A LOW SPERM COUNT OR ERECTILE DYSFUNCTION.
- THE WOMAN'S FALLOPIAN TUBES ARE BLOCKED.
- OVULATION TAKES PLACE RARELY OR IRREGULARLY.
- THE COUPLE IS UNABLE TO HAVE COMPLETE SEXUAL INTERCOURSE.
- THE CERVICAL MUCOUS ATTACKS AND KILLS THE SPERM.
- THE WOMAN DOES NOT MANUFACTURE ENOUGH PROGESTERONE TO CARRY A BABY TO TERM.
- THE WOMAN IS OVER 34 (FERTILITY DECLINES RAPIDLY AFTER THAT AGE).

A SELECTION OF PINK FOODS

GUAVAS

PINK GRAPEFRUITS

SALMON

FIGS

RHUBARB

PRAWNS

RASPBERRIES

EAT PINK FOODS

Pink foods such as pink grapefruit contain the phytonutrient lycopene that not only gives the grapefruit its magnificent colour but also enhances the anti-oxidant content. Eating citrus fruits as part of five or more portions of fruit and vegetables per day is linked to reduced risk of stroke.

Raspberries

Grown on climbing canes, RASPBERRIES are an excellent source of dietary fibre, Vitamin C and folate. They activate the body's natural self-cleansing ability; improving skin, hair and liver functions. They boost energy and encourage efficient metabolism of protein.

Raspberries are available fresh or frozen and can be eaten on their own with cream or made into smoothies, sorbets and preserves.

Nutrition
- Contain soluble fibre, pectin
- A good source of Vitamin C

Good For
- Boosting the immune system
- Acting as a natural diuretic
- Boosting moods
- Energizing

How Much To Eat
- 100g (3 $^1/_2$ oz) provides 75% of RDA Vitamin C
- Eat fresh and raw

Phytonutrients
- Anthocyanidins
- Flavonoids
- Catechins

Rhubarb

RHUBARB is technically a vegetable but is used as a fruit. It is a strange looking plant and originally comes from China and Tibet.

It is a rich source of oxalic acid which helps remove toxins from the body cells and promotes a feeling of general well being. It is important to remember, however, that oxalic acid interferes with the absorption of calcium and can be toxic if eaten in high quantities. Plant foods such as rhubarb, spinach and beetroot are rich in oxalic acid, while chocolate, nuts and tea are moderate sources.

Nutrition
- Vitamin A, C
- Potassium
- Manganese
- Calcium

Good For
- Oxalic acid

How Much To Eat
- 100g (3 $^1/_2$ oz) portion = 7 kcal
- Best eaten lightly stewed

Phytonutrients
- Anthocyanidins
- Anthrones

did you know?

A FEW BANANA SKINS BURIED IN THE SOIL AROUND YOUR RASPBERRY CANES GUARANTEE BRILLIANT RASPBERRIES OF VIBRANT COLOUR AND FLAVOUR.

Figs

The **FIG** from the banyan tree is widely used in Ayurvedic medicine. They make excellent laxatives.

Nutrition
- Iron
- Potassium

Good For
- Boosting energy
- Digestive problems such as constipation
- Anaemia

How Much To Eat
- 100g (3 $\frac{1}{2}$ oz) serving of fresh figs = 43 kcal
- 100g (3 $\frac{1}{2}$ oz) dried fig = 213 kcal (Eat three times a week)

Phytonutrients
- Beta-carotene
- An enzyme called ficin (aids the digestive system by tenderising protein foods)

IN ANCIENT GREECE, OLYMPIC ATHLETES WERE FED A LOT OF FIGS TO BUILD UP THEIR STAMINA.

Pink Grapefruits

PINK GRAPEFRUITS are marginally higher in Vitamin C than white ones. Grapefruits are high in soluble fibre which encourages the body to eliminate surplus cholesterol.

The flavonoid compounds found in pink grapefruits can inhibit a special enzyme in the intestines that is responsible for breaking down antihistamines and statins – drugs for lowering cholesterol.

Nutrition
- Vitamin C
- Potassium

Good For
- Anti-oxidising
- Diabetes
- Sore throats
- Circulatory challenges
- Reducing risk of stroke

How Much To Eat
- Half a medium pink grapefruit weighs 170g (6 oz)

Phytonutrients
- Flavonoids and bio-flavonoids
- Phenolic acid
- Lycopene
- Beta-carotene
- Pectin

DID YOU KNOW?

Both pink and red grapefruits are members of a special group of fruits that contain lycopene. Lycopene are open chained unsaturated carotenoids that give the vibrant red colour to other fruits and vegetables such as tomatoes, blood oranges and watermelons.

Watermelon sellers in a Bolivian market.

Brie, Salmon and Pink Grapefruit Platter

SERVES 4

4 SLICES OF SMOKED SALMON

4 GENEROUS SLICES OF RIPE BRIE
  CHEESE

HALF A PINK GRAPEFRUIT – PEELED
  AND CUT INTO 4 SEGMENTS

GENEROUS HANDFUL OF MIXED GREEN
  LEAVES AND BALSAMIC VINEGAR

SEASON WITH FRESHLY GROUND
  BLACK AND PINK PEPPERCORNS

Arrange the fresh ingredients attractively on a platter and serve chilled with fresh crunchy bread. This is an ideal brunch platter or good to have with wine.

Pink Grapefruit and Walnut Salad

SERVES 4 (AS A SIDE-SALAD)

100G (3 ^{1}/$_2$ OZ) WALNUT HALVES – BROKEN INTO SMALLER PIECES

2 PINK GRAPEFRUITS

4 TBSP WALNUT OIL

140G (5 OZ) ROCKET LEAVES

140G (5 OZ) FETA CHEESE – CRUMBLED

Preheat oven to 200°C (390°F) or gas mark 6.

Tip the walnuts into a baking tray and roast for 5 minutes until the nuts are brown – but watch they don't burn. Put on a plate to cool.

Segment the grapefruit. Slice off the top and bottom of the fruit with a sharp knife, cut off the peel and make sure there is no white pith left. Cut into each segment between the membranes. Do this over a bowl to catch the juices. Halve the fruit segments if they are large.

Now put the walnut oil in the reserved grapefruit juice and fruit segments. Add the rocket leaves, cheese and toasted walnuts and toss gently.

Divide between four side plates.

Raspberry Mousse

SERVES 4

FOR THE BASE:

BUTTER – FOR GREASING

3 EGGS

75G (2 ¹/₂ OZ) CASTER SUGAR

75G (2 ¹/₂ OZ) PLAIN FLOUR –
   SIFTED, PLUS EXTRA

FOR THE FILLING:

675G (1 LB 8 OZ) RASPBERRIES

25G (1 OZ) CASTER SUGAR

JUICE AND GRATED RIND OF ONE
   LEMON

2 TBSP POWDERED GELATINE –
   SOAKED IN 3 TBSP WATER

2 EGG WHITES

150 ML (5 FL OZ) DOUBLE CREAM

150 ML (5 FL OZ) CRÈME FRAICHE

FOR THE DECORATION:

1–2 EGG WHITES

450G (1 LB) MIXED SUMMER FRUITS

CASTER SUGAR – FOR COATING

ALMONDS

GARNISH WITH MINT

THE BASE:

Preheat the oven to 190°C (375°F) or gas mark 5. Grease and flour a 23 cm (9 in) loose
bottom cake tin. Bring a pan of water to the boil, then remove from the heat.

Place the eggs and sugar in a bowl over the hot water; whisk until the mixture is thick and
creamy and forms a lasting trail on the surface when you lift the whisk. Remove from the heat
and continue whisking until cold.

Gently fold in the flour using a metal spoon (do not over-mix). Pour into the tin and bake for about
15–20 minutes until golden. Turn out on to a wire rack to cool.

Slice cake in half horizontally and leave one half back in the clean tin – cut side up.

Raspberry Mousse

THE FILLING:

Place 450g (1 lb) raspberries in a pan with half of the sugar, lemon juice and rind. Cook for 5–7 minutes until the sugar is dissolved and the raspberries are soft.

Spoon two tablespoons of the juice over the sponge. Add the gelatine to the pan. Stir until dissolved, and then press the fruit through a sieve over a bowl.

Top up the juice to 600 ml (20 fl oz) with water if necessary. Set the bowl over iced water and leave to stand; stir occasionally to check if it is setting (this should take about 15 minutes).

Meanwhile, put remaining sugar in a pan with three tablespoons of water and dissolve over a low heat. Wash down the sides of the pan with a clean brush dipped in water and bring the syrup to the boil. Cook without stirring, until it reaches 50°C (119°F) on a sugar thermometer or until a drop of syrup forms a soft ball in cold water. Then remove from the heat.

Whisk the egg whites until stiff. Pour in the sugar syrup in a steady stream, whisking all the time, until cold, thick and glossy. Lightly whip the cream and fold into the crème fraiche, then roughly chop the reserved fruit. When the fruit mixture is just setting, fold in the cream, meringue and fruit. Pour over the sponge and chill until set. Hold a hot damp cloth around the tin for a few seconds; release the cake on to a serving plate. Lightly whip the egg white; dip the fruit in the egg white, then in the sugar to coat. Arrange these and the almonds on the mousse and serve.

Fig and Raspberry Compote

SERVES 4

2 FRESH FIGS

1 TBSP CLEAR HONEY

¼ LEVEL TSP GROUND CINNAMON

200G (7 OZ) FRESH RASPBERRIES

GREEK OR PLAIN YOGHURT FOR SERVING

Preheat the oven to 180°C (350°F) or gas mark 4.

Cut the figs into quarters and put them in a small roasting tin. Drizzle with the honey and sprinkle with cinnamon, then bake for ten minutes until they have softened.

Tip figs into a bowl, with all the juices, and leave to cool. Snip the figs into smaller pieces with scissors, or cut them with a knife.

Add the raspberries to the bowl and mash them with a fork. Spoon yoghurt into glass dishes and top with a couple of spoonfuls of compote.

Note: The compote will keep in a covered bowl in the fridge for up to five days. Not suitable for freezing as they tend to go too mushy due to the high water content.

Rhubarb Brioche Pudding

SERVES 6–8

450G (1 LB) PINK RHUBARB

55G (2 OZ) BUTTER

12 SLICE BRIOCHE LOAF

450 ML (15 FL OZ) CREAM

230 ML (8 FL OZ) MILK

4 LARGE FREE RANGE EGGS – BEATEN LIGHTLY

1 TSP PURE VANILLA ESSENCE

175G (6 OZ) SUGAR

1 X 20CM (1 X 8IN) OVENPROOF DISH

A SHALLOW ROASTING DISH

Cut the rhubarb into $2^1/_2$ cm (1 in) pieces. Put into a dish and sprinkle with sugar. Leave to macerate for an hour.

Butter the brioche and arrange four slices, butter-side down, in one layer in the buttered dish. Scatter half the rhubarb over the bread, and cover with another layer of bread – butter-side down.

Scatter the remaining rhubarb on top and cover with the remaining bread – butter-side down.

Whisk the cream, milk, eggs, vanilla essence and sugar together in a bowl. Pour the mixture through a fine sieve over the bread.

Sprinkle the sugar over the top and let the mixture stand, covered loosely, for at least one hour or refrigerate overnight.

Preheat the oven to 180°C (350°F) or gas mark 4. Bake in a shallow roasting dish (the water should be boiling and come half-way up the sides of the baking dish) in the middle of the preheated oven, for about one hour or until the top is crisp and golden.

Serve the pudding warm with some softly whipped cream.

Raspberry Ripple Ice-Cream

SERVES 4–6

450 ML (15 FL OZ) DOUBLE CREAM

400G (12 OZ) CAN MILK – SWEETENED AND CONDENSED

1 TSP VANILLA ESSENCE

4 TBSP SOFT RASPBERRY JAM

Whisk cream until it becomes thick. Then open the can of condensed milk and stir into the cream.

Slowly add vanilla essence and place into a container in the freezer for 3 hours. Then spoon in the raspberry jam and mix in at random.

Place back into the freezer for another 30 minutes and serve on raspberry shortcake.

Raspberry Brulée

SERVES 4

350G (12 OZ) RASPBERRIES

GRATED RIND OF 1 ORANGE

1 TBSP CASTER SUGAR

150 ML (5 FL OZ) DOUBLE CREAM

150G (5 ½ OZ) THICK GREEK YOGHURT

50G (2 OZ) DEMERARA SUGAR

Divide the raspberries among four ramekin dishes, making sure that you leave sufficient room for the topping. Sprinkle over the orange rind and caster sugar.

Whip the cream until thick and stir in yoghurt. Spread over the raspberries and chill for 30 minutes.

Preheat the grill to 190°C (375°F) or mark 5. Sprinkle the Demerara sugar over the cream to evenly cover.

Place the ramekin dishes on a baking sheet, then place the sheet under the grill for a few minutes until the sugar is golden brown and just starting to caramelise.

Allow the desserts to cool. Chill for at least 1 hour before serving.

Pretty in Pink 'Pavlov-ettes'

MAKES 12

4 EGG WHITES

200G (7 OZ) CASTER SUGAR

1 TSP CORN FLOUR

TINY DROP OF PINK FOOD COLOURING

1 TSP LEMON JUICE

140 ML (4 FL OZ) CREAM

150G (5 1/2 OZ) NATURAL YOGHURT

500G (1LB 2 OZ) FRESH FRUIT

Preheat the oven to 140°C (280°F) or gas mark 1.

Prepare the flat tin by cutting out a piece of grease-proof paper that will fit snugly onto the tin.

Crack each egg carefully into a jug – separating the egg yolk or yellow part from the white jelly part.

Place the egg whites into a large mixing bowl.

Add half the sugar and using an electric mix, whisk until stiff. Gradually add the remaining sugar, whisking all the time. Stir in corn flour, pink colouring and lemon juice.

Spoon onto the baking sheet as one big Pavlova or spoon into 12 small 'Pavlov-ettes'.

Bake for 40–45 minutes.

Put the cream into a clean bowl and whisk until thick. Add natural yoghurt.

Decorate with fresh cream and fresh fruit. A dessert that will really thrill dinner guests!

THE COLOUR gold

GOLD IS MYSTICAL, POWERFUL AND ANCIENT. IT CONJURES UP IMAGES OF PRE-COLUMBIAN INCA ARTEFACTS AND EGYPTIAN SCULPTURES, ALONG WITH SUN-WORSHIPPING. GOLD SIGNIFIES AN ENDLESS SUPPLY; IT RADIATES VITALITY AND ABUNDANCE FOR ALL.

There is a sense of graciousness associated with gold and also knowledge and wisdom. Those who like gold can be highly imaginative individuals. They have an interest in things of an esoteric nature and are spiritual. They may be shy and can come across as aloof. They make loyal and trusting friends and are extremely reliable. This is the friend you can tell your darkest secret to and you can be assured that it will not travel any further.

THE LOVER OF GOLD CAN BE A PERFECTIONIST AND CAN HAVE RIDICULOUSLY HIGH EXPECTATIONS. They always aim high and are big achievers who do not like being second best. They are doers and brilliant planners; they adore making up new projects and are happy to get others to do the nitty-gritty. They can be intolerant when others do not grasp their ideas quickly and are impatient with sloppy workers or work. The leader always has a gold streak in them; there is a depth of self-knowledge that puts him or her in front and the wisdom to put plans in motion.

WHAT IS YOUR COLOUR PERSONALITY? TO FIND OUT TURN TO PAGE 2.

THE GOLD COLOUR PERSONALITY

- KNOWS WISDOM IS TO BE HANDED ON TO OTHERS, NOT TO BE HOARDED
- WELL-HEELED
- ASSOCIATED WITH MONEY AND MATERIAL WEALTH
- GLORIOUS — IT COMES UP TRUMPS WHATEVER THE ODDS AS IT CAN SHAKE OFF ANY PARASITIC ACTIVITY, BOTH EMOTIONAL AND PHYSICAL, THAT MAY HINDER PERFORMANCE AND PREVENT SUCCESS
- ABSORBS FACTS QUICKLY; MINDFUL AND QUICK-THINKING
- FULL OF WISDOM AND FINDS THE SOLUTION THAT YELLOW WAS LOOKING FOR — IT IS LIKE A MATURE YELLOW THAT HAS COME INTO ITS OWN AUTHORITY
- TRUSTS NO ONE
- FEAR OF FAILURE AND CAN PUT OFF DOING THINGS
- UNREAL EXPECTATIONS — ALWAYS IN SEARCH OF FOOL'S GOLD

Mr Gold

The gold male has a vibrant personality, with a charisma that dazzles. He has a hilarious sense of humour and is usually the guy talking and giving the lecture or demonstration. He has an elephant brain and can remember facts, figures and statistics when it is necessary to demonstrate a point or create conversation at the dinner table. He loves everything that is quality: fine food, fine wine, fine restaurants and sparkly people with life stories that are enigmatic and inspirational. The gold male likes independent partners who ooze mystery and energy.

The gold male has an appetite to explore the unknown; he is positively curious. He loves to be adventurous and travel is essential to his well-being. He appreciates great manners and loves you to surprise him with useful gifts – something unusual, unique and different such as tickets to an astrology observation meeting or a 'legends' rock tour. Shopping for this man will keep you on your toes.

Ms Gold

The gold female is positive, active and enjoys her own company. Unlike many other personalities she can spend a few days by herself and tends to need this time to organise the numerous projects she has planned. She adores researching and reading up on new concepts, products or places to go. She is gracious and projects a feeling of well-being. She is rarely ill and likes to take good care of herself.

Ms Gold is a master at taking time out when needed by having a siesta or power nap; this technique energises her to move onto the next pressing project. She loves colours, textures and tastes so she will enjoy spending time in the kitchen cooking, pottering around a food market sampling the local produce and enjoying the splendid fresh cut flowers, plant life and culinary herbs. She also loves art and artistic activities. An ideal day out includes exposure to visual arts and consumption of culinary art. She is very excitable and will keep you on your toes, indoors as well as outdoors.

A difficult darling to get settled as her fiercely independent nature requires someone very special indeed. Once she has given her heart to you, you can be sure that you have found your pot of gold at the end of the rainbow. Life with her will be as colourful as it gets.

Young Gold

The gold child will bring a glow into your life. From the minute they can crawl, they are eager to get cycling, rollerblading or skateboarding – anything that will get them moving. They have a keen interest in things that move and grow. It would be a fantastic idea to get them a small gardening kit and seeds, when old enough, and they will happily play for hours in the garden.

Gold children are extremely artistic and love to play dress-up. They are also inventive and adore making things – from cakes to water bombs! They are enthusiastic students and enjoy the challenges that learning presents. They also like to read and enjoy quiet time alone. They can be shy and can get a little lost if their other siblings are loud or boisterous, so it is really important to let them express themselves.

THE GOLD PARENT

The gold parent is amazed with the new baby and will have read every book available on the subject. They attend every local seminar and are totally into the entire role. The house is colourful and stimulating – buzzing with games and books and stuff that kids love. They are the ones to have the parties and celebrations in their house. Gold parents are able to balance work and parent roles beautifully.

Gold mum and dad put activity and outdoor pursuits high on the things to do list and encourage junior to get involved in all types of team sports and activities. They must be careful not to be too demanding on their child and have expectations that do not suit their child.

Guide To Wearing Gold

Gold makes an ideal colour for accessories: handbags, belts, sunglasses and make-up for eyes and nail varnish for nails. It sparkles up your evening wear and adds a touch of glamour. Summer tans glow with golden footwear.

THE GOLD CAREER

The gold career ideally involves sharing the information and knowledge they have gathered since birth. The gold personality has a spectacular way with words and is talented at presenting new concepts and ideas in a convincing manner. This means they have an uplifting and motivating impact on anyone they come into contact with.They have a magnetic charm and people feel special in their company. They are as smart at networking as they are at communication.As a consequence they naturally make excellent facilitators, humanitarian campaigners, teachers and presenters.

The gold personality is an ideal person to have on any team. They have a magnificent knack of getting to the heart of the issue fast and will be candid and straight-forward when dealing in business. The gold worker works hard and will expect those around them to do the same. They are highly critical and expect high standards at all times, so attention to detail is crucial if you work closely with them.

WHEN TO USE GOLD

When you want to nurture self-worth, gold will help you achieve this by putting value on yourself. Gold is the colour to use when you want to feel like you sparkle and want the world to know it.

WHEN TO AVOID GOLD

Steer clear of gold if you are feeling paranoid as it may aggravate feelings of anxiety and cause you to have irrational fears. In times of doubt, or when you are suspicious of someone or something, avoid gold, as it may exacerbate your feelings. When you are feeling negative, judgemental or over-critical of yourself or others stay away from gold, as it fuels gossip and chatter-box tendencies.

EXERCISE AND LEISURE ACTIVITIES

Gold activities for exercise and leisure include walking and reading. To completely nurture their inquisitive minds, they need information that has substance, so for example they enjoy watching TV programmes that are educational and travel programmes excite them as opposed to soaps. As they are extremely artistic and creative, a hobby that involves creating, developing or designing will work. It is a positive thing for the gold personality to keep a number of activities going at the one time so that they do not become restless or have a daily routine that is too predictable.

A GOLD DAY PLAN

EXERCISE – I WILL BE AWARE OF MY NERVOUS ENERGY TODAY AND FOCUS ON MY BREATHING TO KEEP ANXIETY LEVELS UNDER CONTROL.

CLOTHES – I WILL WEAR SOMETHING GOLD TODAY AND RADIATE VITALITY TO ALL AROUND ME.

FOOD – I WILL EAT SPROUTS, GRAINS AND HONEY.

AFFIRMATION – I AM IN THE GOLDEN ZONE OF MY LIFE TODAY. THIS IS AS GOOD AS IT GETS.

THOUGHT FOR THE DAY

Today I value who I am. I am doing the right thing. I will do my best in all things.

BEST COLOUR PERSONALITY MATCH

Gold personalities are best suited to indigo personalities. Both personalities are drawn to anything of an esoteric nature. They look beyond the obvious and enjoy researching, especially for something that may help unearth new theories. Both enjoy dressing in exquisite clothes and share a passion for design details. They love things of old and are wise and sensible in their dealings with others.

Gold and pink make a sensitive and tender union and can enjoy a very special friendship based on understanding and mutual respect.

WORST COLOUR PERSONALITY MATCH

The gold personality may clash slightly with yellow personalities as both have similar interests, but the gold may already have the answers to what yellow personalities are looking for. In some circumstances gold personalities may steal yellow's thunder. This can be unpleasant and not particularly stimulating for the excited yellow personality, who is all consumed with investigative pursuits.

✚ Gold **Health**

GOLD IS GOOD AT SOOTHING DIGESTIVE IRREGULARITIES, IRRITABLE BOWEL SYNDROME AND RHEUMATICS. THIS IS AN IDEAL COLOUR TO BE AWARE OF AS GOLD FOODS CAN HELP REDUCE INFLAMMATION AND ARE IDEAL FOR THOSE WHO SUFFER FROM ARTHRITIS.

THE GOLDEN YEARS

I often chat with peers and colleagues about health and the issue of growing older sometimes comes up. It makes me laugh when I think about the poor, mistreated cells of my 20s! They sure had a lot to deal with – those party days, late nights, quick foods and nervous energy, not to mention the sun-lounging for hours. What a great mix to accelerate cell overload. As I approached my thirties, I became more aware that a bit of TLC was needed. I began to take it easy, relaxed more and cut down on the partying. Today I strive to lead a more balanced and zestful life. No matter what your age, fitness profile or past experiences, the time is NOW to give yourself a break, lap up the fresh air, eat well and be yourself.

Growing older is not an illness, but the passing years do make the body more vulnerable to disease. Our genes dictate that the body's cells stop dividing after they have divided between 20 and 30 times. New cells must be made to replace those that stop dividing; a process that slows with age. When there are no longer enough new cells to replace the ones that have died or suffered damage, the result is ageing and most scientists agree that the accumulation of free radicals over time is what causes ageing. Studies show that cells stop dividing, change form and release damaging proteins that harm bodily tissues, further contributing to the ageing process. Many researchers maintain that it is our chosen lifestyle that accelerates ageing, rather than genetic or other factors.

A significant number of problems faced by people over the age of 60 may also be attributed to nutritional deficiencies. As we age, our bodies do not assimilate nutrients as well as they once did. Many elderly people experience malabsorption, where the nutrients in food are not properly absorbed from the gastrointestinal tract. As the body ages, its system slows down and becomes less efficient. As we get older good nutrients are more important than ever to support, repair and regenerate cells.

This theory has been subject to a great deal of research in recent years and has been gaining increased acceptance. Free radicals are atoms or groups of atoms that are extremely unstable and highly reactive. If they are present in excessive amounts, they begin attacking the body on a cellular level. Free radicals attack the cell's protective membranes and genetic material – the nucleic acids DNA and RNA – causing damage and malfunction. The immune system may be attacked by the damaged cells, as they act like foreign invaders. This will lead to an impaired immune system.

Free radicals are very chemically reactive. They exist for only one-millionth of a second each which makes it difficult for researchers to study them directly. Remember, however, that even with their short life span they do considerable damage to our cells, especially as people age.

THINGS TO DO TO HELP THE AGEING PROCESS

Choose activities that help you maintain your natural body rhythm – if you move to your own beat you are more than halfway there!

1. Drink water regularly – tepid, with fresh lemon or lime or herbal teas.
2. Eat your colours. Eat plenty of fresh fruit and vegetables. (See next page for more details)
3. Get exercise every day. If you cannot get to it every day, at least take some time out and relax.
4. Breathe well – you expel the greatest proportion of all toxins through breathing.
5. Have a plan for your day – this will help you to be more organised and avoid stressful situations.
6. Have a laugh – it is good for the whole body.
7. Talk to friends and family in person or over the phone. It is great to keep in touch and will help prevent feelings of isolation.
8. De-clutter your life as you go. Get rid of things that are now useless and refrain from putting them all in boxes in the attic; all that stuff is hanging over you. The important memories are already in your heart and mind – otherwise recycle. You will feel a whole lot lighter and it will also help you ditch any 'bag lady' syndrome fears that might be lurking around in your head.
9. Listen to music as this will help release happy endorphins that will help boost your mood.
10. Weather permitting – take a potter in the garden. If you do not have a garden you could plant a window box with some plants of your favourite colour.

FRUITS AND VEGETABLES

In order to enjoy good health and sustain longevity it is necessary that your diet is balanced, varied, colourful and has a combination of raw and cooked fruits and vegetables.

FOUR TIPS FOR EATING RAW FRUITS AND VEGETABLES

1. CHOOSE <u>ORGANIC</u> FRUITS AND VEGETABLES WHEN POSSIBLE. PESTICIDES CAN LEAVE TOXIC RESIDUE ON PLANTS THAT CAN HARM YOUR ORGANS. BE SELECTIVE BUT DEFINITELY BUY ORGANIC ROOT VEGETABLES AS THESE ARE MOST SUSCEPTIBLE TO ABSORBING PESTICIDES AS THEY ARE CLOSEST TO THE SOIL.
2. EAT FRUITS AND VEGETABLES WHEN THEY ARE IN SEASON. THIS WILL ENSURE THAT YOU ARE EATING THE PRODUCE WHEN THEY ARE AT THEIR BEST. (SEE COLOUR STAR PLAN CHAPTER FOR MORE DETAILS.)
3. EAT ALL YOUR COLOURS WHEN CHOOSING RAW FRUITS AND VEGETABLES.
4. RAW FRUITS AND VEGETABLES CONTAIN ENZYMES WHICH HELP YOUR BODY AND PROLONG LIFE. ENZYMES ARE DESTROYED WHEN FOOD IS HEATED OVER 60°C (140°F).

WHAT ARE ENZYMES?

- Enzymes are catalysts that help the body digest food effectively. It is extremely important to have foods rich in enzymes as they can help you overcome digestive lethargy, distress and fatigue.
- Enzymes are small proteins.
- Plant enzymes survive into the intestines and can be absorbed into tissues helping to break down old cooked food residues.
- Metabolic enzymes regulate metabolism and help you stay slim.
- Digestive enzymes are made by the body.
- Food enzymes are found in foods and help digestion.

did you know?

A PERSON WHO EATS RAW FOOD CONTAINS FAR MORE ENZYMES THAN THAT OF A PERSON WHO EATS COOKED FOOD.

A SELECTION OF GOLD FOODS

BUCKWHEAT

CANNELLINI BEANS

SUNFLOWER SEEDS

SESAME SEEDS

PUMPKIN SEEDS

OATS

QUINOA

SPROUTS

ADZUKI BEANS

BUTTER BEANS

MUNG BEANS

ALMONDS

NUTS

PULSES

WALNUTS

ALFALFA

BARLEY

EAT GOLD FOODS

When putting this section together I was thinking of the Sting track – 'Fields of Gold'. This prompted me to compile the list of foods as gold, even though some are not gold in colour. Many may be described as tan or brown, such as those listed in the nut section. But all of the foods listed make a healthy contribution to the diet, provide valuable nutrients and can significantly reduce many illnesses such as certain cancers. There are many studies published that reveal the effects that sprouted seeds can have on bowel health. Many have a low glycaemic rating and introducing them into your diet will make a tasty change to perhaps the tried and tested ingredients that you currently eat regularly. Using some of the gold foods listed you can successfully add variety to your diet.

SPROUTS

Sprouts are 'The freedom food', powerhouse empires that provide the body with anti-inflammatory anti-oxidants. Any seed or bean equipped with the potential to reproduce can sprout. Seeds or beans can be brought to life by soaking them in water to produce a long thin shoot.

Sprouts contain two anti-ageing constituents: RNA – nucleic acids that are only found in living cells and DNA – nucleic acids that contain genetic instructions used in the development and functioning of all known living organisms. Sprouts can be added to many dishes such as stir fries, salads, wraps and omelettes. They are a concentrated source of living enzymes and are easy to digest. For more details on sprouts, log onto www.isga-sprouts.org, the International Sprout Growers Association.

Kids are fascinated with them and will really enjoy sprouting their own – so will you! Have a look at the following guide to discover how you can get started.

HOW TO SPROUT!

You can have home grown sprouts by simply purchasing a sprouting kit and sprinkling water over the seeds or beans or make your own kit.

You will need:

1 large jam jar

A handful of seeds

Water – enough to make the muslin moist

Muslin – sufficient to cover the bottom of the jar

Rinse the seeds well. Place into the jar and cover with some cooled, boiled water (2–3 cm).

Cover with muslin and secure the jar with a rubber seal. Leave overnight in a warm, dark place.

The next day rinse the seeds well and repeat. When you see a little sprout, you can leave the jar out in an open, bright space.

Leave the seeds to sprout for a few hours. Unleash the vitamins and minerals!

GUIDE TO SPROUTS

Type of sprout:	Alfalfa	Spelt	Mung
Culinary uses:	Salad	Juices	Salad/Steam vegetable
Flavour:	Mild flavour	Crunchy and sweet	Crisp and crunchy
Amount needed:	4–5 tbsp	2 cups	1 cup
Time to sprout:	7 days	3 days	4–5 days
You will need:	Tray	Jar	Jar
Sprouting experience:	Beginner	Beginner	Intermediate

Type of sprout:	Sunflower	Adzuki	Buckwheat
Culinary uses:	Salad/Juice	Salad/Steam vegetable	Salad/Juice
Flavour:	Hard	Delicate/Crunchy	Crisp
Amount needed:	5–6 tbsp	1 cups	5 tbsp
Time to sprout:	9 days	4–5 days	10 days
You will need:	Tray	Jar	Tray
Sprouting experience:	Medium	Medium	Advanced

Alfalfa

Mung Beans

Adzuki Beans

ALFALFA contains phenolic acids which block specific enzymes that cause inflammation. It has cholesterol lowering abilities, which are largely due to the saponins.

MUNG beans are packed with a high concentration of anti-oxidants that help the body deal with free radicals. You can grow them at home. (See the table on previous page.)

ADZUKI beans are sweet lentil-shaped and have a nutty taste and texture. You can eat them raw or add them to stir-fries.

Nutrition
- Folic acid
- Iron
- Calcium
- Copper
- Zinc
- Living enzymes
- Fibre

Nutrition
- Folic acid
- Calcium
- Iron
- Copper
- Zinc
- Proteins
- Enzymes
- Fibre

Nutrition
- Folic acid
- Zinc
- Iron
- Calcium
- Proteins
- Enzymes
- Fibre

Good For
- High energy
- Helping regenerate the body
- Helping the body deal with free radicals

Good For
- High energy
- Helping regenerate the body

Good For
- High energy
- Helping regenerate the body
- Helping the body deal with free radicals

How Much to Eat
- An average serving is 2 tablespoons
- Eat at least three times a week, raw or mixed in salads or in sandwiches

How Much to Eat
- An average serving is 40g or 2 tablespoons.
- Aim to eat these at least twice a week.
- They can be eaten in salads and stir-fries.

How Much to Eat
- Eat at least three times a week

Phytonutrients
- Saponins
- Phenolic acids

Phytonutrients
- Coumestrol (See Glossary for more details)
- Saponins

Phytonutrients
- Phenolic acid

This jazz player in Buenos Aires, Argentina was so full of energy he must have eaten a lot of beans!

PULSES

Pulses are edible seeds of certain plants of the legume family and include peas, beans and lentils. Research has shown that beans were among the first plants cultivated when agriculture began. Common beans such as kidney, black and pinto were cultivated in Mexico; lima beans were cultivated in Peru and chickpeas in the Middle East.

Dried pulses are widely available and should be stored in air-tight containers. Keep out of direct light and use within 6 months. Pulses toughen on storage and older ones will take longer to cook. Pulses can be used in a variety of ways – to thicken and enrich soups, stews and casseroles or in a sauce with vegetables, fish, poultry or meat. They can also be cooked and served cold in salads.

Raising the Pulse

Dried beans have been a staple survival food for centuries. They make the second largest contribution to the diet after cereals. There are many advantages attributed to pulses namely that they are inexpensive and have a long shelf life.

Tina's Cooking Tip

Remember that most dried pulses need to be soaked before cooking. Always discard the soaking water, rinse well and cook in fresh water. Changing the water will help to reduce the flatulence some people suffer when eating pulses. Add a pinch of caraway, dill, cumin and fennel seed.

Never use salt or acid when cooking pulses as this toughens the skins though salt may be added in towards the end of the cooking period. Why not check out the recipes for Butter Bean Pasta or Two-Bean Vegetable Goulash at the end of this chapter?

NUTS

Due to their phytonutrient component, adding nuts and seeds to the daily diet will reduce the visible signs of ageing, such as wrinkles and sagging skin. Nuts can also help decrease the risk of heart disease because of their Omega-3 content and the fat present in nuts helps the body to absorb the phytonutrients, vitamins and minerals found in other fruits and vegetables.

Nuts also help with weight control as they are packed full of protein and so make an ideal snack; a handful will keep you full for hours so that you refrain from munching on other types of snacks between meals.

Walnuts

WALNUTS are low in sodium and saturated fat so they help promote a healthy heart.

Nutrition
- Low in sodium and saturated fat
- High in polyunsaturated fats and monounsaturated fats
- Protein
- Small amounts of zinc
- Vitamin E

Good For
- Lowering cholesterol
- Promoting good skin
- Providing a feeling of fullness

How Much to Eat
- Four walnuts will provide a healthy amount of essential Omega-3 fats.
- A 100g portion will provide you with 688 kcals.
- Use in salads or press into oil and use as dressing for salads.

Phytonutrients
- Phytosterols
- Flavonoids

Almonds

ALMONDS are the seeds of a tree related to the peach and plum. They may be bitter or sweet. Bitter almonds contain hydrocyanic acid and are poisonous if eaten in large quantities. The toxins are destroyed by heat but these almonds are used in small quantities to flavour cakes, confectionery and liqueurs, such as Amaretto. Sweet almonds are usually eaten dried. Almonds go well with apricots, chicken and chocolate.

Of all nuts, almonds contain the most calcium. They also contain 20% protein, which is – weight for weight – one third more protein than a medium-sized egg.

Nutrition
- Calcium
- Protein
- Zinc
- Magnesium
- Potassium
- Iron
- High in riboflavin – a B group Vitamin
- Fibre

Good For
- Almond oil is particularly good for the skin.

How Much to Eat
- A palmful of almonds three times a week. It should be eaten with foods that contain Vitamin C for maximum absorption.

Phytonutrients
- Hydrocyanic acid (bitter almonds only) – a toxic prussic acid and should never be eaten raw.

did you know?

TRIALS SHOW THAT INCORPORATING WALNUTS INTO THE MEDITERRANEAN DIET OR JAPANESE DIET CAN LEAD TO DECREASES IN BAD CHOLESTEROL.

SEEDS

Seeds can make a good contribution to the intake of minerals, including many minerals that are not found in quantity in a wide variety of foods such as zinc and selenium. Though high in fat, it is mostly polyunsaturated and some of the most important Omega-3s are present in most seeds. Seeds can be eaten as part of an in-between snack or incorporated into salads and vegetable dishes, in breads and home baking. Eating them raw is more nutritious. Store them in the fridge and eat within a few weeks to ensure the polyunsaturated oils do not oxidise and go rancid. If this is not possible, store them in a cool, dark, dry place.

Sesame Seeds

SESAME SEEDS are rich in phytic acid, which makes up about 5% of their weight. Eat with Vitamin C-rich fruits and vegetables to aid iron absorption.

These seeds are a wonderful source of calcium and they have a reputation for being an aphrodisiac in the Far East! This may be due to the high Vitamin E and iron content.

Nutrition
- Exceptional source of calcium
- Good source of protein
- Magnesium
- Iron
- Vitamin B namely niacin and folate
- Vitamin E

Good For
- Boosting energy
- Boosting sex drive

How Much to Eat
- 1 tbsp sesame seeds: weighs 12g.
- Eat as a snack, on salads, roast or toast them at least three times a week.

Phytonutrients
- Phytic acid
- Lignan – sesaminol – a strong anti-oxidant

Pumpkin Seeds

As PUMPKIN SEEDS are a particularly rich source of zinc they can be very beneficial for men. Zinc is essential for the production of fertile sperm, as well as being a scientifically protective substance for the prostate gland. Zinc is also important for boosting the immune system.

Nutrition
- Good source of fibre
- Magnesium
- Potassium
- Excellent source of iron and zinc
- Contains a small amount of Vitamin E

Good For
- Building immune system
- Helping fertility

How Much to Eat
- 1 tbsp of pumpkin seeds weighs 16g; almost a quarter of their weight is protein.
- Eat at least three times a week in salads or sprinkle over cereals.

Phytonutrients
- Phenolic acids
- Carotenoids
- Lignans
(Refer to Glossary for more details)

SUNFLOWER seeds are extremely nutritious and contain large amounts of protein, B Vitamins and are one of the best sources of Vitamin E that helps promote healthy skin.

Nutrition
- Protein
- Vitamin B – niacin
- Vitamin E
- Selenium
- Potassium

Good For
- Building the immune system
- A healthy heart
- Promoting healthy skin

How Much to Eat
- A palmful three times a week sprinkled on salads or blended in a pâté. (See recipe section for ideas.)

Phytonutrients
- Carotenoids

BUCKWHEAT is a seed, not a grain and delivers more protein than rice, wheat, millet or corn. It is incredibly nutritious and healthy but ranks low on the glycaemic index. It contains arginine and lysine which are two essential amino acids that the body cannot produce itself. The body has to obtain these amino acids from food as they are essential for growth and repair of body cells.

Buckwheat contains no problematic gluten and so can be part of a gluten-free diet. It contains rare carbohydrate-compounds called fagopyritols which can reduce blood sugar levels which makes it beneficial for diabetics.

The fibre in buckwheat is largely soluble and can help reduce cholesterol levels. Buckwheat also contains polyphenols which is a powerful anti-oxidant that helps the body eliminate toxins (especially rutin which reduces blood pressure) and can help prevent haemorrhoids and varicose veins.

Nutrition
- Lysine and arginine (two of the eight essential amino acids)
- Fagopyritols
- Soluble fibre
- Gluten-free
- Zinc
- Copper
- Manganese

Good For
- Helps reduce cholesterol levels due to the soluble fibre
- Helps reduce blood pressure
- Helps prevent haemorrhoids and varicose veins as it supports the walls of the blood vessels

How Much to Eat
- Eat as part of your six portions of cereals a day.

Phytonutrients
- Fagopyritols
- Polyphenols

did you know?

BUCKWHEAT PASTA OR SOBA NOODLES MAKE A DELICIOUS ALTERNATIVE TO DURUM WHEAT PASTA, WHICH IS USED TO MAKE THE REGULAR TYPE OF PASTA. THEY COOK JUST LIKE OTHER PASTAS.

GOLDEN GRAINS

Golden grains are high in fibre and satisfy hunger more readily and for a longer period of time than refined grain products such as white flour, refined breads, pastries and pasta. Golden grains contain indigestible fibre that prevents blood sugar from rising quickly. The outer layer, known as the bran layer, is rich in minerals, polyunsaturated fatty acids and beneficial phytonutrients.

All of the grains listed here include a full nutritional profile and there are a number of easy to follow recipes. It is advisable to alternate with some of the other grain products listed in this chapter to achieve up to six servings of wholegrain cereals, pasta and potatoes a day. Introducing a variety of grains into your diet will make it more interesting.

OATS

Oats, nuts and seeds are packed full of nutrient-rich compounds. They help keep you looking young and fresh and provide long-lasting energy throughout the day. Choose 'whole groats' when purchasing oats as these oats are unprocessed and most natural so that you are getting all the nutrients that the grain has to offer. Oats contain beta-glucan fibres that make them good for cardiovascular health. Beta-glucan is a type of sponge-like soluble fibre that attracts cholesterol-based bile acids in the intestine and carries them out of the body.

Eating porridge helps the brain produce serotonin – a brain transmitter that keeps us focused and our spirits high. The combination of good, readily available calories and B Vitamins in dried fruit bars and oat flapjack bars can help those suffering with anxiety and nervous irritability. They can help you to deal with stress and leave you with more energy to get on and do the things in life that matter most. Oats are also gentle on the digestive system and will not affect people with IBS (Irritable Bowel Syndrome).

Oats contain both soluble and insoluble fibre. Foods rich in soluble fibre help regulate blood glucose levels and appetite which can benefit weight loss and heart disease. Magnesium, also found in oats, is a mineral necessary for slimming as it helps to break down carbohydrates, influence insulin and regulate blood sugar.

Oats

Porridge **OATS** take third place on a scale of 240 foods ranked according to how well they fill you up.

Nutrition
- Magnesium
- Zinc
- Beta-glucan fibres
- Vitamin E

Good For
- Lowering cholesterol
- Boosting the immune system
- Raising energy levels
- Regulating blood glucose
- Cardiovascular health

How Much to Eat
- Eat 5 or more portions of grains per day – 2 tbsp (30g) of oats makes a medium bowl of porridge per day.
- For optimal cholesterol lowering effect 75g or 5 tbsp oats daily is recommended.

Phytonutrients
- Phenolic acids
- Phytosterols
- Protease inhibitors
- Flavonoids – avenanthramides
- Saponins

OATS *(continued)*

The beta-glucan fibres in oats exert beneficial anti-glycaemic effects and lower cholesterol. In a clinical trial published in 2002, it showed that diabetics given oatmeal, oat bran or foods fortified with beta-glucan, registered far lower and slower rises in blood sugar when compared with volunteers who consumed the same amount of white rice and bread.

Oats are high in immunity-boosting Vitamin E and contain unique anti-oxidants called avenanthramides. Tufts University, USA, conducted research and found that this unique anti-oxidant reduces the risk of cardiovascular disease by inhibiting LDL (bad) cholesterol damage. They can also hinder the process underlying the first stage of arteriosclerosis. Avenanthramides work with the minerals zinc, selenium and silica, to keep body cells healthy and boost the immune system.

did you know?

OATS ARE ONE OF THE FIRST CEREALS CULTIVATED BY MAN IN CHINA IN 7000 BC. EGYPTIANS MADE OATMEAL BISCUITS AND THE GREEKS MADE PORRIDGE FROM OATS.

Quinoa

Researchers call QUINOA a nutritionally superior food. The high fibre quinoa seed is rich in unsaturated oils and is an excellent source of calcium, iron, phosphorus and potassium. It contains Vitamin E and several B vitamins, such as riboflavin, thiamine, niacin and B6. It has absolutely no cholesterol. Nutritionists make special reference to the protein content of quinoa as it contains about twice the protein of traditional grains.

Quinoa also has few carbohydrates and an exceptionally high content of lysine (one of the eight essential amino acids necessary for growth and repair of body cells). Lysine is thought to be deficient in most cereal grains. Coeliacs and people with gluten intolerant diets can also eat quinoa and it's now available in all good health food shops worldwide.

Nutrition
- Vitamin E
- B Vitamins – riboflavin, thiamine, niacin and B6
- Iron
- Magnesium
- Calcium
- Zinc
- Fibre
- Protein
- Phosphorus
- Potassium
- Lysine

Good For
- Coeliacs and people with gluten intolerance
- Boosting the immune system
- Lifting spirits as it's a 'Good Mood Food' due to the high levels of essential amino acids present
- Combating stress and fatigue
- Helping promote healthy nails, skin and hair
- Assisting constipation, thrush, fertility problems, varicose veins and menstrual problems

How Much to Eat
- Eat at least twice a week – 50g portion

Phytonutrients
- Saponins

DID YOU KNOW?

Quinoa (the Chenopodium Quinoa) was a sacred food of the pre-Colombian Inca Empire and its history spans over 3,000 years. The Ancient Incas called quinoa the "mother grain" and they ceremoniously opened the first quinoa furrow with a golden implement each year, offering it to the Gods during religious feasts and festivals.

Quinoa is native to the high arid regions of the Andes and has been cultivated since antiquity, from Colombia to Chile. It thrives in harsh climatic conditions and rural Andean peasants of Peru and Bolivia still rely heavily on quinoa as a dietary staple. They grind the seed into flour for tortillas and porridge or use it to add bulk to stews, soups and casseroles. It can even be popped like popcorn. In recent days, quinoa has been reintroduced into the "nouveau Andean cuisine" and features heavily in dishes served at fashionable restaurants, for example in the Pantagruel Restaurante located in the Miraflores district, Lima, Peru.

WHILE STAYING WITH A LOCAL FAMILY ON THE ISLAND OF AMANTANI ON THE SHORES OF LAKE TITICACA IN BOLIVIA, I SAMPLED QUINOA PREPARED IN NUMEROUS WAYS. QUINOA RESEMBLES A MILLET SEED AND HAS A SLIGHTLY NUTTY FLAVOUR. IT KEEPS INDEFINITELY AND COOKS LIKE RICE – BUT IN HALF THE TIME. AFTER COOKING, QUINOA EXPANDS AND THE TEXTURE IS SIMILAR TO TAPIOCA. IT SWELLS BECAUSE THE STARCH GRAIN HAS BURST AND HAS ABSORBED THE WATER.

Barley

BARLEY has soluble fibre that helps regulate appetite and blood glucose levels. Pot barley or flakes are more nutritious than refined pearl barley.

Nutrition
- Soluble fibre
- Vitamin E
- Magnesium
- Selenium
- Folate

Good For
- A healthy heart
- Helping regulate appetite and blood glucose levels

How Much to Eat
- 40g or 2 tbsp
- 1 slice of rye bread
- Include these grains at least once a week.

Phytonutrients
- Phenolic acids
- Phytoestrogens
- Lignans – help prevent inflammation

Tina's Tip

WHOLEGRAINS SATISFY HUNGER FAR BETTER THAN REFINED FLOUR PRODUCE. THEY APPEAR TO INCREASE INSULIN SENSITIVITY AS THE INDIGESTIBLE FIBRES IN WHOLEGRAINS PREVENT BLOOD SUGAR FROM RISING QUICKLY. 80% OF A WHOLEGRAIN'S ANTI-OXIDANT CONTENT IS IN THE BRAN AND GERM. THESE LAYERS ARE REMOVED WHEN THE GRAINS ARE REFINED. WHEAT-BRAN'S ANTI-OXIDANT CAPACITY IS 20 TIMES HIGHER THAN THAT OF REFINED WHEAT FLOUR. SO YOU NEED TO DITCH WHITE BREAD, BAGELS, CROISSANTS AND DANISH PASTRIES!

DRESSINGS

Tina's Oil Dressing Tips:
- A dressing of oil: one tablespoon of extra-virgin oil contains 14g of fat. That is more than enough to drizzle over your salad or cooked vegetable like broccoli or asparagus.
- As a general rule, a good dressing needs – three parts oil to one part acid. Season well.
- The acid in a dressing can be vinegar or citrus (lemon, lime or orange). Try a flavoured vinegar such as sherry, cider, tarragon or raspberries for a taste boost.
- Save your best extra-virgin oil for dressings.
- Nut oils, such as walnut and sesame, and flavoured oils, such as lemon and chilli, add an interesting twist to dressings.
- Dressings can be stored at room temperature away from strong light (which dulls the flavour) or in the fridge. Oils solidify in the fridge, so bring them back to room temperature and shake well before serving.

Five of the Best Dressings
Basic: Lightly whisk 3 tablespoons extra-virgin olive oil, 1 tablespoon white wine vinegar, a little mustard and a pinch of sugar. Season.

Italian-style: 3 tablespoons extra-virgin olive oil, one tablespoon balsamic vinegar, one teaspoon sun-dried tomato paste, 1 crushed garlic clove, a few torn fresh basil leaves and seasoning.

French-style: 1 1/2 tablespoons walnut oil, 1 1/2 tablespoons vegetable oil, zest and juice of 1 small orange, small handful chopped fresh tarragon leaves and seasoning.

Moroccan-style: 3 tablespoons extra-virgin olive oil, juice of 1 small lemon, 1/2 teaspoon red chilli, 1 teaspoon crushed and toasted cumin seeds, small handful chopped fresh flat leaf parsley and mint.

Oriental-style: 1 1/2 tablespoons toasted sesame oil, 1 1/2 tablespoons sunflower oil, 1 tablespoon rice wine vinegar, splash of light soy sauce and 2 teaspoons honey.

Adzuki Bean Slice

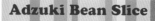

MAKES 15–20 SQUARES

200G (7 OZ) ADZUKI BEANS, SOAKED
OVERNIGHT IN THREE TIMES THEIR
    VOLUME OF WATER

180G (6 ½ OZ) CASTER SUGAR

2 TBSP HONEY

1 TSP NATURAL VANILLA EXTRACT

150G (5 ½ OZ) UNSALTED BUTTER,
    PLUS EXTRA FOR GREASING

100G (3 ½ OZ) PLAIN FLOUR

100G (3 ½ OZ) GROUND ALMONDS

100G (3 ½ OZ) RICE FLOUR

PINCH OF SALT

Drain the beans, put them into a saucepan, cover them with water and bring to the boil. Drain them again, put them back in the saucepan with the same amount of fresh water, then turn the heat down and simmer the beans for about 1 1/2 hours until they are very soft. Keep adding water if they start to dry out.

When the beans are completely soft, drain them and put them back in the saucepan. Add 100g (3 1/2 oz) of the sugar, the honey and vanilla extract. Stir over a low heat for about 5 minutes until the sugar has dissolved.

Put into a food processor and process till smooth, or put through a sieve until the beans are paste-like in texture. Set aside to cool.

Preheat the oven to 180°C (350°F) or gas mark 4. Butter a 20 x 28 cm (8 x 11 in) baking tin and line it with parchment paper.

If you are using a food processor – process the flour, ground almonds, rice flour, butter, the remaining sugar and the salt until the mixture is quite crumbly. Otherwise, cut the butter into small pieces.

Mix the dry ingredients together and rub the butter into them with your fingers. If the mixture is too dry add a little more butter.

Press half the mixture into the prepared tin. Spread the adzuki paste evenly over the top and sprinkle with the remaining flour and almond mixture (like a crumble).

Bake for 25–30 minutes, until the topping is golden and crisp. Cool in the tin.

When cold, cut into squares. Take the slices out of the tin carefully as the topping tends to crumble (because of the rice flour).

Pine Nut Pesto

SERVES 2

1 TBSP PINE NUTS

50G (2 OZ) TOFU

½ CUP PACKED FULL WITH BASIL
  LEAVES

1 TBSP LEMON JUICE

1 TBSP WATER

Combine all the ingredients together in a blender and whiz until you have a smooth paste.

Serve with fresh pasta or drizzle over a salad.

Hummus

SERVES 4

400G (12 OZ) CANNED CHICKPEAS –
  RINSED WELL AND DRAINED

2 TBSP TAHINI (SESAME SEED PASTE)

2 CLOVES GARLIC – CRUSHED

2 TBSP FRESH LIME JUICE

GROUND BLACK PEPPER

Blend the chickpeas, tahini, garlic and lime juice in a blender until smooth and creamy. Season with ground black pepper.

Serve with vegetable crudites.

did you know?

CHICKPEAS PROVIDE A RICH
SOURCE OF FIBRE, CALCIUM,
IRON AND ZINC.

Two-Bean Vegetable Goulash

SERVES 4

100G (3 ½ OZ) CANNELLINI BEANS – SOAKED
    OVERNIGHT

100G (3 ½ OZ) BLACK BEANS – SOAKED
    OVERNIGHT

1 TBSP OLIVE OIL

1 ONION – FINELY CHOPPED

4 STICKS CELERY – IN CHUNKS

1 COURGETTE – IN CHUNKS

2 CARROTS – PEELED AND CUT INTO CHUNKS

1 CAN TOMATOES – CHOPPED

300 ML (10 FL OZ) VEGETABLE STOCK

1 TBSP PAPRIKA

PINCH CARAWAY SEEDS

SALT AND PEPPER

1 TBSP CORNFLOUR

2 TBSP WATER

TINA'S TIP

Do not cover the pot with a lid. The beans remain very tender, as the skin does not tend to toughen.

Heat oil in a frying pan and fry the onions, celery, courgette and carrots quickly over a high heat until browned. Pour in tomatoes. Stir in paprika, caraway seeds, salt and pepper. Pour in vegetable stock.

Cover and simmer for 20 minutes until the vegetables are tender.

Stir in the cooked beans. Blend the cornflour in with the water and add to the pan. Bring to the boil; stirring until the sauce thickens. Simmer for 10 minutes.

Serve with boiled brown rice.

COOKING THE BEANS: Drain the beans and rinse really well. Put them into two separate pots and cover with water. Boil for 10 minutes; then lower the heat and simmer for 1 hour. Drain, rinse well and set aside.

did you know?

THIS FAMOUS GOULASH WAS ORIGINALLY SOUP.
TODAY BEANS, MEAT, POTATOES AND NOODLES
ARE ADDED MAKING IT EDIBLE AS A MAIN COURSE.

Four Seed Bread

MAKES 1 LOAF – 10 SLICES

300G (10 ½ OZ) SELF-RAISING
   WHITE FLOUR

100G (3 ½ OZ) WHOLEMEAL
   FLOUR

1 LEVEL TSP POPPY SEEDS

1 TBSP SESAME SEEDS

1 TBSP SUNFLOWER SEEDS

1 TBSP PUMPKIN SEEDS

25G (1 OZ) DRIED APRICOTS OR
   SULTANAS

1 DSTSP BLACK TREACLE

350–375 ML (11–12 FL OZ) WARM
   WATER

MARGARINE OR WHITE FAT AND
   KITCHEN PAPER FOR GREASING

PINCH OF SALT

3 TSP BAKING POWDER

TOPPING: SESAME SEEDS

Preheat oven to 200°C (390°F) or gas mark 6.
Grease tin.

Sieve white flour, salt and baking powder into a
bowl.

Add wholemeal flour, all the seeds and chopped
apricots or sultanas. Pour hot water into a jug or
cup and dip the dessertspoon into the hot water
and then dip into the treacle; the hot spoon will
help the treacle to drop from the spoon easily. Then
add to the flour. Add the warm water to the dry
ingredients and mix to a soft consistency. Knead on
a floured board and place into tin. Now wet the
top with a little water. Sprinkle some sesame seeds.
Bake for 45–50 minutes until nicely browned.
Remove from the tin using oven mitts. Test by
tapping the bottom of the loaf. It will sound hollow
if it is cooked.

Cool on a wire tray. Do not cut until it is cold.

Walnut Pâté

SERVES 2

150G (5 ½ OZ) WALNUTS – SOAKED OVERNIGHT

50G (2 OZ) LEEKS – FINELY CHOPPED

2 TBSP OLIVE OIL

1 TBSP MIXED HERBS

Blend all the ingredients together until creamy.

Use extra oil and water if it looks too dry.

Serve with wholegrain brown bread or crackers.

Pumpkin Seed Pâté

SERVES 2

150G (5 ½ OZ) PUMPKIN SEEDS – SOAKED OVERNIGHT

50G (2 OZ) SUN-DRIED TOMATOES – SOAKED OVERNIGHT

2 TBSP EXTRA-VIRGIN OLIVE OIL

1 TBSP FRESH PARSLEY – CHOPPED

1 TBSP LEMON JUICE

1 TSP FRESH OREGANO

1 TSP FRESH THYME

(OPTIONAL: 2 GARLIC CLOVES CRUSHED)

Blend all the ingredients together in a blender until smooth.

You can add garlic if you like.

This will keep for one day and is an ideal dip with vegetable crudités of your choice.

Buckwheat Noodle and Pink Prawns

SERVES 4

750G (26 OZ) LARGE FRESH PRAWNS,
   TAILS ON – PEELED
400 ML (13 FL OZ) CAN COCONUT
   MILK
1 TBSP FISH SAUCE
1 TBSP LIGHT SOY SAUCE
2 CLOVES GARLIC
2 TBSP FRESH GINGER – GRATED
1 TBSP FRESH CORIANDER –
   CHOPPED, PLUS EXTRA LEAVES TO
   GARNISH
1 TBSP GROUND CUMIN
2 FRESH RED CHILLIES
2 TSP LEMONGRASS – CHOPPED
400G (12 OZ) FRESH BUCKWHEAT NOODLES OR PASTA
VEGETABLE OIL – TO TOSS
GARNISH WITH FRESH COCONUT SHAVINGS OR LIME
1 TSP SUGAR

Preheat the oven to 180°C (350°F) or gas mark 4.
Place the prawns in a baking dish. Put the coconut
milk, fish sauce, soy sauce, garlic, ginger, coriander,
cumin, chillies, sugar, and lemongrass in a food
processor and blend until smooth. Pour over the
prawns and bake for 10 minutes.

Pick out the prawns and put on to a plate. Put the
sauce in a small pan and reduce by half over a
medium heat on the hob.

Cook the noodles according to packet instructions,
drain well and toss with a little oil.

Serve topped with prawns, sauce, coriander and
lime/fresh coconut (optional).

TINA'S TIP

Quinoa may be added
into many types of
bread, savoury cakes,
soups and stuffing. It
can be mixed with flour
and used for breaded
fish. It is absolutely
delicious as a crust with
lamb cutlets. Dabble
with this wondrous little
Andean ingredient and
check out its versatility!

Barley Bread

MAKES 1 LOAF – 10 SLICES

1 TBSP YEAST

2 TBSP BROWN SUGAR – DIVIDED

150 ML (5 FL OZ) WARM WATER – DIVIDED

2 CUPS BARLEY FLOUR – DIVIDED

1 TBSP OIL

1 TBSP SALT

1/3 CUP BEAN FLOUR

Preheat oven to 180°C (350°F) or gas mark 4 and grease baking sheet.

Put yeast into small bowl. Add 1/2 tbsp sugar and 75 ml warm water. Put in a warm place to rise.

Pour remaining 75 ml (3 fl oz) water into large mixing bowl. Add 1 cup barley flour and mix vigorously. Add remaining 1 1/2 tbsp brown sugar, oil and salt, and mix well. Add softened yeast and beat briskly. Then add bean flour and enough remaining barley flour to make dough that can be kneaded.

Place on a floured board and knead until smooth and elastic.

Shape into two round loaves on greased baking sheet and slash diagonally across tops. Let rise until double in bulk. Oil tops lightly, if desired, for more crispness. Bake for one hour. Remove from tin and turn onto wire rack and cool.

Butter Bean Pasta

SERVES 4

2 TBSP OLIVE OIL

2 RASHERS – CHOPPED

1 ONION – CHOPPED FINELY

1 CLOVE GARLIC – CRUSHED

300G (10 ½ OZ) BUTTER BEANS – DRAINED
   AND RINSED WELL

400G (12 OZ) CAN TOMATOES – CHOPPED

1 TBSP NATURAL YOGHURT

1 TBSP CHILLI SEASONING – CHOPPED

500G (17 OZ) BUCKWHEAT PASTA

TO GARNISH:

GRATED PARMESAN CHEESE

CHOPPED PARSLEY

TINA'S TIP

This dish has a straight-forward earthy taste and is ideal for parties. Serve with a selection of toppings, such as: finely grated cheddar cheese, Greek style yoghurt or fresh slices of avocado.

Heat the oil in a large frying pan.

Sauté bacon, onion and garlic over a medium heat until onion is tender.

Stir in tomatoes, butter beans, natural yoghurt and chilli seasoning.

Heat gently, stirring occasionally.

Toss sauce through hot cooked buckwheat pasta.

Serve immediately topped with Parmesan cheese and parsley.

did you know?

BUTTER BEANS ARE ALSO CALLED
LIMA BEANS AND IT IS THOUGHT
THAT THEY ORIGINATED IN PERU.

Quinoa Pilaff Stir-Fry

SERVES 4

850 ML (1 LB 12 OZ) WATER

350G (12 OZ) QUINOA

2 TBSP OLIVE OIL

100G (3 ½ OZ) CARROT – GRATED

100G (3 ½ OZ) BROCCOLI FLORETS

100G (3 ½ OZ) YELLOW PEPPERS

100G (3 ½ OZ) MUNG BEAN SPROUTS

3 TBSP TOMATO PURÉE

1 ONION – FINELY CHOPPED

2 CLOVES GARLIC – CRUSHED

1 TSP GROUND BLACK PEPPER

BUNCH FRESH CORIANDER

Boil the water in a saucepan. Add the quinoa. Boil and then simmer for 15 minutes. Drain well. Heat the oil in a wok/saucepan. Add the onion and garlic and stir-fry for 3–4 minutes. Then add the remaining ingredients, inserting the coriander near the end.
Serve in small bowls.

Quinoa Salad

SERVES 2

75G (2 ½ OZ) DRY QUINOA

450 ML (14 FL OZ) WATER

1 LARGE RIPE AVOCADO – CHOPPED

100G (3 ½ OZ) LIMA BEANS/GREEN
  BEANS – COOKED AND CHOPPED

3 SPRING ONIONS – CHOPPED FINELY

3 CLOVES GARLIC – CRUSHED

CHOPPED FRESH MINT

SALT AND COARSE GROUND PEPPER
  TO TASTE

Rinse quinoa in a sieve thoroughly (10 to 15 quick rinses) with cold water.
Heat water to boiling point. Add quinoa, cover and reduce heat to low. Simmer for 15–20 minutes until the water is absorbed and the quinoa is tender. Set aside to cool. Prepare the remainder of the salad in a medium-sized bowl and when quinoa is cool, mix it with the rest of the salad.

Honey, Garlic and Lemon Chicken

SERVES 4

3 LEMONS

50G (2 OZ) BUTTER

3 TBSP CLEAR HONEY

1 GARLIC CLOVE – FINELY CHOPPED

SALT AND PEPPER

4 ROSEMARY SPRIGS – LEAVES STRIPPED FROM THE STALKS

8 CHICKEN PIECES – SUCH AS THIGHS AND DRUMSTICKS

750G (26 OZ) POTATOES – CUT INTO SMALL CHUNKS

GREEN SALAD – TO SERVE

Preheat oven to 200°C (390°F) or gas mark 6.

Squeeze the juice from two lemons and put in a small pan with the butter, honey, garlic, rosemary and plenty of salt and pepper. Heat gently until the butter melts.

Arrange the chicken in one layer in a shallow roasting tin. Put the potatoes around the chicken.

Drizzle the lemon butter over the chicken and potatoes; turning the potatoes until evenly coated.

Cut the remaining lemon into eight wedges and nestle among the potatoes.

Roast the chicken for 50 minutes to 1 hour; stirring a couple of times, until the chicken is cooked and the potatoes are crisp and golden.

Serve with a green salad of your choice (See The Colour Green chapter for recipes).

Quinoa and Coriander Stuffing

SERVES 2

50G (2 OZ) BROWN BREADCRUMBS
(SPELT/RYE/BUCKWHEAT BREAD)
50G (2 OZ) COOKED QUINOA
LARGE BUNCH OF CORIANDER –
FRESHLY CHOPPED
SALT AND PEPPER
50G (2 OZ) BUTTER
2 TBSP OF ONION – FINELY CHOPPED
RIND AND JUICE OF 1 LIME
1 EGG – BEATEN

Mix the breadcrumbs and quinoa together with the seasoning.

Melt the butter in a saucepan and brown onions. Add the crumb mixture with the lime juice and beaten egg and blend to a moist consistency.

Stuff the chicken or turkey meat and pan fry or oven bake.

Quinoa, Asparagus and Carrot Loaf

SERVES 4

1 SMALL ONION – CHOPPED FINELY
100G (3 ½ OZ) GROUND ALMONDS
100G (3 ½ OZ) QUINOA FLAKES
150 ML (5 FL OZ) WATER
2 EGGS
FRESHLY GRATED NUTMEG
HANDFUL FRESH CORIANDER
HANDFUL FRESH PARSLEY – CHOPPED
250G (9 OZ) TRIMMED ASPARAGUS –
COOKED
250G (9 OZ) BABY ORGANIC CARROTS
– COOKED

Preheat the oven 190°C (375°F) or gas mark 5 and grease a 450g (1 lb) loaf tin.
Combine the onion, almonds, eggs, quinoa and water together in a bowl. Season with the fresh herbs and nutmeg and place a layer in the loaf tin.
Put a layer of asparagus on top.
Place another layer and then some carrots.
Continue until all the ingredients have been placed in the tin.
Bake for 30 minutes until firm in the centre.
Cool the tin, then slip a knife around the edges and carefully turn out.
To vary the vegetables in this loaf, simply choose a selection of vegetables of your chosen colours.
Ensure that you have approx. 500g (17 oz) of vegetables in all.
This loaf makes a terrific lunch-time option with salad.

Roasted Chicken Drumsticks with Honey, Parsley and Garlic

SERVES 4

1 TBSP OLIVE OIL

4 TBSP BUTTER

3 TBSP HONEY

SALT AND PEPPER

12–16 CHICKEN DRUMSTICKS

3 GARLIC CLOVES – FINELY CHOPPED

2 TBSP FRESH PARSLEY – CHOPPED

1 TBSP LEMON JUICE

Heat a large, heavy-based lidded casserole or frying pan over a moderate heat.

Add the oil and half the butter. Generously season the drumsticks with salt and pepper. When the butter is foaming; drop in the drumsticks and fry until lightly browned all over. Now spoon honey over the dish.

Cover the casserole with a lid and leave the drumsticks to fry gently for 20–25 minutes, turning regularly. Remove the lid and add the remaining butter, along with the garlic, parsley and lemon juice.

Take the casserole off the heat and leave the flavours to infuse for a few minutes before serving.

Tortillas

SERVES 2–4

25G (1 OZ) GRAM FLOUR (CHICKPEA)

100G (3 1/2 OZ) CORNFLOUR

2 TBSP TAPIOCA FLOUR

1/2 TSP SALT

2 EGGS

360 ML (12 FL OZ) WATER

OIL FOR BRUSHING THE FRYING PAN

GREASEPROOF PAPER

Place the flours and salt in a mixing bowl and mix together thoroughly. Add the egg and beat until smooth and then slowly beat in the water. Cover with cling film and refrigerate for 30 minutes.

Heat a medium-sized frying pan until very hot and then brush with oil. Making sure the pan is still very hot, pour in enough batter to just cover the bottom of the pan. Cook over a high heat until the bottom of the tortilla is golden brown and the edges begin to curl up. Flip the tortilla over and cook on the other side for 30 seconds only; until barely cooked.

Transfer the tortilla onto greaseproof or parchment paper and repeat with the remaining batter; stacking each cooked tortilla between greaseproof paper.

Allow to cool and refrigerate or freeze until ready to use. They are great with all types of sandwiches and Mexican food.

Vegetable Burger

SERVES 2

1 MEDIUM POTATO

1 SMALL CARROT

HANDFUL OF PEAS

2 SCALLIONS

1 STICK CELERY

HALF A RED PEPPER – OPTIONAL

1 CLOVE GARLIC – CRUSHED

50G (2 OZ) BUTTER/MARGARINE

30G (1 OZ) PORRIDGE
    OATS/BREADCRUMBS

1 TSP WORCESTERSHIRE SAUCE

50 ML (1 ³/₄ FL OZ) WATER

¹/₂ TSP CURRY PASTE OR POWDER

¹/₂ TSP SALT

1 TBSP OIL TO FRY

GARNISH WITH LETTUCE, CHEESE
    AND TOMATO

Dice the celery, scallions and pepper.
Peel garlic and chop finely.
Wash, peel and grate the carrots and the potato.
Melt the margarine and sauté all vegetables very gently over a low heat for 3 minutes.
Stir in oats, water, Worcestershire sauce, salt, pepper and curry paste or powder.
Cook; stirring for 3 minutes. Then spread the mixture on a plate. Leave to cool and set.
Divide into 4 pieces and form into burgers using a little flour. Fry burgers in 1 tbsp oil over medium heat until brown – 6 minutes on each side.
Drain on kitchen paper and serve.

Honey-Glazed Almond Bread

SERVES 8

100G (3 ½ OZ) ALMONDS

350G (12 OZ) FLOUR

350G (12 OZ) STRONG WHITE FLOUR

1 PACKET EASY-BLEND DRIED YEAST

2 TSP SALT

1 TBSP BLACK TREACLE

500 ML (16 FL OZ) WARM MILK

2 TBSP GOOD QUALITY OLIVE OIL

100G (3 ½ OZ) SUNFLOWER SEEDS

FOR THE GLAZE

1 TBSP BEATEN EGG

1 TBSP CLEAR HONEY

Preheat oven to 200°C (390°F) or gas mark 6. Grease two baking sheets.

Coarsely chop the almonds by hand; keep the pieces quite large; then set aside.

Combine the flours, yeast and salt in a large bowl. Add the treacle, milk and olive oil.

Stir to form a dough, adding a little more milk if necessary so that it does not stick to the sides of the bowl. Turn the dough onto a lightly floured surface and knead for about 10 minutes. When ready, the dough should be smooth and elastic.

Clean your hands and then add the seeds and nuts into the dough. Divide the dough in half, and then shape each piece until smooth and round in shape and place centrally on the baking sheets. Enclose each sheet in a large plastic bag, sealing a little air inside so that the plastic is not in contact with the bread.

Leave aside in a warm place for 30–45 minutes or until doubled in bulk.

To glaze the loaves mix the egg and honey and gently brush over the surface of the dough. Bake for 20–25 minutes or until the loaves are a good conker brown and sound hollow when tapped on the base. Cool on a wire rack.

Savoury Gram Flour Pancakes

SERVES 2

100G (3 ½ OZ) GRAM FLOUR (CHICKPEA)

½ TSP SALT

½ TSP CAYENNE PEPPER

BLACK PEPPER TO SEASON

330 ML (11 FL OZ) ICED WATER

OIL FOR FRYING

FOIL

Preheat the oven to 140°C (280°F) or gas mark 2.

In a large mixing bowl, mix the flour, salt, cayenne and black pepper together. Gradually add the iced water, beating well, until you get a smooth batter. Add a little more water if necessary. Heat a little oil in a frying pan.

Add a quarter of the batter, swirling it around the base to coat evenly and cook, until the edges are crispy and brown and the top has dried out.

Transfer to a warm plate, cover loosely with foil and keep warm in the oven whilst you cook the remaining pancakes.

Serve with a savoury filling of your choice.

Pumpkin, Poppy Seed and Lemon Loaf

MAKES 1 LOAF - 10 SLICES

225G (8 OZ) PUMPKIN – PEELED AND
    DESEEDED OR BUTTERNUT SQUASH –
    CUBED
4 TBSP FULL CREAM MILK
1 LARGE EGG
175G (6 OZ) SELF-RAISING FLOUR
1/2 TSP BAKING POWDER
1/2 TSP BICARBONATE OF SODA

150G (5 1/2 OZ) CASTER SUGAR
1 1/2 TSP MIXED SPICE
1/2 TSP NUTMEG – GRATED
50G (2 OZ) UNSALTED BUTTER – CUT
    INTO SMALL PIECES
2 TBSP POPPY SEEDS
ZEST OF 1 SMALL LEMON – GRATED

Preheat the oven to 180°C (350°F) or gas 4 and grease a 900g loaf tin and line with baking paper or greaseproof paper, then grease well once more.

Cook the pumpkin in boiling water for 10–15 minutes, until tender. Drain well and leave until the steam dies down, then blend to a smooth purée in a food processor.

Scoop into a mixing bowl and mix in 3 tbsp milk and the egg.

Sift the flour, baking powder, bicarbonate of soda, sugar, mixed spice, nutmeg and seasoning into the cleaned bowl of the food processor.

Add the butter and process until the mix looks like fine breadcrumbs.

Add to the purée and stir until just mixed; adding the remaining milk if the mixture seems dry.

Stir in the poppy seeds and grated lemon zest.

Spoon the mixture into the loaf tin and bake for 45 minutes until well risen and golden.

Remove the cake from the tin and cool on a wire rack.

Take off the paper and serve cut into slices.

Almond Shake

MAKES 1

2 CUPS WATER
1 CUP ALMONDS – SOAKED OVERNIGHT
1 TSP FLAXSEED OIL
1 TSP CINNAMON
1 TSP VANILLA EXTRACT

Blend all the ingredients in a blender.
Strain and serve the shake immediately.
Serve chilled.

Honey Cake

SERVES 8

225G (8 OZ) BUTTER – SOFTENED

225G (8 OZ) LIGHT
    MUSCAVADO SUGAR

GRATED ZEST OF 1 LEMON

4 EGGS

100 ML (3 FL OZ) HONEY

350G (12 OZ) SELF-RAISING FLOUR

2 TSP BAKING POWDER

1/2 TSP GROUND GINGER

50G (2 OZ) WALNUTS – CHOPPED

FOR THE FILLING AND TOPPING

450 ML (15 FL OZ) DOUBLE CREAM

2 TBSP HONEY

ZEST OF LEMON – SHREDDED

Preheat the oven to fan 160°C (315°F) or gas mark 3 and lightly grease the cake tin and line the base with a circle of non-stick baking parchment.

Put all the ingredients for the cake (except the walnuts) into a large mixing bowl and mix well until evenly blended – an electric mixer is best for this (or use a wooden spoon). Then stir in the chopped walnuts.

Spoon the mixture into the prepared cake tin and level the surface. Bake for 1–1 1/2 hours, until well risen, golden and springy to the touch.

Allow to cool slightly, then turn cake out onto a wire rack, peel off the lining paper and leave to cool completely.

MAKING THE FILLING AND TOPPING: Whip the cream until it just holds its shape and then fold in the honey.

Split the cake horizontally into three and fill and cover with the cream, using a small pallet knife to smooth it evenly over the top and sides. Decorate the top with the shredded zest.

Golden Caramel Squares

MAKES 16

100G (3 ½ OZ) BUTTER –
 DICED, PLUS EXTRA FOR
 GREASING

225G (8 OZ) DIGESTIVES –
 HALVED

50G (2 OZ) PLAIN
 CHOCOLATE – BROKEN
 INTO CHUNKS

1 EGG – BEATEN

1 TBSP PREPARED STRONG
 COFFEE

100G (3 ½ OZ) DESICCATED
 COCONUT

40G (1 OZ) PECAN NUTS – CHOPPED

FOR THE FILLING

175G (6 OZ) ICING SUGAR – SIFTED

40G (1 OZ) BUTTER

1 ½ TBSP CUSTARD POWER

1 TSP VANILLA EXTRACT

5 TSP MILK

FOR THE TOPPING

100G (3 ½ OZ) PLAIN CHOCOLATE –
 BROKEN INTO CHUNKS

1 TBSP BUTTER

Preheat the oven to 180°C (350°F) or gas mark 4 and lightly butter a 20 cm (8 in) square tin.

Put the biscuits into a food processor or a blender and process to fine crumbs.

Place butter, chocolate, egg and coffee in a pan. Cook over a low heat until the butter and chocolate has just melted. Be careful not to over-cook.

Then remove from the heat and stir in crumbs, coconut and nuts.

Spoon the mixture into the tin and spread level with the back of a spoon. Bake for ten minutes.

Remove and leave until cold. Beat filling ingredients in a bowl until smooth.

Spread over the base. Chill for 1 hour or until firm.

Make the topping: melt the chocolate and butter in a small heatproof bowl over a pan of simmering water.

Remove from heat, cool slightly and then spread over the filling. Chill until set.

Cut into squares and store in the fridge.

Oat Bars

MAKES 12

150G (5 ½ OZ) PORRIDGE

25G (1 OZ) COCONUT –
 DESICCATED

150G (5 ½ OZ) APRICOTS –
 DRIED AND CHOPPED

50G (2 OZ) RED APPLE –
 CHOPPED

2 TBSP VEGETABLE OIL

2 TBSP CRUNCHY PEANUT
 BUTTER

3 TBSP CLEAR HONEY

50G (2 OZ) RAW SUGAR
 CANE – SOFT BROWN
 SUGAR

½ TSP CINNAMON

Preheat oven to 180°C (350°F) or gas mark 4.

Put the oil, peanut butter and honey into a bowl and heat over a pan of hot water until the ingredients have softened and are easy to stir together.

Add all of the remaining ingredients to the mixture and stir until they are all mixed well.

Place into a greased tin and bake for 20 minutes.

Slice into bar size of your choice.

Allow to cool and for an extra special treat melt chocolate and spread over the bars.

Almond Milk

MAKES 750 ML (24 FL OZ)

250G (9 OZ) BLANCHED ALMONDS

100G (3 ½ OZ) SUGAR

800 ML (26 ½ FL OZ) WATER

Grind the almonds and sugar in a blender with 400 ml (12 ½ fl oz) of water. This will make a thick paste. Leave for 1 hour.

Add the remaining 400 ml (12 ½ fl oz) water. Shake the mixture through a sieve. To squeeze out any excess liquid; press hard on the solids.

Serve chilled.

Note: *This is a lactose-free recipe and can be used to make ice-cream, smoothies and puddings.*

THE COLOUR
black

BLACK SUGGESTS MYSTERY; IT POINTS TO MAGIC AND ESOTERIC KNOWLEDGE. IT SYMBOLISES A SENSE OF POWER AND PROMISE. LIKE THE LIGHT AT THE END OF THE TUNNEL OR TURNING THE CORNER, IT SUGGESTS THAT THINGS ARE CHANGING. THERE IS NOTHING WEAK ABOUT BLACK, WHICH IS PROBABLY WHY SOME PEOPLE FEAR IT.

Black becomes negative when depression sets in because of disappointments in life. Like everything, this darkness has its time, but then something happens to change the elements. If you are blind-folded, you cannot see. But remove the blind-fold, come out of the blackness and the world of colour opens up before your eyes. **BLACK INDICATES THAT SOMETHING IS LYING DORMANT OR BURIED.** It is the colour at the bottom of a barrel, the deepest part of a water well or a badly burnt pot. You have to fill the barrel up again, climb up out of the water well or clean the black from the pot, and start afresh.

THOUGHT FOR THE DAY
I am a powerful person in my own space.

A BLACK DAY PLAN

EXERCISE – I WILL FIND MY RHYTHM AND GET MOVING.

CLOTHES – I WILL WEAR BLACK TODAY SO THAT I HAVE A FEELING OF PERSONAL STRENGTH AND A SENSE OF BEING IN CONTROL.

FOOD – I WILL EAT BLACK FOOD AND PERHAPS HAVE A HALF OF STOUT/GUINNESS.

AFFIRMATION – I WILL BE IN COMPLETE CONTROL.

Guide To Wearing Black

People who wear a lot of black may be hiding something or trying to maintain a state of control. In more extreme cases they can be control freaks or generally heavy in mood and spirit. Black is the absorber that gives nothing out. Watch out for those who wear black or a black and white combination – women in particular – as they do not want to be visible. Who or what is this person hiding from – their partner or their bad habits? The challenge for anyone in black is to let their true self be seen by the world.

Black is seductive which explains the emphasis on black evening wear – the little black number or black lingerie. When black is worn with another colour, it intensifies that colour. If you want to assess the mood of anyone wearing black, check what colour they are wearing with it, as the accent colour reveals their mood (See Colours that Go With Black for more details).

Black is a colour often associated with mourning. Coco Chanel is thought to have designed many of her clothing lines wearing black, as she mourned the death of her lovers.

Be careful of wearing black, as it can bring out the worst aspects of power; encouraging harsh behaviour, treachery and deceit. Black in its negative is the fear of what is next.

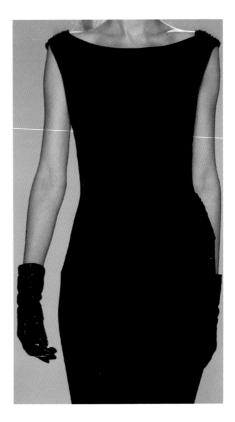

COLOURS THAT GO WITH BLACK

All colours go with black. It is the way that they are worn, however, which is crucial to whether the outfit will work or not. It is usually better to wear the other colour underneath the black dress or suit.

Remember the skin loves to breathe light so make sure that you don't always wear black underwear. Add a little splash of colour now and then.

WHEN TO WEAR BLACK

BLACK can be worn in the evening time when you want to take on a more secretive or intriguing character. Remember wearing black from head to toe is rather uninspiring – so be sure to add some colour for finesse and personal touch. Wearing a decorative necklace, for example, will show that you have great taste and an eye for detail.

It's well known that wearing black can make a person look more slender and it's ideal for evening wear. **IT'S ALSO A USEFUL COLOUR WHEN YOU WANT TO PLAY IT SAFE.**

When teenagers start to wear black they are letting the world know that they are ready to take control. If black is worn obsessively by people in their 20s and 30s, it can indicate that something has brought the person's life to a halt or they are putting their life on hold. Often it can be suggestive of a person feeling trapped. **ACCORDING TO COLOUR GURU LILIAN VERNER-BONDS, PEOPLE IN THEIR 40S WEAR BLACK BECAUSE THEY HAVE COME TO TERMS WITH POWER AND CONTROL IN THEIR LIVES.**

WHEN NOT TO WEAR BLACK

BLACK accessories are generally heavy and unappealing – so avoid at all costs. While black evening gloves are great for fancy dress parties they need to remain in the dressing-up box. When attending a summer wedding never wear black. **ALSO NEVER WEAR BLACK WHEN YOU ARE FEELING LUSTRELESS AS IT WILL ACCENTUATE THE CONDITION.**

BLACK does not suit every skin tone – pale-skinned, fair-haired people with light eye colouring for example. Black may make the wearer appear older and have a 'pinched' look. If black does not suit your skin tone, or washes you out, only wear it from the waist down or wear it in the evening time and select soft fabrics that have a sense of movement.

✚ Black Health

DEPRESSION

The negative side of black is that it can cause you to turn in on yourself. This can have a powerful and energy-zapping effect on the body. Depression is one of the deadliest diseases of the 21st century. For many years it was a hidden disease as people would not talk about it. Fortunately there are now many knowledgeable individuals out there who are prepared to speak candidly about the illness and we are all benefiting from this information and gaining a greater understanding of depression.

Depression is an illness that affects the whole body; the nervous system, moods, thoughts and behaviour. It affects the way you eat and sleep, the way you feel about yourself and the way you react to and think about the people and things around you. People with depression typically withdraw and hide from society. They lose interest in everything around them and become incapable of experiencing pleasure.

There are many types of depression, with variations in the number of symptoms, their severity and persistence. Symptoms include chronic fatigue, sleep disturbances (either insomnia or excessive sleeping), changes in appetite, headaches, backaches, digestive disorders, restlessness, irritability, quickness to anger, loss of interest or pleasure in hobbies, and feelings of worthlessness and inadequacy. Many think of death and consider suicide,

DID YOU KNOW?

Most depressive disorders are categorised as either unipolar or bipolar. Unipolar disorders are characterised by depressive episodes that most often recur at least several times during a person's life. Bipolar disorders usually begin as depression, but as they progress, they involve alternating episodes of depression and mania. As a result, bipolar depression is commonly known as manic depression.

Perhaps the most common type of depression is a chronic low-grade depression called dysthymia. This condition involves long-term and/or recurring depressive symptoms that are not necessarily disabling but keep a person from functioning normally and interfering with social interactions and their enjoyment of life. Research has found that this type of depression often results from (unconscious) negative thinking habits. Double depression is a variation of dysthymia where a person with chronic low-grade depression periodically experiences major depressive episodes, then returns to his or her "normal", mildly depressed state.

especially around the holiday season. Things appear bleak and time seems to pass slowly. Symptoms can last for weeks, months or years.

A person with depression may be chronically angry and irritable, sad and despairing or display little or no emotion at all.

The causes of depression are not fully understood, but they are many and varied. Depression may be triggered by many things including: tension, stress, a traumatic life event, chemical imbalances in the brain, thyroid disorders, nutritional deficiencies, poor diet, the over-consumption of sugar, glandular fever, lack of exercise, endometriosis or any serious physical disorders or allergies. Hypoglycaemia (low blood sugar) is another common cause of depression.

Heredity is another significant factor in this disorder. Research has proven that for up to 50% of people suffering from recurrent episodes of depression, one or both of the parents also experience depression.

Whatever the factors that trigger it, depression begins with a disturbance in the part of the brain that governs moods. Most people can handle everyday stresses – their bodies readjust to these pressures. When stress is too great for a person and their adjustment mechanism doesn't respond, depression may be triggered.

SAD (Seasonal Affective Disorder)

SOME PEOPLE BECOME MORE DEPRESSED IN THE WINTER MONTHS WHEN THE DAYS ARE SHORTER AND DARKER. THIS TYPE OF DISORDER IS KNOWN AS SEASONAL AFFECTIVE DISORDER (SAD). PEOPLE WHO SUFFER FROM SAD LOSE THEIR ENERGY, HAVE ANXIETY ATTACKS, GAIN WEIGHT AS A RESULT OF CRAVING THE WRONG FOODS, SLEEP TOO MUCH, AND HAVE A REDUCED SEX DRIVE. IT'S CAUSED BECAUSE OF PROBLEMS WITH THE REGULATION OF THE PINEAL GLAND IN THE BRAIN. THIS GLAND MODULATES THE PRODUCTION OF MELATONIN AND SEROTONIN.

THE HORMONE MELATONIN IS PRODUCED AS IT GETS DARK, MAKING US FEEL SLEEPY. THIS IS A HEALTHY STATE OF AFFAIRS, AS IT HELPS TO RESTORE THE BODY'S BALANCE AND LONGEVITY. BUT WHEN IT GETS BRIGHT AND WE START TO WAKE UP, MELATONIN PRODUCTION SHOULD FALL. RESEARCHERS HAVE PROVEN THAT A CHEMICAL REACTION IS CAUSED WHEN BRIGHT LIGHT ENTERS OUR EYES. THESE REACTIONS CONTROL OUR DAILY RHYTHMS AND MOODS. DURING THE WINTER MONTHS, HOWEVER, WHEN THERE IS NOT ENOUGH LIGHT TO STIMULATE THE PINEAL GLAND, MELATONIN LEVELS CAN REMAIN HIGH THROUGHOUT THE DAY, CAUSING FEELINGS OF LETHARGY AND DEPRESSION.

THE OPPOSITE CONDITION IS CALLED REDUCED MELATONIN AND IS CAUSED BY THE USE OF STRONG, ARTIFICIAL LIGHT. MELATONIN HAS A SEXUALLY INHIBITIVE EFFECT ON PEOPLE, SO IF A PERSON SUFFERS FROM REDUCED MELATONIN, THEIR SEX DRIVE INCREASES AND IT CAN LEAD TO THE EARLY ONSET OF PUBERTY IN CHILDREN.

WOMEN ARE MORE LIKELY TO SUFFER FROM SAD THAN MEN. A SIMPLE AND PROVEN REMEDY IS TO SIT IN FRONT OF BRIGHT LIGHT (10,000LUX) FOR ABOUT HALF AN HOUR, MORNING AND EVENING.

DIET AND DEPRESSION

A poor diet, especially one with a lot of junk food, is a common cause of depression. Foods greatly influence the brain's behaviour. The chemicals, called neurotransmitters, in the brain, which regulate our behaviour and are commonly associated with mood are: dopamine, serotonin and norepinephrine. When the brain produces serotonin, tension is eased. When it produces dopamine or norepinephrine, we tend to think and act quickly and are generally more alert.

At the neurochemical and physiological level, neurotransmitters are extremely important. These substances carry impulses between nerve cells. Serotonin, for example, plays a role in modulating mood, sleep and appetite. Low levels of serotonin can lead to depression, anxiety and sleep disorders. The consumption of the amino acid tryptophan increases the amount of serotonin made by the brain. So, eating complex carbohydrates such as wholegrains, spelt, buckwheat and rice (not simple carbohydrates such as sugary foods and refined carbohydrates such as pastries and cakes) raises the level of tryptophan in the brain and has a calming effect. High-protein foods, such as eggs, fish and pulse vegetables, on the other hand, promote the production of dopamine and norepinephrine, which promote alertness.

A SELECTION OF **BLACK** FOODS AND DRINKS

TEA

OLIVES

CAVIAR

TREACLE

BLACKBERRIES

LIQUORICE

BLACK BEANS

EAT BLACK FOODS

Many black foods, such as liquorice and blackberries, contain very healthy elements, as does black tea and perhaps that most famous black drink of all – Guinness – which is well-known for its rich iron content.

Blackberries

BLACKBERRIES are a good source of salicylate – a hydroxybenozic phenolic acid that plants produce to fight infection. The anti-inflammatory painkilling drug, aspirin, is produced from salicylate, which was originally extracted from a willow tree. Dietary salicylate may reduce the risk of heart disease. Blackberries are high in Vitamin E but wild varieties have a higher concentration than the cultivated varieties. A blackberry is sometimes called a "fingerberry" or "black haw". Eat them raw or baked in muffins; put in crumbles or eat in jam.

Nutrition
- Vitamin C
- Vitamin E
- Pectin (Soluble fibre that aids elimination of waste from the body)
- Potassium

Good For
- Providing a low fat source of Vitamin E
- Easing aches and pains
- Combating heart disease

How Much To Eat
- 15 blackberries = 75g (2 $^1/_2$ oz) per serving
- Eat in season where possible and include them in your diet as part of your five servings per day

Phytonutrients
- Flavonoids
- Lignans
- Phenolic acid
- Salicylate

TO BUY

Choose plump, almost dark purple, shiny blackberries. If the blackberries still have a stem attached it indicates that the berries are immature and have been picked too early. They are best eaten on the day of purchase but they will keep in the fridge for a day or so. They can also be frozen so you can make sure you have them all year round.

Black Tea

BLACK TEA has an anti-oxidant function – boosting the body's natural defence mechanisms and improving blood flow to coronary arteries, helping people to avoid and/or recover from heart attacks. When brewed properly, black tea has a much higher caffeine content compared to other teas (50–65% of coffee, depending on the type and brewing technique).

Nutrition
- Flavonols – good anti-oxidants.

Good For
- Bone health
- Reducing the risk of heart disease

How Much To Eat
- 1–5 cups daily

Phytonutrients
- Flavonoids
- Phenolic acids
- Xantine
- Alkaloids

Storing Your Tea

There are four things that can harm tea: **AIR, LIGHT, MOISTURE AND EXCESSIVE HEAT**. So it is advisable to store your tea in an airtight, lightproof container away from moisture or heat. The bags that some tea comes in are good storage containers. As long as the bag is tightly shut, with air expelled, it should be 98% airtight. Tightly closing jars can also be good storage containers, as long as they are stored out of the light. Your tea will keep best, however, in a metal tin. Tea can be best kept for a longer period if stored at room temperature, in a dry place, closed within the packaging and away from strong smells. **BE CAREFUL ABOUT STORING YOUR TEAS WITH YOUR SPICES AS TEA IS EXTREMELY ABSORBENT AND WILL ABSORB THE AROMAS OF WHATEVER IS AROUND IT.**
Never store tea in the fridge or freezer. Under the conditions recommended, tea should last for at least a year. Tea kept well should not spoil but may lose flavour over time. The type of tea also makes a difference to how long it will last – the tighter the roll of the leaf, the longer the shelf life of the tea. A green powder tea will last longer for this reason. Generally, flavoured teas, like Earl Grey or jasmine tea, have the shortest shelf life, followed by green tea, oolong and then black teas.

Did You Know?

IN A RECENT STUDY PUBLISHED BY THE EUROPEAN FOOD INFORMATION COUNCIL, IT WAS DISCOVERED THAT ONE CUP OF BLACK TEA SUPPLIES AROUND 200 MG (0.007 OUNCE) OF FLAVONOIDS WHICH ARE RELEASED IN THE FIRST FEW MINUTES OF BREWING. MAKE SURE YOU BREW TEA FOR AT LEAST A MINUTE TO MAXIMISE THE RELEASE OF FLAVONOLS.

TYPES OF TEA

BLACK TEA is allowed to wither and then it's rolled. Oxidation then takes place during which water evaporates out of the leaf and the leaf absorbs more oxygen from the air. Black teas usually undergo full oxidation/fermentation. Then the leaves undergo firing (rapid heating). The results are the characteristic dark brown and black leaf, and the more robust and pronounced flavours of black teas.

OOLONG TEA is partially withered and partially oxidised which is why it is called a semi-green or semi-fermented tea. China and Taiwan are the main producers of this type of tea. Leaves for oolong must be picked at exactly the right time and processed immediately afterwards. Some are withered in direct sunlight and then shaken in bamboo baskets to bruise the edges of the leaves. Others are dried in drying chambers, which is more cost effective as the process is faster.

There will be a certain amount of oxidation on the parts of the leaf that have been broken to develop a fuller, richer flavour after the natural juices have been exposed to oxygen. Experience is required to identify the best time to stop oxidation which is when the leaves are 30% red and 70% green. The leaves are then taken indoors to dry over charcoal-fired stoves. Oolong teas have a fruity or perfumed aroma and a smooth but complex flavour, with a hint of peach or apricot.

GREEN TEA is allowed to wither only slightly after being picked. Then the oxidation process is stopped very quickly by firing the leaves. In Japan the leaves are first steamed and then cooled, rolled, pressed, sorted, polished and dried.

Green teas tend to have less caffeine (10–30% of coffee). A recent study in the UK found that chemicals in this tea also shut down a key molecule which plays a significant role in the development of cancer.

WHITE TEA is the most delicate of all teas. White tea is named after the tiny white or silver hairs that cover the bud as it develops at the tip of each shoot. They are usually made from just the unopened bud, gathered before it can start to unfurl. They are then steamed and dried.

When brewed they give a very pale, champagne colour and have a light and sweet flavour. White teas have the lowest caffeine content of all teas.

YELLOW TEA is made from new buds and then piled and left out. The heat generated from the natural oxidation process dries them out to prevent any further decomposition. The caffeine content is higher than green teas and the taste has a delicate sweetness.

HERBAL TISANES/HERBAL TEAS such as jasmine, elderflower and camomile are made from flowers, herbs and fruits, and are all naturally caffeine free. Some of them have added natural flavouring, for example camomile, honey and vanilla tea.

Black Bean and Pepper Salad

SERVES 4

100G (3 ½ OZ) BULGHAR WHEAT

1 RED PEPPER – SEEDED AND CUT INTO QUARTERS

1 YELLOW PEPPER – SEEDED AND CUT INTO QUARTERS

400G (12 OZ) COOKED BLACK BEANS – DRAINED

25G (1 OZ) RAISINS

50G (2 OZ) PINE NUTS – TOASTED

2 TBSP FRESH PARSLEY – CHOPPED

MIXED SALAD LEAVES – TO SERVE

FOR THE DRESSING

2 TOMATOES – PEELED, SEEDED AND DICED

1 GARLIC CLOVE – CRUSHED

¼ TSP EACH CHILLI POWDER AND PAPRIKA

1 TBSP OLIVE OIL

1 TBSP FRESH LEMON JUICE

GROUND BLACK PEPPER

Place the bulghar wheat in a heatproof bowl. Pour over 600ml (20 fl oz) of boiling water and leave to soak for 20 minutes. Rinse the wheat in cold water and drain well.

Place the peppers skin side up in a grill pan and cook under a hot grill for about 10 minutes until the skins have blackened and charred. Leave to cool a little, then peel off the skins.

MAKING THE DRESSING: Place the tomatoes, garlic, chilli powder, paprika, oil, lemon juice and seasoning in a small bowl and whisk until well combined.

Mix together the peppers, bulghar wheat, black beans, raisins, pine nuts and parsley. Arrange on a bed of salad leaves. Then drizzle over the dressing.

Stir-fried Squid with Peppers and Black Bean Sauce

SERVES 4

450G (16 OZ) CLEANED SQUID

6 SHITAKE/CHESTNUT MUSHROOMS – WIPED

3 TBSP VEGETABLE OIL

1/4 INCH ROOT GINGER – FINELY CHOPPED

1 GARLIC CLOVE – FINELY CHOPPED

1 SMALL GREEN CHILLI – SEEDED AND
   FINELY SLICED

8 SPRING ONIONS – THICKLY SLICED

1/2 RED PEPPER – SEEDED AND CUT INTO
   DIAMONDS

1/2 GREEN PEPPER – SEEDED AND CUT
   INTO DIAMONDS

FOR THE SAUCE

1 TBSP BLACK BEAN PASTE

1 TSP CORNFLOUR

2 TBSP SAKE OR DRY SHERRY

1 TBSP SOY SAUCE

1/2 TSP SUGAR

Slit open the squid. Peel off any purple membrane and rinse thoroughly. Score the outside into diamonds, then cut into wide strips. Pat dry on kitchen paper and set aside.

Remove the stalks from the mushrooms and slice thickly. Whisk together all of the ingredients for the sauce with two tablespoons of water.

Heat the oil in a wok and quickly fry the squid in batches. Then remove with a slotted spoon and set aside.

Add a little more oil if necessary, then stir-fry the ginger, garlic, chilli and spring onions. Add the peppers and mushrooms for 2 minutes. Return the squid to the wok and add the sauce. Bring to the boil and cook for about a minute; stirring until thickened. Then serve.

Goats' Cheese and Black Olive Pancakes

SERVES 4-6

MAKES 14-16

2 TBSP FRESH SNIPPED CHIVES

2 TBSP TORN FRESH BASIL

25G (1 OZ) STONED BLACK OLIVES – CHOPPED

2 TBSP TAPENADE (SEE PAGE 203 FOR RECIPE)

2 X 100G (2 X 3 ½ OZ) PACKS FIRM GOATS'
   CHEESE – CUBED

2 SPRING ONIONS – FINELY CHOPPED

SUNFLOWER OIL FOR FRYING

DRESSED MIXED SALAD LEAVES – TO GARNISH

PANCAKES:

250G (9OZ) PLAIN FLOUR

1 TSP BAKING POWDER

PINCH OF SEA SALT

375 ML (12 FL OZ) WATER

1 EGG

1 TSP GOLDEN HONEY

3 TBSP OIL

ADDITIONAL OIL FOR
   COOKING

Preheat the oven to 140°C (280°F) or gas mark 2. In a large mixing bowl, mix the flour, baking powder, salt, herbs, olives and eggs together.

Gradually add the water, beating well, until you get a smooth batter. Add a little more water if necessary.

In another bowl, mix the tapenade with the goats' cheese and spring onion.

Heat a little oil in a large frying or griddle pan on a medium heat and spoon the batter on. Before turning, spoon a heaped tablespoon of cheese mixture on to the uncooked side. Then flip over and cook for one minute. Keep warm while you use up the batter.

Finally put 2 to 3 pancakes on each plate. Garnish with salad leaves and serve.

Black-Eye Bean Salad

SERVES 4

200G (7 OZ) BLACK-EYE BEANS – COOKED

LITTLE GEM LETTUCE – CHOPPED

SPRING ONIONS – CHOPPED

1 TBSP FRESH MINT – CHOPPED

2 TBSP OF FRESH LEMON JUICE

2 GARLIC CLOVES – CRUSHED

5 TBSP OF GROUNDNUT OIL

SALT AND PEPPER

Black-eye beans must be soaked overnight, and then boiled for 30–45 minutes to cook them.
Then mix 200g cooked black-eye beans with one chopped little gem lettuce, three chopped
spring onions and chopped fresh mint.

Place lemon juice, garlic cloves, groundnut oil and some seasoning in a screw-topped jar and
shake until well combined.

Drizzle over the salad and toss to coat. Serve at room temperature.

Blackened Fish

SERVES ANY NUMBER

1 TBSP EACH CAYENNE, PAPRIKA, FENNEL SEEDS, MUSTARD POWDER, GROUND
  BLACK PEPPER

1 TSP DRIED BASIL

1 TSP THYME

4 TSP SALT

1–2 FISH FILLETS – PER PERSON

A LITTLE OIL

Mix the spices, herbs and salt together. Brush fillets with oil and press mixture over them; coating well. Fry fillets in oil for 2 minutes on each side. Serve.

Black Bread in Flower Pot

SERVES 6

25G (1 OZ) BLACK TREACLE

225G (8 OZ) STRONG WHITE BREAD FLOUR

225G (8 OZ) RYE FLOUR

1 TSP SALT

1 SACHET EASY-BLEND DRIED YEAST

1/2 TSP POTATO FLOUR

CRUSHED OATS – TO FINISH

300 ML LUKEWARM WATER

Blend treacle with 300 ml (10 fl oz) lukewarm water. Mix the flours and salt in a large bowl. Stir in the yeast.

Now make a well in the centre and pour in the liquid. Mix to a soft dough. Knead on a floured surface for 5–10 minutes until smooth and elastic. Place in a bowl, cover with oiled polythene and leave to rise in a warm place for an hour or until doubled in size.

Knock back the dough and shape to fit a well-greased, well-seasoned flowerpot. Cover with oiled polythene and leave in a warm place for about 20 minutes.

Preheat oven to 220°C (425°F) or gas mark 7. Mix the potato flour with 150 ml (5 fl oz) hot water and brush over the loaf. Sprinkle with oats and bake for 30–40 minutes until well risen. Cool on a wire rack.

Black Olive Pâté (Tapenade)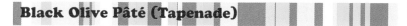

SERVES 2

100G (3 ½ OZ) PINE NUTS – SOAKED

100G (3 ½ OZ) BLACK OLIVES

125 ML (4 FL OZ) WATER

1 AVOCADO

FRESH PARSLEY – CHOPPED

1 VINE TOMATO – DICED

Place all the ingredients into a blender and mix until creamy.

Black Tapenade and Goats' Cheese Parcels

MAKES 32

375G (12 OZ) PACKET READY-ROLLED PUFF PASTRY – THAW IF FROZEN

3 TBSP TAPENADE (BLACK OLIVE PÂTÉ)

350G (11 OZ) CHERRY TOMATOES – SLICED

100G (3 ½ OZ) FIRM GOATS' CHEESE – CHOPPED

SALT AND PEPPER

Preheat the oven to 220°C (425°F) or gas mark 7.

Unroll the pastry and cut into eight pieces crossways and four lengthways.

Arrange the squares, a little apart, on two dampened baking sheets. Spread a little of the tapenade on each square. Place a few of the tomato slices on top, followed by a little cheese. Sprinkle with salt and plenty of freshly ground black pepper, then bake for 12–15 minutes until puffed up and golden. Serve warm or cold.

Black Pudding on Toast with Carrot and Black Onion Seed Purée

MAKES 24

225G (8 OZ) BLACK PUDDING – CUT
   INTO 24 SLICES
6 LARGE SLICES WHOLEMEAL BREAD
GROUND BLACK PEPPER
BUTTER – FOR BUTTERING TOAST
225G (8 OZ) CARROTS – CHOPPED
1 TBSP OLIVE OIL
1 TSP BLACK ONION SEED
PINCH OF SUGAR
3 TBSP FRESH APPLE JUICE
2 TBSP THICK GREEK YOGHURT

THE PURÉE: Place carrots, oil, black onion seed, sugar and apple juice in a pan. Bring to the boil, cover and cook for 12–15 minutes until carrots are tender.

Pour carrots and pan juices into a food processor and process until smooth. Add the yoghurt and mix well. Return to the pan and keep warm.

THE PUDDING: Place the black pudding on a grill pan and grill on both sides for 5–6 minutes until cooked. Toast the bread, then butter lightly and stamp each slice into four rounds with a small cutter.

To assemble, place a piece of black pudding on each round of bread and top with a little carrot purée. Sprinkle with pepper and serve warm.

Black Caviar and Dill Blinis

SERVES 12

200G (7 OZ) SMOKED TROUT FILLETS
100 ML (10 FL OZ) CRÈME FRAICHE
1 TBSP CHOPPED FRESH DILL, PLUS
   EXTRA – ROUGHLY CHOPPED TO
   GARNISH
2 TBSP FRESH LEMON JUICE
6 READY-MADE LARGE BLINIS OR 18
   SMALL ONES
SMALL JAR OF BLACK HERRING ROE
   (CAVIAR)

Break the smoked trout into bite-size pieces. Mix together the crème fraiche, chopped dill and lemon juice in a small bowl, then season with salt and pepper.

Just before serving, toast the blinis on each side. Put one on each plate and top with a spoonful of the crème fraiche mixture, then some trout pieces, then a spoonful of the black herring roe.

Garnish with roughly chopped dill and serve immediately.

Black Poppy Seed and Treacle Tray

MAKES 1

75G (2 ¹/₂ OZ) BUTTER

2 TBSP BLACK TREACLE

350G (11 OZ) WHOLEWHEAT FLOUR

2 TBSP POPPY SEEDS

150 ML (5 FL OZ) WATER

Preheat the oven to 200°C (390°F) or gas mark 6. Heat the butter, treacle and 150 ml (5 fl oz) water together until the butter has melted.

Bring to the boil, then remove from the heat and beat in the flour to form a soft dough. Reserve a quarter of the dough and roll out the remainder to a 30 cm (12 in) square; trimming the edges if necessary.

Transfer to a greased baking sheet. Roll out the reserved dough and cut into thin strips. Brush the edges of the large square with water and arrange strips around the edge in a wavy line. Sprinkle poppy seeds around the edge.

Bake for 15–18 minutes until crisp and lightly coloured. Serve on a tray with nibbles on top.

Black Treacle Bread

MAKES 1 LOAF

300G (10 ¹/₂ OZ) SELF-RAISING
    WHITE FLOUR

100G (3 ¹/₂ OZ) WHOLEMEAL
    FLOUR

1 TBSP SPROUTED SESAME
    SEEDS

1 TBSP SPROUTED POPPY SEEDS

1 TBSP SPROUTED SUNFLOWER
    SEEDS

1 TBSP PUMPKIN SEEDS

1 DSTSP BLACK TREACLE

350 ML (11 FL OZ)
    WARM WATER

Preheat the oven to 200°C (390°F) or gas mark 6. Sieve the white flour into a mixing bowl. Add wholemeal flour and all the seeds, keeping some for later. Heat the water and dip the dessertspoon into the warm water and measure out the treacle. Put the treacle into the warm water and stir.

Next pour into the flour and seeds. Stir all around. Turn the mixture onto a floured board. Then knead with your hands and place into the tin.

Sprinkle seeds on top and sprinkle with water, so the seeds stick. Bake for 40–45 minutes.

It should sound hollow when you tap the underneath. Cool on a wire tray.

Blackberry and Raspberry Sorbet

MAKES 1 LITRE

550G (18 OZ) BLACKBERRIES

250G (9 OZ) RASPBERRIES

150G (5 ½ OZ) SUGAR

GRATED ZEST AND JUICE OF 1 LEMON

2 TBSP FRAMBOISE

1 EGG WHITE – BEATEN

This makes a scrumptious treat on a sunny summer's day! Place the berries, lemon juice, zest and sugar in a saucepan. Bring slowly to the boil and simmer for about 3 minutes.

Remove from the heat.

Strain into a measuring jug, pressing as much fruit as possible through the sieve. If necessary add water to achieve 1 litre (34 fl oz) of pulp.

Cool completely and stir in the framboise. Taste and add extra sugar if desired. Chill.

Fold in the beaten egg white and serve immediately with fresh raspberries. Freeze any leftovers.

Black Poppy Seed Cake

SERVES 10

175G (6 OZ) SOFTENED BUTTER

175G (6 OZ) CASTER SUGAR

3 EGGS – BEATEN

250G (9 OZ) SELF-RAISING FLOUR

50G (2 OZ) POPPY SEEDS

GRATED RIND OF TWO ORANGES

GRATED RIND OF TWO LEMONS

4 TBSP NATURAL YOGHURT

FOR THE TOPPING

1 SMALL ORANGE

1 LEMON

250G (9 OZ) CARTON MASCARPONE
   CHEESE

3 TBSP ORANGE OR LEMON CURD

Preheat the oven to 150°C (300°F) or gas mark 2. Grease and line a deep 20 cm (8 in) round cake tin.

Using a wooden spoon, beat together the butter, sugar, eggs, flour, poppy seeds, citrus rinds and yoghurt until smooth. Spread the mixture in the tin and bake for 45–50 minutes until just firm. Cool in the tin for 10 minutes, then turn out and cool on a wire rack. Peel off the paper.

Meanwhile, pare the rind from the orange and lemon and set aside. Mix the mascarpone cheese with enough orange juice to make a spreadable icing. Lightly swirl in the curd to give a marbled effect. Roughly spread over the top and sides of the cake and scatter over the pared rind.

Black Forest Snow Peak Mountain

SERVES 2

100G (3 ¹/₂ OZ) SHOP BOUGHT
    INDIVIDUAL CHOCOLATE SPONGE
    SLAB CAKE
1 TBSP BRANDY
400G (12 OZ) PITTED BLACK CHERRIES
    IN SYRUP
2 LARGE EGGS – SEPARATED
100G (3 ¹/₂ OZ) CASTER SUGAR,
    PLUS 2 TBSP

¹/₂ TSP WHITE WINE VINEGAR
2 X 100 ML TUBS VANILLA ICE-CREAM
75 ML (2 ¹/₂ FL OZ) MILK
¹/₄ TSP VANILLA ESSENCE
2 TSP ARROWROOT
JUICE OF HALF A LEMON
MINT SPRIGS – TO DECORATE
ICING SUGAR – FOR DUSTING

Preheat the oven to 230°C (450°F) or gas mark 8. Line the base of two 10 cm (4 in) loose-bottomed flan tins with baking parchment.

Cut the sponge into four slices, then cut the slices in half diagonally and use them to line the bottom of the tins; pressing down firmly to ensure they form a solid base.

Sprinkle the brandy on top. Drain the cherries, reserving the syrup for the sauce. Arrange 6–8 cherries around the edge of each base.

Place the egg whites in a clean bowl and whisk until stiff. Whisk in 50g (2 oz) of the caster sugar, 1 tablespoon at a time; then carefully fold in all but 2 tablespoons of the remaining sugar, followed by the vinegar.

Run a knife around the edge of each ice-cream tub, then turn out the ice-cream onto the sponge bases. Completely cover the ice-cream and sponge with the meringue; making sure there are no gaps. Then decorate by swirling the meringue with a fork. Bake for about 5 minutes until the meringue is golden brown.

MAKING THE CRÈME ANGLAISE: Heat the milk in a small pan. Whisk the egg yolks with the remaining 2 tablespoons of caster sugar and the vanilla essence. Pour in the hot milk, whisking continuously. Then pour back into the pan and continue to cook over a low heat until thickened.

MAKING THE CHERRY SAUCE: Blend the arrowroot with 2 tablespoons of the syrup from the cherries, and place in a small pan. Add the lemon juice and the remaining cherries and syrup. Bring to the boil – stirring all the time, then reduce to a simmer and cook until clear. Spoon some crème anglaise and cherry sauce on to opposite sides of two serving plates. Carefully remove the black forest snow peak from the tins and transfer to the plates. Decorate with mint sprigs, dust with icing sugar and serve at once.

Dark Prune and Marzipan Tart

SERVES 8

FOR THE PASTRY

175G (6 OZ) PLAIN FLOUR

100G (3 ¹/₂ OZ) BUTTER

 – CUT INTO CUBES

50G (2 OZ) CASTER SUGAR

1 EGG YOLK

FOR THE FILLING

200G (7 OZ) PITTED PRUNES

 – READY TO EAT

175G (6 OZ) MARZIPAN

50G (2 OZ) CASTER SUGAR

85G (3 OZ) BUTTER

25G (1 OZ) PLAIN FLOUR

2 EGGS

5 TBSP APRICOT JAM

Preheat the oven to 200°C (390°F) or gas mark 6. Combine the flour and butter together and mix into crumbs (or use a food processor). Add the sugar and mix briefly. Add the yolk, 1–2 tablespoons of cold water and pulse or mix briefly to form a firm dough. Wrap in plastic film and chill for 30 minutes.

THE FILLING: Chop the marzipan into small pieces and put in the food processor with the sugar and butter. Work until soft. Then add the flour and eggs.

Roll out the pastry to line a 23–24 cm (9 ¹/₂ in) flan tin. Trim edges, place paper beans on pastry and bake for 10 minutes.

Remove paper and beans and bake for 5 minutes more. Next remove from oven and let cool slightly. Reduce oven to 180°C (350°F) or gas mark 4. Spread 2 tablespoons of jam over the pastry. Spread the marzipan cream over the top. Arrange the prunes evenly over the filling. Bake for 30–35 minutes until risen and golden.

Cool in the tin and transfer to a large serving plate. Heat the remaining jam; stirring until syrupy. Brush over the tart and serve warm or cold.

THE COLOUR
white

WHITE CONTAINS ALL THE COLOURS OF THE SPECTRUM AND IT IS THE HOSTESS TO ALL THE COLOUR STARS. IT REFLECTS LIGHT AND IS ASSOCIATED WITH SPIRITUALITY AND GOODNESS – THE WHITE KNIGHT IS ALWAYS READY TO SAVE THE DAMSEL IN DISTRESS.

White is an important colour for your health. The collective functioning of the endocrine system is governed by white. The eyeball is also white and can be a very useful indicator of how healthy you are.

White is a symbolic colour. Health professionals and people working in the food industry often wear white coats to convey **CLEANLINESS** and **EFFICIENCY**, while the judge in the courtroom wears a white wig to symbolise **IMPARTIALITY**.

THE KEY WORDS ASSOCIATED WITH WHITE ARE:

- PEACE
- TRANQUILLITY
- INNOCENCE
- PURITY
- ORDER

Guide to Wearing White

There are no shades or tints of white in colour therapy but in fashion and interior design there are numerous shades from snow white to creamy whites to 'off-whites'. White is a great colour to use when you are moving through a stressful situation as it can restore anything that is pinched or stretched; it can break the ice and help people to open up. Pearl white can help digestion as it promotes a dislike for fatty foods. Gallstones symbolise that your emotional life has been upset or disturbed.

WHEN TO WEAR WHITE

When you have a hangover, wear white to calm the body and mind. When starting a new exercise or de-tox programme white helps to cleanse the system. Choose white when you want to open up and share your feelings. Of course it is also a good choice for wedding days!

WHEN TO AVOID WHITE

White gives the impression of perfection which is something life is not. Mae West sums it up well in her line: "I used to be snow white, but I drifted".
White can show life in an unrealistic way. People return to white time and time again for purification but living in a white world would be stark. It is really important not to wear or have an over-abundance of white in the interior décor of your home as it can feel somewhat clinical and detached.

A WHITE DAY PLAN

EXERCISE – TODAY I WILL GET OUT INTO THE FRESH AIR AND WALK BESIDE WATER.

CLOTHES – I WILL WEAR WHITE AS A SYMBOL THAT I AM OPEN AND WILLING TO ABSORB THE NEXT OPPORTUNITY THAT PRESENTS ITSELF TO ME.

FOODS – I WILL EAT PLENTY OF WHITE FOOD TODAY TO HELP ME ELIMINATE THAT WHICH I NO LONGER NEED.

AFFIRMATION – I AM STARTING A NEW STORY TODAY.

THOUGHT FOR THE DAY

I am clear and emotionally detached today.

⊕ White Health

WHILE EACH GLAND HAS A SPECIFIC COLOUR THAT GOVERNS IT, THE COLLECTIVE FUNCTIONING OF THE ENDOCRINE SYSTEM IS WHITE.

WHITE CAN ACT AS AN ANTISEPTIC AND MANY THERAPISTS MAY USE WHITE IN COLOUR HEALING TO HELP THE CLIENT OPEN UP. WHITE CAN HELP THEM BECOME LESS DENSE AND MAY TRIGGER THE PROCESS OF MELTING THE ICE .

WEARING WHITE CAN HELP MAKE THE SKIN LOOK MOIST, SUPPLE AND LOOK SOFTER AS OPPOSED TO WEARING BLACK, WHERE THE SKIN CAN LOOK PINCHED. REFER TO THE YELLOW CHAPTER FOR MORE SKIN HEALTH DETAILS.

did you know?

SULPHUR PLAYS A MAJOR ROLE IN AIDING BILE FLUID, BRAIN FUNCTION, CONNECTIVE TISSUE, HAIR, NAILS AND SKIN. IT IS RANKED AS THE 8TH OR 9TH MOST ABUNDANT MINERAL IN THE BODY AND IS STORED IN EVERY CELL.

FOODS WITH SULPHUR

GREEN	WHITE	GOLDEN SEEDS	RED
CABBAGE	GARLIC	PUMPKIN	RED HOT
BROCCOLI	ONION	HEMP	CHILLI
BRUSSEL	CAULIFLOWER	SEEDS	PEPPERS
SPROUTS			
KALE			

EAT WHITE FOODS

White foods included in this section are represented by the vegetables, fruit and poultry group of that colour. It is worth remembering that a colourful plate each meal time will ensure that you are getting a wide and varied selection of phytonutrients.

If you are a pasta lover, for example, and choose to eat a carbonara dish, include some green peas to add a splash of colour. If you have a sweet tooth and the dessert choices include a meringue or creamed rice then your meal choices are all a little white. You may find that you feel stodgy or bloated after this type of starchy meal. If you mix your colours each time this won't happen.

MILK

Milk is a complete or whole food for the young, containing high biological protein and calcium. These macronutrients and micronutrients are essential for bone development and growth. It is necessary to include at least three servings of calcium in the diet daily to help reduce the risk of developing osteoporosis. Teenagers can afford to have up to five servings per day.

Milk contains Conjugated Linoleic Acids (CLA) which is a fatty acid found in the fatty portion of milk. CLA is a powerful anti-oxidant and has been rated as three times more powerful an anti-oxidant than Vitamin E. CLA is present in small quantities in milk, creating much debate among food researchers as to the nutritional contribution it can make to the diet due to the small amounts present.

An interesting development in combating the symptoms of premenstrual syndrome (PMS), that almost three quarters of all women experience at some point in their lives, uses a combination of calcium and Vitamin D. Senior Dieticians at Hammersmith Hospital and Queen Charlotte's Menopause and Women's clinic in London have devised the Double-D anti-PMS Diet. D stands for dairy which is a good source of calcium and Vitamin D. The ratio recommended for daily consumption is 1,500 milligrams of calcium to 20 micrograms of Vitamin D. For example:

150g tub low fat yoghurt = 285 mg calcium
75g edam cheese = 578 mg
300 ml semi-skimmed milk = 360 mg calcium

Vitamin D content of fish
100g canned salmon = 12 mg Vitamin D
100g sardines in tomato sauce = 7.5 mg Vitamin D

Other good sources of calcium include green leafy vegetables, baked beans, soya milk and soft-boned fish.

A SELECTION OF WHITE FOODS

GARLIC

ASPARAGUS

PEARS

COD

MILK

POPCORN

COCONUT

HADDOCK

RICE

CHICKEN

ROOT VEGETABLES

LEEKS

CAULIFLOWER

ONIONS

WHITING

Garlic

GARLIC, leeks, spring onion, chive and onions are all related and belong to the allicin family. Allicin is a special compound found in these foods that has an anti-bacterial and an anti-inflammatory function. Garlic also contains many sulphur-rich compounds.

Nutrition
To activate the allicin, garlic must be crushed. It may be destroyed in cooking so to maximise the powerful effect, it is best to eat garlic raw.

Good for
- Blood pressure
- Promoting a healthy heart

How much to eat
- One clove weighs 4g ($^1/_8$ oz)
- $^1/_2$–3 cloves per day
- Many people take 1 garlic capsule a day

Phytonutrients
- Key source of allylic sulphides which are sulphur compounds that have been shown to induce enzymes that detoxify body cells
- Flavonoids

Asparagus

ASPARAGUS is a member of the lily family. It is most commonly green but can also come in white form – when it is cut below the ground – or purple which turns green when cooked. Drink the water you cook asparagus in for its diuretic value or add it to soups or stocks.

For women, it is an excellent vegetable to eat around the time of your period as it acts as a mild sedative and can reduce any discomfort. Asparagus is also a good source of fructo-oligosaccharides, a special type of dietary fibre that can promote the growth of beneficial lactobacilli bacteria in the colon – bacteria that are essential for healthy colon activity.

Nutrition
- Folate
- Vitamin E
- Fructo-oligosaccharides

Good for
- Colon health
- Premenstrual cramping
- Mood boosting

How much to eat
- 5 asparagus spears per serving

Phytonutrients
- Flavonoids
- Carotenoids
- Saponins

Pears

One **PEAR** a day provides 11% of the desired amount of Vitamin C and 10% of the desired amount of copper. Both help to stimulate the white blood cells which fight infection so pears help to boost the immune system. Pears are also one of the few foods least likely to trigger an allergic reaction so are often used as part of an exclusion diet to investigate food intolerances.

Researchers at the State University in Rio de Janeiro noted in the scientific journal *Nutrition* that pears appear to accelerate weight loss in women. Overweight women who added 300g (10^1/2 oz), or three small pears a day, to a reduced calorie daily meal plan lost more weight than women who did not. One reason may be that pears are low in energy density so they leave us feeling full for longer.

Nutrition
- Vitamin C
- Vitamin A
- Potassium
- Dried pears – Protein, Iron & Vitamin A

Good for
- Providing hydroxycinnamic acids which act as good antioxidants
- Boosts the immune system by stimulating the white blood cells

How much to eat
- A medium pear weighs 160g per serving (eat as part of five to nine portions a day diet)

Phytonutrients
- Flavonoids
- Condensed tannins

Chicken

CHICKEN is good eaten grilled, roasted, in a casserole or used in soup. Remember most of the fat is contained in the skin, so remove this part. It is good for building general resistance and contains the anti-viral amino acid lysine which is helpful for suppressing the cold sore virus. Chicken provides easily absorbed iron and zinc – twice as much in the dark meat as in the breast – which makes chicken an excellent food during pregnancy. Chicken breast contains high quality Vitamin B6, double the amount found in dark meats – this makes it useful for PMS.

Nutrition
- Iron
- Zinc
- Protein
- Vitamin B6
- Lysine

Good for
- Pregnancy
- PMS
- Building up the body's general resistance
- Resistance to colds

How much to eat
- Good to eat once a week

Phytonutrients
None

Leeks

LEEKS are in the allicin family and are full of healing properties. The Ancient Greeks used leeks for throat and voice challenges. Many singers today use them everyday to improve their singing voices.

Nutrition
- The green part is a good source of Vitamin A

Good for
- Natural diuretic

How much to eat
- Average portion size 75g (2^1/2 oz) per serving

Phytonutrients
- Flavonoids
- Fructo-oligosaccharides

did you know?

THE LEEK IS THE SYMBOL OR NATIONAL EMBLEM OF WALES.

Mini Leek Quiches

MAKES 8

450G (1 LB) PLAIN FLOUR

PINCH SALT

350G (12 OZ) BUTTER – CUBED

2 EGG YOLKS

3 TBSP WATER

FILLING:

50G (2 OZ) BUTTER

5 LEEKS – THINLY SLICED

HANDFUL FRESH CORIANDER

5 EGGS

300 ML (10 FL OZ) SINGLE CREAM

SALT AND PEPPER

1 TBSP FRESH ROSEMARY

Preheat the oven to 180°C (350°F) or gas mark 4.

MAKING THE PASTRY: Sift the flour into a bowl. Add the salt. Rub in the butter and bind with the egg yolks and water, then wrap and chill for 10 minutes. Roll out the pastry and line 8 small flan rings; place on a baking sheet. Line the pastry with grease-proof paper and weigh down with baking beans. Bake in a preheated oven for 15 minutes.

MAKING THE FILLING: Meanwhile melt the butter for the filling in a saucepan. Add the leeks and sauté gently. Remove from the heat and cool. Mix the fresh coriander through the leeks and divide them evenly into the pastry cases. Beat the eggs together and stir in the cream. Season with salt and pepper.

Pour the liquid evenly into the cases. Garnish with fresh rosemary and bake for 20 minutes. Serve with a crispy mixed leaf salad.

Leek, Potato and Rocket Soup

SERVES 4-6

50G (2 OZ) BUTTER

1 ONION – CHOPPED FINELY

3 LEEKS – CHOPPED

2 POTATOES – DICED

900 ML (30 FL OZ) VEGETABLE STOCK

2 LARGE HANDFULS OF CHOPPED ROCKET

150 ML (5 FL OZ) CREAM

SALT AND PEPPER

ROCKET HAS A WONDERFUL PEPPERY
TASTE AND IS GREAT WITH THIS SOUP.
IT IS TERRIFIC TO EAT AT LUNCH TIME
AS IT IS WARMING AND FILLING.

Melt the butter in a pot and lightly sauté the vegetables. Cover and leave for about 15 minutes.

Next pour in the stock, cover with a lid and simmer for 20 minutes; until the vegetables are tender. Pour the soup into a blender and purée. Return the soup into the pot. Add the rocket and stir in the cream. Season with salt and freshly ground black pepper. Ladle the soup into warmed bowls and serve with a spelt roll.

Sweet Potato and Leek Soup

SERVES 4-6

15G (½ OZ) BUTTER

4 MEDIUM LEEKS – THINLY SLICED

800G (1 LB 12 OZ) SWEET POTATOES
   – PEELED AND CUBED

1 MEDIUM WHITE POTATO – PEELED
   AND CUBED

600 ML (20 FL OZ) CHICKEN STOCK

SALT AND FRESHLY GROUND PEPPER

FRESHLY GRATED NUTMEG

150 ML (4½ FL OZ) CREAM

3 TBSP CHOPPED CHIVES

Melt the butter in a saucepan and add the vegetables. Sauté for 10 minutes.

Add the chicken stock and allow the stock to come to the boil; then simmer until the vegetables are tender. Transfer the mixture into a blender and purée. Return to the saucepan and season well.

Next add the fresh nutmeg. Stir in the cream and serve with some freshly chopped chives and wholemeal brown bread.

A fabulous smooth and creamy soup with an elusive flavour that is hard to identify.

Leek, Courgette and Carrot Loaf

SERVES 4-6

2 TBSP OLIVE OIL

200G (7 OZ) LEEKS – SLICED THINLY

1 COURGETTE – GRATED

225G (8 OZ) CARROTS – GRATED

1 CLOVE GARLIC – CRUSHED

4 EGGS

600 ML (20 FL OZ) MILK

SALT AND PEPPER

1 TBSP CHIVES – CHOPPED

225G (8 OZ) POTATOES – PEELED
    AND CHOPPED

LOAF TIN

Preheat the oven to 180°C (350°F) or gas mark 4. Heat the oil in a saucepan and add the garlic and leeks. Sauté for 5 minutes. Add the courgettes and grated carrots and sauté for another 5 minutes.

Beat the eggs and milk together in a bowl and season well.

Add the vegetables from the saucepan. Place half the mixture into the loaf tin.

Place the sliced potato on top and add the remaining mixture. Sprinkle chopped chives on top. Bake for 40 minutes and serve with a portion of crispy garlic and olive potatoes.

Roasted Root Vegetables

SERVES 4

2 CARROTS – PEELED, CUT IN HALF
    LENGTHWAYS

2 PARSNIPS – PEELED, CUT IN HALF
    LENGTHWAYS

1 BABY FENNEL – CUT INTO 2 CM THICK SLICES

2 TBSP OLIVE OIL

2 TBSP HONEY

1 TBSP WHOLEGRAIN MUSTARD

1 TBSP BOILING WATER

4 GARLIC CLOVES – PEELED

1 BUNCH FRESH CORIANDER LEAVES

Preheat oven to 200°C (390°F) or gas mark 6.

Cut the carrots and parsnips into 10 cm (4 in) lengths. Place into a greased roasting dish with the fennel.

Combine olive oil, honey, wholegrain mustard and water. Pour over the root vegetables and ensure they are well coated. Sprinkle over the coriander leaves and whole garlic cloves.

Roast for 35–40 minutes; tossing every 15 minutes until golden brown.

Serve with a piece of oven baked fish or chicken.

Garlic Potatoes with Olives

SERVES 4

900G (2 LB) POTATOES – SLICED

2 ONIONS – SLICED

2 TBSP OLIVE OIL

4 GARLIC CLOVES – CRUSHED

1 TBSP FRESH ROSEMARY

2 TBSP FRESH PARSLEY – CHOPPED

SALT AND PEPPER

12 PITTED BLACK OLIVES – HALVED

300 ML (10 FL OZ) DOUBLE CREAM

125G (4 1/2 OZ) GRATED GRUYERE CHEESE

Preheat the oven to 200°C (390°F) or gas mark 6.

Boil the potatoes for about 10 minutes. Heat the oil in a pan and sauté the onions and garlic. Add the seasoning and herbs.

Remove the pan from the heat and add the cream and cheese.

Layer the par-cooked potatoes with olives and the garlic creamy sauce. Bake for 40 minutes.

Serve immediately with Leek, Courgette and Carrot Loaf or a meat or fish dish of your choice.

Sweet Fish Cakes

SERVES 2

1 TIN TUNA FISH IN BRINE

1 SWEET POTATO – COOKED AND MASHED

1 SPRING ONION – FINELY CHOPPED

1 ROSEMARY SPRIG – FINELY CHOPPED

Blend the fish, sweet potato and spring onion together.

Add chopped rosemary.

Using your hands make even-sized ball shapes.

Place on a baking sheet and heat in the oven for 10–15 minutes at 180°C (350°F) or gas mark 4.

Serve with tomato and basil salsa or mixed leaf salad.

Chicken, Red Pepper and Smoked Mozzarella Quesadillas

SERVES 4

2 READY-TO-EAT COOKED CHICKEN BREASTS – FINELY DICED

½ SMALL RED PEPPER – DESEEDED AND FINELY DICED

4 SPRING ONIONS – TRIMMED AND FINELY CHOPPED

200G (7 OZ) SMOKED MOZZARELLA – FINELY DICED

FEW FRESH SAGE LEAVES – FINELY CHOPPED

8 SOFT FLOUR TORTILLAS

OLIVE OIL – TO GREASE

SALSA

Put the chicken, pepper, spring onions, mozzarella and sage into a bowl. Season and mix together. Lay a tortilla flat; scatter a quarter of the chicken mixture over it. Top with another tortilla and press together. Make 3 more quesadillas in the same way.

Grease two large frying pans with a little olive oil and put over a medium heat. Put one quesadilla into each pan and cook for 2 minutes, until golden. Invert onto a plate, then slide back into the pan and cook for 2 minutes until the filling is hot and the cheese is melting. Set this one aside while you cook the other two.

Cut each quesadilla into 4 and serve with salsa.

Chicken Noodle Stir-Fry

SERVES 4

200G (7 OZ) DRIED MEDIUM EGG NOODLES (ABOUT 3 BLOCKS)

VEGETABLE OIL FOR COOKING

4 TBSP UNSALTED CASHEW NUTS

1 TBSP ICING SUGAR

2 CHICKEN BREASTS – SKINNED AND CUT INTO LITTLE STRIPS

BUNCH OF FRESH CORIANDER – LEAVES PICKED AND STALKS FINELY CHOPPED

2 BIG GARLIC CLOVES – THINLY SLICED

THUMB-SIZE PIECE OF GINGER – PEELED AND THINLY SLICED

8 SPRING ONIONS – THINLY SLICED

HANDFUL OF BEAN SPROUTS

2 TBSP SOY SAUCE

1 TBSP FISH SAUCE

1 GEM LETTUCE

SALT AND PEPPER

1 FRESH CHILLI – DESEEDED AND SLICED TO GARNISH

FEW SPRIGS WATERCRESS (OPTIONAL)

1 LIME – TO GARNISH

1 TBSP WATER

Cook the noodles in boiling salted water according to packet instructions. Drain and refresh under cold water. Drain again. Then toss in a little oil and put to one side.

Toss the cashews nuts in a tablespoon of water with the icing sugar. Drop into a hot saucepan and cook; shaking and tossing constantly, until the nuts turn sticky then golden. Tip onto a baking tray to cool, then crush with a pestle and mortar.

Heat a frying pan or wok big enough to hold all the ingredients. Season the chicken with salt and pepper and stir-fry in a little vegetable oil for 2–3 minutes, until almost cooked.

Add the coriander stalks, garlic, and ginger and cook for a further minute. Add the spring onions and nearly all the bean sprouts and stir-fry for a few seconds.

Then add the cooked noodles and coriander leaves. Keep stir-frying until the noodles are warmed through. Season with the soy and fish sauces and remove from the heat.

Serve in bowls and decorate with the rest of the bean sprouts, gem leaves, watercress sprigs (if desired) and the nuts.

Garnish with sliced chilli and lime wedges.

Japanese Herring Fish Cakes with Ginger and Spring Onion

SERVES 2

4–6 HERRING – DEPENDING
   ON THEIR SIZE, SCALED
   AND FILLETED (YOU NEED
   ABOUT 500G/17 OZ
   FILLET IN TOTAL)

4 CM (1 1/2 IN) PIECE FRESH
   GINGER – VERY FINELY
   CHOPPED

3 FAT SPRING ONIONS –
   FINELY CHOPPED

4 CHESTNUT MUSHROOMS – FINELY CHOPPED

LITTLE OIL FOR FRYING

100G (3 1/2 OZ) ROCKET

2 TSP DARK SOY SAUCE

1 TSP ROASTED SESAME SEED OIL

PINCH OF CASTER SUGAR

Pin-bone the herring (to do this, run your finger down the length of each fillet and where you feel a line of fine hair-like bones and pull each one out with tweezers). Cut the herring lengthways into long, thin strips. Now bunch these strips up together and cut across into small pieces (you don't want to work the fish into a very fine paste here, nor do you want it to become too coarse or it won't hold together).

Put the fish into a bowl with the ginger, onion and mushrooms. Add salt and pepper. Mix together well, and then divide the mixture into eight. Shape with slightly wet hands into patties.

Heat a lightly oiled non-stick frying pan over a medium heat (mid-way on the hob dial). Add the fish cakes and fry for about 1 1/2 minutes each side; until golden brown.

Put on warmed plates and pile some of the rocket alongside. Whisk together the remaining ingredients and drizzle over the rocket.

TINA'S TOP TIP

Herring are also splendid coated in flour or oatmeal; then fried and served with crispy bacon. This recipe works well with all types of oily fish, such as: herring, mackerel and salmon (you will need to skin the salmon first).

Chicken and Coconut Curry

SERVES 4

6 TBSP SOY SAUCE

2 TBSP GROUND CUMIN

3 TBSP MILD CURRY PASTE

1 TBSP GROUND TURMERIC

2 GARLIC CLOVES – CRUSHED

4 TBSP SWEET CHILLI SAUCE

3 STICKS LEMON GRASS – FINELY
   CHOPPED

4 CHICKEN BREASTS – CUT INTO
   2 CM PIECES

5 TBSP CRUNCHY PEANUT BUTTER

300 ML (10 FL OZ) COCONUT MILK

2 FRESH KAFFIR LIME LEAVES

CHOPPED COCONUT TO GARNISH

Combine the soy sauce, cumin, curry paste, turmeric, garlic, sweet chilli sauce and lemon grass in a bowl. Add the chicken and stir well.

Cover and refrigerate for 6–8 hours (or overnight) to marinate.

Put the marinated chicken, peanut butter, coconut milk and lime leaves in a pan and cook over a low heat, stirring occasionally. Allow to cook until the meat is tender.

Garnish with chopped coconut.

Serve with rice.

Sushi Rice

SERVES 10 AT A PARTY

Wash 750g (1lb 10 ^{1}/$_2$ oz) sushi (short grain) rice until the water runs clear. Leave the rice to dry for 1 hour.

Put the rice and an equal volume of cold water into a rice cooker or deep pot, with a 5 cm (2 in) piece of dulse or nori. If using a pot, bring to the boil, then cover. Boil for 2 minutes, then simmer for 20 minutes, by which time the rice should be cooked and all the water absorbed (the absorbency of the rice will vary from brand to brand and according to how old it is).

Cool the rice in a special wooden tub or non-metallic bowl, tossing it with a rice paddle and fanning it. Add 150 ml (4 ^{1}/$_2$ fl oz) sushi vinegar as you cool the rice; just enough to make the rice grains stick together slightly.

Nori Sushi Rolls

SERVES 10 AT A PARTY

750G SUSHI RICE – AS ABOVE

450 ML (15 FL OZ) VEGETABLE
   PATÉ OR SOFT MASHED
   AVOCADO

250 ML (8 FL OZ) RAW
   NORI SHEETS

250 ML (8 FL OZ) CUCUMBER
   – DICED

250 ML (8 FL OZ) SMALL CARROT PIECES

250 ML (8 FL OZ) ALFALFA SPROUTS (OR CLOVER OR SUNFLOWER SPROUTS)

1 ONION – CHOPPED FINELY

A FEW SPRIGS OF FRESH DILL

FRESH PICKLED GINGER AND SOY SAUCE TO SERVE

Spread the paté or avocado mash onto nori sheets. Leave 2 ^{1}/$_2$ cm (1 in) of nori sheet exposed at one end to help seal the roll. Spread a layer of sushi rice over paté or avocado mash.

Across the centre, place a row of cucumber, then a row of carrot, a row of sprouts, onions, add a thin row of dill.

Roll nori from the bottom; squeezing tightly. When rolled, it should be firm and strong.

Cut into mouth size pieces and arrange on a plate with some fresh pickled ginger and soy sauce. You can put fresh fish in the nori rolls also if desired.

Basic Popcorn

Popcorn is cheap to make – a big bowl costs less then 25 cents – but it can be quite unimaginative. I recommend that you use this basic recipe and then follow with my special flavourings.

SERVES 4–6

2 TBSP COOKING OIL

50G (2 OZ) POPCORN

Heat the oil in a heavy 1 ³/₄ litre (3 pints) pan. Before it starts smoking; add the corn which should just cover the base in an even layer. Cover and wait for the popping to stop; shaking the pan occasionally.

Now remove from the heat with the lid on, and add one of the flavourings suggested below while it is still hot. Then serve at once.

Italian Popcorn

1 TBSP OLIVE OIL

50G (2 OZ) PARMESAN – GRATED

1 TBSP FRESH BASIL – CHOPPED

1 TSP FREEZE-DRIED OREGANO

PINCH OF GARLIC POWDER

Sprinkle all of the ingredients over the hot popcorn and toss well together.

Mexican Popcorn

1 TBSP CORN OIL

1 TSP CHILLI POWDER

PINCH EACH OF CAYENNE PEPPER, CUMIN, CINNAMON AND GARLIC POWDER

FRESHLY MILLED SEA SALT

Combine all the ingredients (except the salt) and drizzle over the hot popcorn. Then sprinkle over some salt and toss well together.

Pear and Almond Crumble

SERVES 4

75G (2 ½ OZ) SELF-RAISING FLOUR

60G (2 OZ) GROUND ALMONDS

90G (3 OZ) SOFT DARK BROWN SUGAR

60G (2 OZ) BUTTER

4 RIPE PEARS – CORED AND SLICED LENGTHWISE

JUICE OF 1 LIME

2 TBSP FLAKED ALMONDS

Preheat the oven to 220°C (425°F) or gas mark 7.

Put the flour, ground almonds, sugar and butter into a food processor and process until the mixture resembles breadcrumbs.

Place the sliced pears in a butter ovenproof dish – about 20 x 18 x 5 cm (8 x 7 x 2 in) in size and sprinkle with the lime juice.

Cover the pears with the crumble mix, sprinkle on the flaked almonds. Bake in the preheated oven for 20 minutes.

Coconut Fruit Sushi

MAKES 20

300G (10 ½ OZ) SUSHI
    RICE

100G (3 ½ OZ) CASTER
    SUGAR

200 ML (6 ½ FL OZ)
    COCONUT MILK

1 SMALL MANGO – SLICED

2 KIWI FRUITS – SLICED
    AND HALVED

100G (3 ½ OZ)
    STRAWBERRIES – HULLED
    AND HALVED

1 SMALL PAPAYA – SLICED

LIME WEDGES – TO SERVE

Combine the rice, sugar, coconut milk and 400 ml (12½ fl oz) water in a heavy saucepan.

Bring to boil, stirring constantly to stop the rice from sticking. Reduce to the lowest possible heat and simmer gently for 20 minutes, stirring occasionally. Once the rice has absorbed most of the liquid, cover the pan and leave on the lowest heat for another 10 minutes or until the rice is tender.

Line a 20 x 15 cm (8 x 6 in) shallow tin with cling film. Tip in the rice and spread it out evenly to a depth of 2 cm (½ in). Smooth the top and leave to cool. Cover with cling film and chill for 1–2 hours.

Once chilled, turn the rice out on to a cutting board, remove the cling film and cut into sushi-like fingers, about 8 x 3 cm (1 x 3 in).

Top with the sliced fruit and serve with lime wedges.

Banana Cake

MAKES 1 LOAF

125G (4 1/2 OZ) BUTTER

125G (4 1/2 OZ) CASTER SUGAR

1 EGG

3 VERY RIPE BANANAS

150G (5 1/2 OZ) SELF-RAISING FLOUR

1/2 TSP BREAD SODA

3 TBSP MILK

BUTTER FOR GREASING

Preheat oven to 170°C (325°F) or gas mark 3.

Grease tin(s) generously with butter. Mash bananas. Dissolve bread soda in milk.

Cream butter and sugar until light and fluffy. Beat in the egg well; then the bananas.

Sieve flour into mixture; fold in, and finally stir in the milk. Spoon into tin.

Bake for 40 minutes until golden brown.

Cool in tin for 5 minutes and then carefully turn out. Cool on a wire tray.

Serve as a snack or in a lunch box.

Easy Coconut Cake

SERVES 8

4 EGGS

225G (8 OZ) CASTER SUGAR

100G (3 1/2 OZ) UNSALTED BUTTER

100G (3 1/2 OZ) FLAKED ALMONDS

100G (3 1/2 OZ) DESICCATED COCONUT

GRATED ZEST OF 1 LEMON

GRATED ZEST AND JUICE OF 1 ORANGE

125 ML (4 FL OZ) COCONUT MILK

150G (5 1/2 OZ) SELF-RAISING FLOUR – SIFTED

WHIPPED CREAM – TO SERVE

FRESH PASSION FRUIT PULP – TO SERVE

Preheat oven to 180°C (350°F) or gas mark 4.

Put the eggs, sugar, butter, almonds, coconut, zest and juice, coconut milk and flour in a food processor and blend until combined.

Pour into a buttered 28 cm (11 in) round cake tin.

Bake for 45–55 minutes until golden.

Cool then chill for one hour.

Serve with cream and passion fruit pulp.

Pear and Ginger Juice

SERVES 1

450G (1LB) 2 MEDIUM PEARS – CUT INTO WEDGES

2 CM (1 IN) FRESH GINGER

Feed the fruit and ginger into a juice extractor.

Stir to combine and serve.

THE COLOUR
brown

BROWN IS ASSOCIATED WITH STABILITY, SECURITY AND INDUSTRIOUSNESS. LOVERS OF BROWN APPRECIATE COMFORT AND SIMPLICITY; A SETTLED EXISTENCE IS IMPORTANT. PERSONAL SAFETY, STRONG ROOTS AND A HAPPY HOME LIFE ARE ALL BROWN REQUISITES. BEIGE LOVERS MAY HAVE SIMILAR QUALITIES BUT ARE LESS INTENSE.

BROWN IS THE COLOUR ASSOCIATED WITH THE EARTH. Brown nourishes and promises regeneration – just like when you place a seed in the soil, the seed is placed in darkness but from there grow the roots, shoots and leaves. It is a good colour to have around you if you want to become more focused as it will help stabilise you so that you focus on the job at hand.

This colour will help you to be logical, practical and down-to-earth. Stability, security and reliability are key words associated with brown. People who are drawn to brown may well reflect these qualities.

People who wear brown a lot tend to strive hard to do well and are reliable characters, with a subtle sense of humour. They are loyal friends, with strong views and are also good money managers. People who love brown can try to make life safe by keeping it still and static.

THOUGHT FOR THE DAY
I WILL GO ABOUT MY BUSINESS TODAY IN A LIGHT AND CHEERFUL WAY.

A BROWN DAY PLAN

EXERCISE – I WILL DO STOMACH STRETCHES TODAY.

FOOD – I WILL EAT GREAT QUALITY CHOCOLATE TODAY.

CLOTHES – I WILL WEAR SOMETHING BROWN AND SHOW THE WORLD I AM/FEEL SAFE AND SURE-FOOTED.

AFFIRMATION – IT IS SAFE FOR ME TO GO TO GROUND TODAY AND DIG MY ROOTS IN DEEPER.

Guide to Wearing Brown

Brown is exquisite and luxurious; silk and satin evening wear have heads turning. Brown, neutral and beige are all safe colours to combine together and look terrific in summertime, particularly in linen separates.

The colour brown suits you if your colouring can be described as warm and dark and your complexion golden or beige. It is best to avoid wearing it next to your face if you have a fair complexion with blue undertones, but brown accessories can be worn if desired.

The Brown Career

Working for an established institution may suit people with an affinity for brown best, as the security and routine creates a calm environment for them to work in. The established working hours also help them to plan their other activities more effectively. People who are drawn to brown can become so absorbed in work that they are consumed by the task and withdraw into themselves.

WHEN TO WEAR BROWN

Brown acts like a security blanket in times of stress, as it is soothing. Wear it when you feel like time is passing you by too quickly.

WHEN TO AVOID BROWN

Brown may act like a cloak that keeps you hidden away when you need your true colours to be seen, so in that type of situation, it is best to avoid brown. It is advantageous not to have too much of this colour in your home or wardrobe as it can make you feel afraid or unwilling to try new challenges or activities because of the fear of failing.

Children in Peru are given responsibility at a young age and take it very seriously!

➕ Brown Health

CONSTIPATION

Constipation is the term used to describe a person's difficulty in passing stools at all, or the infrequent passage of hard, dry stools, as a result of food moving slowly through the large intestine. In most cases, constipation arises from insufficient amounts of fibre and fluids in the diet. Fibre is found in plant foods, such as wholegrains, fruits and vegetables. Fibre that is soluble in water takes on a soft texture and helps soften the stools. Insoluble fibre passes through the intestines largely unchanged, and adds bulk to stools, which in turn helps to stimulate bowel contractions.

Other factors that can cause constipation include inadequate exercise, advanced age, muscle disorders, structural abnormalities, bowel diseases, neurogenic disorders and a poor diet (especially heavy consumption of junk food). Constipation may be a side effect of iron supplements and some drugs, such as painkillers and anti-depressants. It is also common during pregnancy.

Regular bowel movements are an important mechanism for removing toxins from the body. The colon serves as a holding tank for waste matter and the non-removal of this waste can cause health problems. Antigens and toxins from bowel bacteria and undigested food particles may play a role in the development of diabetes mellitus, meningitis, thyroid disease, candidiasis, chronic gas and bloating, migraines, fatigue and ulcerative colitis.

People can have bowel movements as infrequently as three times a week and still not be constipated, although there are some health practitioners who maintain that it is important to have a bowel movement every day.

Most people experience constipation from time to time, but usually lifestyle changes and better eating habits can help relieve the symptoms and prevent recurrences.

DID YOU KNOW?

Constipation can give rise to many different ailments including: appendicitis, bad breath, body odour, coated tongue, depression, diverticulitis (a condition where sac-like protrusions occur on the intestinal wall, symptoms include cramping, bloating and tenderness on the left side of the abdomen), fatigue, gas, headaches, haemorrhoids (piles), hernia, indigestion, insomnia, malabsorption syndrome, obesity and varicose veins. It may even be involved in the development of serious diseases, such as bowel cancer.

A SELECTION OF **BROWN** FOODS AND DRINKS

COFFEE

BEEF

CHOCOLATE

BROWN RICE

SHIITAKE MUSHROOMS

BROWN SPELT

CARDAMON

CINNAMON

EAT BROWN FOODS

Brown is always associated with the earth where a lot of fruit and vegetables originate. Also, rich, fibre-filled foods are brown. It is healthy to have 20–25g of fibre daily, yet research indicates that we only have 12g on average a day. A diet rich in fibre promotes internal health and helps maintain regular bowel activity. This means that brown foods, such as spelt, rice and wholegrain cereals are an essential component to the weekly diet.

Shitake Mushrooms

SHITAKE MUSHROOMS are the source of traditional Chinese medicine remedies for the treatment of depressed immune function. They also contain extracts of lentinan which are reputed to have many health benefits and are used extensively in Japan.

The flavour of shitake mushrooms intensifies when they are dried. If bought dried, they can be reconstituted by soaking them in warm water for 30 minutes or simmer them with a little sugar for 15 minutes. They add a rich meaty flavour to soups, stir-fries and pasta dishes.

Nutrition
- Good amounts of Vitamin B
- Soluble fibre
- Polysaccharide – lentinan

Good For
- Anti-cancer and anti-viral benefits
- Boosting the immune system
- Increasing resistance to bacterial and viral infections

How Much to Eat
- An average serving is 50g (2 oz) – about 5 mushrooms

Phytonutrient
- Monoterpenes – a phytonutrient also found in citrus fruit pith, peel and juice.

Coffee

COFFEE can be traced back to as early as the 9th century, when it appeared in the highlands of Ethiopia. From there, it spread to Europe and, as colonies were formed in the Americas, it migrated there. The main plant species are *coffea arabica* and *coffea canephora* (*robusta*). *Robusta* contains about 40–50% more caffeine and can be cultivated in environments where *arabica* will not thrive. When it first reached the South American colonies it wasn't that popular as it was found to be a poor substitute for alcohol.

A study that followed the diet and health of 8,000 Japanese-American men for 25 years found that men who drank five 150ml (4 $^1/_2$ fl oz) cups of coffee a day were five times less likely to develop Parkinson's disease compared to those who drank no coffee. Research is on-going in this area. Smokers eliminate caffeine from their bodies twice as quickly as non-smokers. This may explain why some smokers can consume copious amounts of coffee.

Nutrition
• None – see phytonutrients

Good For
• Some asthmatics, as caffeine is quite similar to theophylline, an effective anti-asthma drug
• Restricting blood flow to the brain as part of anti-migraine medication (referring to pure caffeine and not instant coffee)
• Stimulation when tired

BUT

• Caffeine can interfere with vitamin and mineral absorption
• It increases the insulin produced by the pancreas leading to hypoglycaemia
• It can seriously affect the digestive system
• Caffeine affects blood pressure as it increases heart rate and boosts adrenaline
• Increases the chances of developing osteoporosis

How Much To Drink
• There are serious health implications associated with over-consumption as mentioned above. The average cup of coffee is 150 ml. Up to 4–5 cups per day is considered moderate.
• It takes 300 ml of water to flush 3 ml of coffee through your system.
• Those on medication and pregnant women should drink less or avoid completely.

Phytonutrients
• Flavonoids
• Phenolic acids
• Xanthine Alkaloids

Effects of Coffee on the Body

If you are allergic to caffeine there is a good reason why your body is challenged. There are two types of caffeine metabolisers – rapid and slow. This explains why some people can consume coffee and function well and why others become tired, agitated, irritable, nervous and get upset stomachs. The drug metabolising enzymes (called DME) in the liver are responsible for the breakdown of coffee. The longer it takes to breakdown, the greater the impact on the heart, cholesterol levels and so on. One half to two thirds of people have effective DME function and can metabolise caffeine. The remainder do not and therefore coffee is best avoided as it will have a negative impact on the body.

did you know?

DO YOU THINK THAT DECAFFEINATED COFFEE IS BETTER FOR YOU? IT MAY NOT BE AS DECAFFEINATED COFFEE IS TREATED WITH A SOLVENT CALLED 'METHALYENE CHLORIDE', A CHEMICAL THAT INTERFERES WITH NUTRIENT ABSORPTION.

DIARY

A natural lover of coffee and chocolate, my days in Cartagena, Columbia, were spent rambling around the busy markets and basking on the sun-drenched beaches, consuming large quantities of rich Colombian chocolate and sipping shots of rich roast coffee.

In Columbia, droves of coffee and 'aromatica' dealers walk the streets. The coffee is deep brown, strong smelling and already has the sugar mixed through it. Forget the standard serving you'd get in Europe; they serve half that and it's powerful, sweet and velvety. The health benefits it provided might be questionable but the pleasure benefits were sublime!

Columbian food is a delight! Their famous dish '*Comidia del dia*' consists of brown rice, plantain and fresh fish. They serve a lot of coconut with the rice and *patacon* which are potato cakes made from yucca. The finished dish is called '*pescado frito con patacon*'. They serve beans, avocado and tomatoes as vegetable sides, along with *pan de maiz* or cornbread.

Maize is a staple food and street vendors make *dedito*, sausage-shaped snacks filled with cheese and deep-fried, from maize flour. Sugar is a widely used ingredient and Colombian biscuits and fudge are superb.

The roasting beans gave off such a lovely aroma, they led me to this small coffee manufacturer just off one of the main streets in Cartagena.

Chocolate

CHOCOLATE and cocoa are made from the same bean. Chocolate is made by grinding the beans to make a paste and sugar is then added. High quality chocolate contains at least 50% cocoa and does not contain vegetable fats.

Some researchers suggest that flavonol contribution, found in chocolate containing 70% cocoa solids, has a very mild aspirin-like effect that can have a beneficial impact on circulation, so it is important to choose this type of chocolate. Laboratory and human studies have shown that consuming flavonol-rich cocoa can inhibit platelet activation – when tiny blood cells in the body play a role in blood clotting by clumping together.

Nutrition
- Iron
- Magnesium
- Loaded with calories

Good For
- A healthy heart
- White and milk chocolate provide more calcium

How Much To Eat
- A portion of 40g (1 $1/2$ oz) of milk chocolate is reported to have a similar level of phenolic anti-oxidants as a glass of red wine.
- Chocolate is high in fat and should be eaten in moderation. You need to walk briskly for 50 minutes to burn off a 40g (1 $1/2$ oz) bar of chocolate!

Phytonutrients
- Flavonols

did you know?

THE COCOA TREE IS THOUGHT TO HAVE ORIGINATED IN THE FOOTHILLS OF THE ANDES IN THE AMAZON AND ORINOCO BASINS OF SOUTH AMERICA. COCOA WAS AN IMPORTANT COMMODITY IN PRE-COLUMBIAN MESOAMERICA. SPANISH CHRONICLERS RELATE THAT WHEN THE EMPEROR OF THE AZTECS DINED, HE TOOK NO OTHER BEVERAGE THAN CHOCOLATE, SERVED IN A GOLDEN GOBLET, AND HE ATE IT WITH A GOLD SPOON. IT WAS FLAVOURED WITH VANILLA AND SPICES AND WHIPPED INTO A FROTH THAT DISSOLVED IN THE MOUTH. 50 PITCHERS WERE PREPARED FOR HIM DAILY AND MORE THAN 2,000 OR MORE FOR THE NOBLES OF HIS COURT.

Brown Rice

Eaten for centuries, **BROWN RICE** has long been a staple of the East. You should always choose brown rice over white rice as Vitamin B1, Thiamine, whose function is to convert carbohydrates into energy for the body, is lost in the processing of white rice. Brown rice contains all the nutrients from the germ and outer layer of the grain.

Nutrition
- Low in fat
- Gluten-free
- Vitamin B group, except it is lacking in B12
- Fibre
- Protein
- Zinc

Good For
- Brain power
- Nervous system
- Building muscles
- Skin, hair and immune system

How Much to Eat
- Include in your diet at least three times a week.
- 100g portion (dry weight) is a portion size.

Phytonutrients
- None

THE DIFFERENCE BETWEEN LONG AND SHORT GRAIN RICE

Long grains are about five times as long as they are wide, while short grain is much more rounded. Long grain rice can be used for most dishes and is best cooked in hot water. Short grain rice is best suited for stuffing and risotto.

Short and long grain rice have a similar flavour but if you are looking for something a little different why not cook some of the rice types listed below.

TYPES OF RICE

ITALIAN RICE: Arborio rice – used to make risotto; smooth and creamy, with a nutty flavour.

INDIAN RICE: Basmati rice – aromatic flavour.

JAPANESE RICE: Short, shiny rice – used to make sushi.

THAI RICE: Flavoured with jasmine.

SWEET RICE: Short and sweet, becomes very soft during cooking.

BROWN RICE: This will take about ten minutes longer to cook than white.

COOKING RICE

The Absorption Method
This method uses a specific amount of water, which is completely absorbed by the time the rice is cooked. One measure of rice and two and a half measures of cold water.

1 cup of rice = 175g in dry weight

1 cup measure of water = 250 ml

1 cup of rice to 2.5 cup measures of water = 625 ml water

The Hot Water Method
Rice + Boiling water + Stir + Simmer = cooked and then drain the water away

From the Bronze Age to Medieval times, **SPELT** was an important wheat species in parts of Europe. Today it has found a new niche in the market and is widely sold in health shops as a popular alternative to wheat. It's the only grain to contain mucopolysaccharides which stimulate the immune system and can be used to make bread, cakes and pasta. It is also sold as a pale bread, similar in colour and texture to light rye breads, with a slightly sweet and nutty flavour.

Spelt is closely related to wheat and it is not a suitable substitute for people with coeliac disease.

Nutrition
- Contains mucopolysaccharides
- Good source of carbohydrates
- Protein – gluten
- Fat
- Zinc

Good For
- Providing fibre which promotes bowel health
- Lowering cholesterol
- Boosting the immune system

How Much To Eat
- As part of your six portions of cereals a day
- An average portion is 40g

Phytonutrients
- Phytosterols – helps lower cholesterol

This aromatic seed pod has a strong and unique taste. It is used primarily in Indian cooking and is one of the most expensive spices by weight. It's best stored in its pod form, as once the seeds are ground they quickly lose their flavour. Chewing a few cardamom seeds cleans the mouth and disguises the odour of bad breath.

Varieties of the **CARDAMOM** seed are used in traditional Chinese and Indian medicines. The most common form of cardamom – green cardamom – is a popular flavouring for coffee and tea, primarily in the Middle East.

Good For
- Stimulating appetite
- Aiding digestion
- Freshening breath

This popular spice was first imported to Egypt from China as early as 2000 BC, and is mentioned in the Bible. A recent study found that half a teaspoon of **CINNAMON** a day significantly reduces blood sugar levels in Type II diabetics. This spice also encourages the release of digestive enzymes to start the break down of carbohydrates so it can aid digestion. For many years it has been linked with combating the common cold.

Good For
- Using as a bactericide or antiseptic
- Stabilising blood sugar
- Stimulating digestion
- Helping combat the fatigue that accompanies an infection

TINA'S TIP

In winter when you feel cold and stiff because of bad weather, treat yourself to a warm bath. Sprinkle in cinnamon and a teaspoon of sugar. This will warm you up and help combat the onslaught of colds and flu.

Risotto

SERVES 2 – MAIN PORTION

SERVES 4 – STARTER PORTION

2 STREAKY RASHERS

1 LARGE CHICKEN FILLET

1 MEDIUM ONION

1 CLOVE GARLIC

1 GREEN PEPPER

1 RED PEPPER

3 TBSP OLIVE OIL

200G (7 OZ) LONG GRAIN RICE

500 ML (16 FL OZ) STOCK (YOU
    CAN USE A GOOD QUALITY
    STOCK CUBE IF DESIRED)

100G (3 ³/₄ OZ) MUSHROOMS

1 LEVEL TSP SALT

BLACK PEPPER

FRESH PARSLEY

PARMESAN SHAVINGS – OPTIONAL

Peel, slice and dice onion finely. Peel and crush garlic. Cut peppers, de-seed, wash, dry and dice finely. Wash and slice mushrooms.

Wash, dry and dice chicken fillet into 2 cm pieces. De-rind the rasher and snip into small pieces. Make stock with boiling water.

Heat oil in saucepan and fry rashers until brown. Add onions; soften for 1 minute. Add chicken and fry for 3 minutes. Add peppers, mushrooms, garlic, rice and stir over the heat until the rice is covered with oil. Then add stock and seasoning and bring to the boil; stirring all the time.

Reduce heat to lowest setting, cover tightly and simmer gently for 25 minutes until the rice is soft and the stock has been absorbed. Stir the bottom of the pot occasionally to prevent sticking. Add more water if necessary – 50 ml (1¹/₂ fl oz) at a time.

Wash, dry and chop parsley for garnish. Grate the cheese or use Parmesan shavings.

Spelt Pasta with Creamy Chicken and Shitake Mushrooms

SERVES 2

2 CHICKEN BREASTS, CUBED

250G SPELT PASTA

2 TBSP LEMON JUICE

8 BASIL LEAVES

1 ONION – FINELY CHOPPED

1 CLOVE GARLIC – CRUSHED

6 SHITAKE MUSHROOMS – SLICED
   THINLY

2 TBSP SWEETCORN

HANDFUL FRESH BASIL – ROUGHLY
   CHOPPED

SALT AND PEPPER

1 TBSP OLIVE OIL

BASIL LEAF – TO GARNISH

PARMESAN CHEESE SHAVINGS

SAUCE

25G (1 OZ) BUTTER

25G (1 OZ) FLOUR

350 ML (11 FL OZ) MILK

100 ML (3 FL OZ) WHITE WINE

SALT AND PEPPER TO SEASON

TINA'S TOP COOKING TIP

You can add additional vegetables –
for example, peppers if desired. A
couple of dessertspoons of fresh
cream added at the end will give the
dish an extra creamy twist.

TO COOK THE SPELT PASTA: Place in boiling water with salt for seasoning and simmer
for 15 minutes until tender. Drain in a colander to remove water.

Place the chicken in a bowl and season well with salt and pepper. Mix in the lemon juice and
basil and place in the fridge.

FOR THE SAUCE: Melt the butter in a saucepan and add the flour. The two ingredients
should form a ball. Remove the saucepan from the heat and little by little stir in the milk. Blend
really well to avoid lumps forming. The trick is to make a really smooth roux sauce. Add the white
wine and blend well. Set aside.

Heat olive oil in a pan. Add the chicken and brown. Add the onion and garlic. Sauté gently
and then add the mushrooms and sweetcorn. Pour in the sauce and blend well.

Serve with spelt pasta, fresh basil leaf and Parmesan cheese.

Spelt Pasta with Asparagus

SERVES 4

500G (1LB) SPELT PASTA, COOKED AND DRAINED

1 BUNCH ASPARAGUS – TRIMMED AND BLANCHED

3 BEATEN EGGS

90G (3 1/2 OZ) BUTTER

200 ML (6 FL OZ) FRESH CREAM

100G (3 1/2 OZ) GRATED PARMESAN CHEESE

SALT AND FRESHLY GROUND PEPPER

4 SLICES PANCETTA – CHOPPED LIGHTLY

FRESH CHOPPED CHIVES

Place hot pasta into a saucepan.

Quickly toss all the ingredients, except pancetta, into the pasta.

Allow the cream and eggs to warm and serve immediately with the pancetta and chopped chives.

Spelt Pancakes

SERVES 4

250G (9 OZ) SPELT FLOUR

1 TSP BAKING POWDER

PINCH OF SEA SALT

375 ML (12 FL OZ) WATER

1 EGG

1 TSP GOLDEN HONEY

3 TBSP OIL

ADDITIONAL OIL FOR COOKING

Mix all the dry ingredients together in a bowl.

Mix all the liquids together in a jug and add to the dry mixture and blend well.

Heat the additional oil in a pan on a medium heat on the hob and spoon the batter on to make 4–6 pancakes.

Serve immediately with some fresh fruit of your choice or drizzle some honey and lemon juice on top.

Spelt Muffins

MAKES 12

300G (10 ½ OZ) SPELT FLOUR

300 ML (10 FL OZ) MILK

40G (1 ½ OZ) CASTER SUGAR

3 EGGS

1 TSP BAKING POWDER

1 TBSP OIL

50G (2 OZ) RAISINS

50G (2 OZ) CHOPPED APRICOTS

Preheat the oven to 190°C (375°F) or gas mark 5.

Combine all the dry ingredients together in a bowl.

Add the milk, eggs and oil and mix well.

Add the fruit and spoon mixture into a muffin tin.

Bake for 15–20 minutes.

Turn out onto a wire tray and serve for breakfast if desired.

Ultimate Chocolate Cake

SERVES 8

225G (8 OZ) SELF-RAISING FLOUR

150G (5 ¹/₂ OZ) CASTER SUGAR

50G (2 OZ) COCOA OR DRINKING
   CHOCOLATE

25G (1 OZ) GROUND ALMONDS

3 EGGS

1 TSP VANILLA ESSENCE

5 TBSP MAYONNAISE/PLAIN YOGHURT

100 ML (3 FL OZ) WATER

1–2 TBSP JAM OF YOUR CHOICE

**RICH CHOCOLATE FILLING/ICING –
OPTIONAL**

25G (1 OZ) BUTTER

75G (2 ¹/₂ OZ) COOKING CHOCOLATE

150G (5 ¹/₂ OZ) ICING SUGAR

1 TBSP WATER

1 TBSP MILK OR CREAM

Preheat oven to 180°C (350°F) or gas mark 4. Grease cake tins and line the bottoms only with parchment paper.

Whisk eggs and caster sugar until thick and creamy. Gently stir in mayonnaise or yoghurt. Sieve flour, cocoa and ground almonds into the mixture. Fold in lightly. Then finally fold in the water. Turn this runny mixture into the tins, bake for 20–25 minutes.

Check with a skewer. Allow to cool for 3 minutes in the tin and then turn out gently onto a wire tray.

THE FILLING: Chop chocolate roughly and melt butter with water in a saucepan, by stirring over a gentle heat. Then remove from heat and add the chocolate. Allow to melt, return to heat if necessary.

Sieve icing sugar into bowl, beat in the chocolate mixture and finally add the milk or cream to soften if necessary. Cover and allow to cool.

When the cakes have cooled, spread jam on one half, spread a third of the filling on the other and sandwich together. Ice the top with remaining filling. Use a hot knife to smooth the surface.

Chocolate Muffin Truffle

MAKES 3

3 CHOCOLATE MUFFINS

142 ML (4 FL OZ) CARTON OF WHIPPING CREAM

5 TBSP TIA MARIA OR AMARETTO, PLUS MORE FOR SPRINKLING

250G (9OZ) TUB OF MASCARPONE (SOFT ITALIAN CHEESE)

150G (5 ¹/₂ OZ) DARK CHOCOLATE

Have three wine glasses ready.

Crumble the muffins lightly into a bowl. Melt the chocolate over hot water and leave to cool slightly.

Whip the cream until stiff, adding the 5 tbsp of liqueur towards the end. Combine the cream and mascarpone, using a whisk in a cutting action, or the beaters of an electric whisk (without actually turning it on). Pour the cooled chocolate over and lightly fold together until rippled.

Divide half of the muffin crumble between the wine glasses. Sprinkle each lightly with some of the liqueur. Spoon or pour over half the chocolate mix. Then repeat the layers.

Chocolate Coated Prunes

MAKES 24

24 FRENCH PRUNES – PITTED

100G (3 ¹/₂ OZ) PLAIN CHOCOLATE

100G (3 ¹/₂ OZ) WHITE CHOCOLATE

1 ORANGE – HALVED

Melt the plain and white chocolate in bowls over pans of gently simmering water. Using a cocktail stick, skewer a prune and dip into the plain chocolate. Push the other end of the cocktail stick into a halved orange (skin-side up) to set.

Repeat with a further 11 prunes – dipping them into the plain chocolate and then pushing into the orange half to set. Use the same method for the white chocolate and remaining prunes.

Once set, use a teaspoon to drizzle prunes with melted chocolate of a contrasting colour. (You may have to gently warm the chocolate so it melts again.)

Note: You can dip any fruit or nut into the chocolate.

Chunky Chocolate Brownies

MAKES 18

400G (12 OZ) PLAIN CHOCOLATE – BROKEN INTO CHUNKS

225G (8 OZ) UNSALTED BUTTER OR MARGARINE

225G (8 OZ) LIGHT MUSCOVADO SUGAR

6 EGGS

75G (2 ¹/₂ OZ) SELF-RAISING FLOUR

175G (6 OZ) PECAN NUTS – ROUGHLY CHOPPED

175G (6 OZ) MILK CHOCOLATE – CHOPPED INTO LARGE CHUNKS

Preheat oven to 190°C (375°F) or gas mark 5. Grease and line a 25 cm x 18 cm (10 in x 7 in) shallow baking tin.

Melt the plain chocolate with the butter or margarine in a heatproof bowl over a pan of simmering water.

Beat together the eggs and sugar. Then beat in the melted chocolate mixture. Sift the flour over the bowl and stir in. Add the pecans and milk chocolate chunks; stir until just combined.

Turn the mixture into the prepared baking tin and spread into the corners.

Bake for about 45 minutes until slightly risen and crusty.

Leave to cool in the tin; then cut into squares and serve.

Chocolate and Chestnut Ice-Cream

SERVES 6-8

250G (9 OZ) CAN SWEETENED
  CHESTNUT PURÉE
150G (5 ½ OZ) PLAIN CHOCOLATE –
  CHOPPED
2 TBSP BRANDY
600 ML (20 FL OZ) DOUBLE CREAM

Turn the chestnut purée into a bowl and stir
until fairly smooth. Add the chocolate and
brandy and mix well.
Whip the cream until it just holds its shape.
Then lightly but thoroughly fold into the
chestnut mixture.
Turn into a rigid container and freeze for
3–4 hours until firm.

Irish Coffee Sundaes

SERVES 6

2 X 500 ML (2 X 16 FL OZ) TUBS GOOD QUALITY VANILLA ICE-CREAM
300 ML (10 FL OZ) VERY STRONG HOT FRESH COFFEE
4 TBSP IRISH WHISKEY
1 TBSP DEMERARA SUGAR

Just before eating, put two or three scoops of ice-cream into each serving bowl, then simply mix
together the coffee, whiskey and sugar and pour over. Serve at once.

Cappuccino Cup

SERVES 4

300 ML (10 FL OZ) WHIPPING CREAM

1 TBSP POWDERED GELATINE

225G (8 OZ) PLAIN CHOCOLATE

HANDFUL OF ICE CUBES

300 ML (10 FL OZ) FROMAGE FRAIS

50G (2 OZ) CASTER SUGAR

1 TBSP INSTANT COFFEE POWDER – PLUS
    EXTRA FOR DUSTING

Pour half the cream into a pan. Sprinkle the gelatine over it and leave to soften for about 5 minutes. Heat gently until the cream just begins to simmer and the gelatine has melted, stirring constantly.

Break up 175g (6 oz) of the chocolate into pieces, place in a food processor with the cream mixture and whiz until the chocolate has melted. Add the ice cubes, fromage frais, sugar and coffee powder and mix until smooth. Pour into cups. Cover and chill until set.

Whip the remaining cream and pare curls from the remaining chocolate with a vegetable peeler. Swirl the cream on the "cups". Dust with coffee powder and decorate with the curls.

Serve chilled.

Cappuccino Jelly

SERVES 6

5 TBSP POWDERED GELATINE

600 ML (20 FL OZ) COLD
    STRONG BLACK COFFEE

100G (3 1/2 OZ) RAW CANE
    BROWN SUGAR, SUCH AS
    LIGHT OR DARK
    MUSCOVADO OR DEMERARA

4 TBSP TIA MARIA OR CRÈME
    DE CACAO

150 ML (5 FL OZ) DOUBLE
    CREAM

In a pan, soak the gelatine in about a quarter of the cold coffee until spongy, and then add another quarter of the coffee and the sugar. Heat the mixture and stir constantly – until the gelatine has dissolved completely. Remove the pan from the heat and allow to cool. Stir in the rest of the cold coffee and the liqueur. Pour into individual coffee cups or glasses and put in the fridge until set. Leave enough room for the decoration.

Whip the double cream into soft peaks, then spoon into a piping bag fitted with a small plain nozzle and pipe a swirl on top of the jelly (or just spoon a little over each).

Tiramisu

SERVES 8

1 GENEROUS TSP COFFEE

85 ML (3 FL OZ) BRANDY

2 EGGS

65G (2 OZ) CASTER SUGAR

250G (9 OZ) MASCARPONE
    CHEESE

300 ML (10 FL OZ) DOUBLE
    CREAM

75G (2 ¹/₂ OZ) CHOCOLATE CHIPS

1 PACKET TRIFLE SPONGES

Line a 20–23 cm (8–9 in) loose-bottomed, round cake tin with non-stick baking parchment.

Dissolve the coffee in 120ml (4 fl oz) boiling water and mix with the brandy. Beat the eggs in a bowl. Add the sugar and whisk on high speed until thick and frothy – it should leave a trail as for a whisked sponge.

Mix half of this mixture with the cheese in another bowl. Then stir in the remaining egg and sugar mixture.

Whisk the double cream until thick and then fold into the egg and mascarpone.

Coarsely chop the chocolate chips in a food processor to give chocolate bits and powder.

Split the sponge cakes and line the tin with half of them. Sprinkle half the instant coffee mixture, one third of the chocolate and half of the mascarpone mixture over it.

Add the second layer of sponge, then the remaining instant coffee mixture and another third of the chocolate.

Cover with the rest of the mascarpone mixture, and then sprinkle the surface with the remaining chocolate.

Chill for 4 hours. Then turn out of the tin, remove the lining paper and serve cold.

Mincemeat

MAKES 12 PIES

2 COOKING APPLES – SUCH AS
    BRAMLEYS – PEELED

2 LEMONS

450G (1 LB) BEEF SUET – SHREDDED

100G (3 ½ OZ) CANDIED MIXED
    PEEL – CHOPPED

2 ROUNDED TBSP ORANGE
    MARMALADE

200G (7OZ) CURRANTS

450G (1 LB) RAISINS

200G (7 OZ) SULTANAS

900G (2 LB) MUSCOVADO SUGAR

5 TBSP IRISH WHISKEY

Preheat the oven to 180°C (350°F) or gas mark 4. Stew apples. Grate the rind from the lemons and squeeze out the juice. Mix this into the apple pulp; then add the other ingredients, one by one, until everything is mixed thoroughly together.

To sterilise jars, wash them well in hot, soapy water. Then rinse well.

Fill them with the mixture and place on a rack in the oven at 140°C (280°F) or gas mark 1 for 25–30 minutes. Take care when handling hot jars.

Mincemeat and Almond Slice

MAKES 18 SLICES

175G (6 OZ) BUTTER

250G (9 OZ) PLAIN FLOUR

100G (3 ½ OZ) LIGHT MUSCOVADO SUGAR

400G (14 OZ) MINCEMEAT

75G (2 ½ OZ) CHOPPED MIXED NUTS

Preheat oven to 190°C (375°F) or gas mark 5.

Rub the butter into the flour until the mixture resembles fine breadcrumbs and stir in the sugar.

Sprinkle half the crumble mix evenly over a greased 18 x 28 cm (7 x 1 in) shallow oblong tin. Press down lightly with the back of a metal spoon.

Spoon mincemeat evenly over the top, spreading it out carefully. Add the nuts to the remaining crumble mix and then sprinkle evenly over the top.

Bake for 30–35 minutes until crisp and light golden brown.

Cool in the tin for 10 minutes, then cut into three lengthways and six widthways to make 18 slices.

Coffee Éclairs

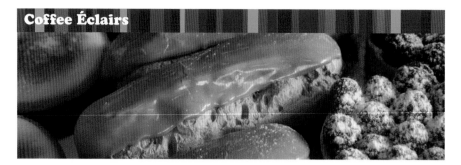

MAKES 12

100G (3 ¹/₂ OZ) BUTTER – PLUS EXTRA
    FOR GREASING
140G (5 OZ) PLAIN FLOUR
4 EGGS

FOR THE VANILLA CREAM

1 VANILLA POD
540 ML (18 FL OZ) DOUBLE CREAM
1 TBSP CASTER SUGAR

FOR THE CHOCOLATE ICING

100G (3 ¹/₂ OZ) PLAIN CHOCOLATE
KNOB OF BUTTER

Preheat the oven to 200°C (390°F) or gas mark 6. Grease two baking sheets.

Sift the flour onto a sheet of greaseproof paper. Cut the butter into pieces and put in a medium-sized pan with 300 ml (10 fl oz) water. Bring to the boil. As soon as it begins to boil, tip in the flour all in one go (the greaseproof paper helps make sure it all goes in the pan), stirring with a wooden spoon as you do so.

Remove from the heat and beat vigorously until the mixture forms a soft ball of dough that doesn't stick to the sides of the pan. This will take a minute or so. Let the dough cool in the pan for 5 minutes.

In a bowl, lightly beat the eggs together with a fork and then beat them into the dough, a little at a time. Beat well until you have a smooth, glossy paste.

Spoon the mixture into a piping bag with a 2 cm (³/₄ in) plain nozzle.

Shape 8 cm (3 ¹/₄ in) long éclairs, place onto the baking sheets, leaving room between each to allow them to spread.

Bake for 25–30 minutes, swapping the baking sheets around on the oven shelves after 15 minutes so all the éclairs cook evenly. Then remove the baking sheets from the oven.

Using a small sharp knife slit each éclair about halfway along one side to let the steam out.

Return to the oven for a further 5 minutes to allow the insides to dry out. The éclairs should be pale golden brown and very crisp.

Transfer them to a wire racks to cool completely.

FOR COFFEE ICING:

Pour 2 tablespoons of boiling water over 2 tablespoons of instant coffee in a small bowl or cup, and mix well. Cool slightly.

Put 200g (7 oz) icing sugar in a bowl and add the coffee mixture. Stir into the sugar to make a glossy icing, adding a splash of water if necessary.

Spoon the icing over the filled éclairs and leave to set.

Christmas Pudding

MAKE 3 PUDDINGS (2 LBS EACH)

225G (8 OZ) PLAIN FLOUR

1 TSP BAKING POWDER

225G (8 OZ) FRESH WHITE BREADCRUMBS

225G (8 OZ) SUET – SHREDDED

100G (3 $^1/_2$ OZ) ALMONDS – GROUND

500G (16 OZ) DARK MUSCOVADO SUGAR

1 TSP MIXED SPICE – GROUND

$^1/_2$ TSP NUTMEG – GRATED

$^1/_2$ TSP CINNAMON – GROUND

175G (6 OZ) PRUNES – STONED

175G (6 OZ) CARROTS – PEELED AND
    FINELY GRATED

750G (1 LB 10 $^1/_2$ OZ) MIXED
    CURRANTS, SULTANAS AND RAISINS

50G (2 OZ) MIXED PEEL

2 APPLES – PEELED, CORED AND
    ROUGHLY CHOPPED

GRATED ZEST AND JUICE OF 1 LEMON

GRATED ZEST AND JUICE OF 1 ORANGE

5 EGGS

4 TBSP BLACK TREACLE

4 TBSP GOLDEN SYRUP

500 ML (16 FL OZ) STOUT/GUINNESS

Sift the flour with the baking powder. Add the breadcrumbs, suet, ground almonds, sugar and spices.

Purée the prunes in a food processor and add to the mix with the carrots, dried fruit, mixed peel, apples and lemon and orange zest.

Beat the eggs and stir into the mix with the lemon and orange juices, treacle, golden syrup and stout/Guinness.

You should now have a pudding mixture of approximately 3 kg (7 lbs) in total weight. It will have a reasonably moist and loose texture but if it appears dry, add some more stout. Then taste it to check for flavour and richness. If it's a bit bland, add more spices to liven it up.

TO COOK THE PUDDINGS: Butter and lightly flour three 900g (2 lb) pudding basins. Fill each one $^3/_4$ full with the mix. Top with a circle of greaseproof paper, and then cover the basin. Steam at temperature 2–3 on hob (turning down the heat if necessary) over boiling water for 4–6 hours (6 hours will make the puddings even richer). Don't forget to top up the water from time to time. Leave the puddings to cool before refrigerating or storing them in a cold, dark place until needed.

THE COLOUR
silver

SILVER GLISTENS, SPARKLES AND REFLECTS THE LIGHT. SILVER LIGHTS CAN HELP US TO RELAX AND FEEL COMFORTABLE AND ENCOURAGE US TO BE REFLECTIVE ON THE PAST, LEARNING LESSONS FROM PAST MISTAKES. AS YOU LOOK INTO WATER, A MIRROR OR STAINLESS SILVER, YOU WILL SEE A REFLECTION. SOME PEOPLE AVOID LOOKING IN MIRRORS AS THEY ARE UNHAPPY WITH WHAT THEY SEE; OTHERS ADORE THEIR OWN REFLECTION. SILVER ILLUMINATES OR ALLOWS US TO SEE THE TRUTH.

Silver has a sense of magic about it. It can help promote your imagination and intuition. **WE ASSOCIATE SILVER WITH THE MOON AND MANY PEOPLE BELIEVE THAT BATHING IN THE LIGHT OF THE MOON HELPS YOU TO ABSORB SILVER ENERGY**. Not only is this extremely therapeutic, it can also help restore tranquillity. Making love under the moon is said to be an unforgettable experience – to be tried at least once in a lifetime!

But sliver has a negative side – it is not a winning colour and is associated with being a runner-up or second best. Some forms of silver may also be seen as insipid, dismal, cold and uninteresting. Flat or dirty silver looks like grey and can be a depressing colour. Silver can also signify illness. It governs a small energy centre at the back of the knees and is known to affect the balance of body fluids.

A person drawn to silver is looking for the ideal emotional relationship. Silver is protective which is a key factor in why many people wear silver jewellery. To get the full benefit of this positive attribute, it is important to keep your silver jewellery in good shape.

THOUGHT FOR THE DAY

I accept the changes that life presents today. Just like the tides – things come and go.

A SILVER DAY PLAN

CLOTHES – I WILL WEAR SOMETHING SILVER TO PROTECT MY SENSITIVE NATURE. THE INCAS OF PERU BELIEVED THAT SILVER WAS THE COLOUR THAT PROTECTED A PERSON'S SPIRIT.

FOOD – I WILL EAT FISH AND SEA VEGETABLES TODAY.

AFFIRMATION – I TRUST MY INNER FEELINGS AND I MOVE WITH GRACE, EASE AND ELOQUENCE.

EXERCISE – I WILL DO KNEE STRETCHES AND HANG IN THE YOGA POSE OF 'THE DOG'. THIS POSE WILL HELP ME LET GO OF ALL THE STRESSES OF THE DAY, STRETCH OUT THE KNEES AND COMPLETELY RELAX.

Guide To Wearing Silver

Silver is an ideal colour for accessories – particularly in summer. When you fancy sparkling in a bold and bright way, use silver belts, handbags and jewellery as they add a touch of magic, without overloading you. If you would like to create a wild look, then wearing silver fabrics is the way to go. Silver will show you have an individual streak and enjoy expressing this sense of being different and unique.

When To Wear Silver

Silver is a good colour to wear when you want to remain impartial or when solving disputes. When you need to go with the flow – choose silver. It is useful to use when you need to reflect on matters.

When you are feeling indecisive and torn between choices in life, silver will bring clarity. So when you can't quite put your finger on what you need to do next, reflect on it with the colour silver. It is reflective and can help strengthen your intuition; when we trust our intuition we rarely make mistakes. If you are working alongside someone who appears to be two-faced, silver will reflect their true face. Turn to silver if you find yourself confused over fantasy and reality, as it will help to clear the mist away and bring calmness into your life again.

When To Avoid Wearing Silver

Avoid wearing silver when you are emotionally shattered or upset as the colour has a tendency to promote wallowing in emotions.

✚ Silver Health

The fish markets in Patagonia, Chile, help people to maintain a healthier lifestyle

Marrows are a popular vegetable for sale in the markets in Argentina.

Silver is the colour that governs knees and body fluids. The body is composed of almost 65% water so it is vital that we keep the body system in balance. Drinking water assists hydration, helps the body to eliminate unwanted salts and maintains blood pressure at normal, healthy levels. As people age they may find that their knee joints can become stiff and sore. Sometimes the weather can exacerbate the pain – particularly cold and damp weather – and foods can also have an effect. Foods such as acidic wheat and drinks such as coffee, tea and alcohol can be offenders, as the acidic nature of these foods and drinks can cause stiffness in joints. So it is imperative to eat a diet rich in fresh fruit and vegetables, mixed with a varied supply of fish and pulse vegetables. The body is then supplied with nutritious sources of vital phytonutrients that help it to maintain optimum energy levels and strengthens immune function.

Silver health also relates to high blood pressure and osteoarthritis.

Arthritis

Arthritis is the inflammation of one or more joints. It is characterised by pain and stiffness (especially in the morning or after exercise), swelling, deformity, and/or diminished range of motion. Bone growths or spurs may develop in the affected joints; increasing pain and decreasing mobility. There may be audible cracking or grating noises when the joint moves.

Arthritis is not a modern ailment; in fact it has been with us since the beginning of time. Archaeologists have discovered evidence of the disorder in the skeletons of Neanderthals and other prehistoric mammals, even dinosaurs. Despite the length of time this disorder has plagued human kind, conventional medicine remains confounded as to why it occurs.

It is a condition that can affect the body's moveable (or synovial) joints at the knees, wrists, elbows, fingers, toes, hips and shoulders. In healthy joints, the synovial membrane is thin, the cartilage that covers the bones is smooth, and a thin layer of synovial fluid covers the bone surfaces. A problem in any of these areas, however, can result in arthritis – a thickening of the synovial membrane, an increase in the secretion of synovial fluid, enlargement of the bones, or some combination of these factors and swelling and deformity of the joints can be the result.

Arthritis may appear suddenly or come on gradually. Some people feel a sharp burning or grinding pain, while others compare the pain to toothache. Moving the joint usually hurts, although sometimes there is only stiffness.

Osteoarthritis

Osteoarthritis (also called "degenerative joint disease") involves deterioration of the cartilage protecting the ends of the bones. It is sometimes caused by injury or an inherited defect in the protein that forms cartilage. More commonly, **it is as a result of the wear and tear of ageing, diet and lifestyle.** The cartilage begins to break down, and the normally smooth sliding surfaces of the bones become pitted and irregular; resulting in friction. It affects the weight-bearing joints – the knees, hips and back – most severely, but it also commonly affects the hands and knuckles. The tendons, ligaments and muscles holding the joint together become weaker, and the joint becomes deformed, painful and stiff. There is usually some stiffness and pain (more stiffness than pain at first), but little or no swelling. Any resulting disability is most often minor. However, because osteoarthritis makes the bone brittle, fractures become an increasing risk. As osteoarthritis advances, bone outgrowths called osteophytes tend to develop. Often referred to as "spurs," osteophytes can be detected by x-ray and develop near degenerated cartilage in the neck or in the lower back. This condition does not change a person's appearance.

did you know?

OSTEOARTHRITIS RARELY DEVELOPS BEFORE THE AGE OF 40, BUT IT AFFECTS NEARLY EVERYONE PAST THE AGE OF 60. IT MAY BE SO MILD THAT A PERSON IS UNAWARE OF IT UNTIL IT APPEARS ON AN X-RAY. NEARLY THREE TIMES AS MANY WOMEN AS MEN HAVE OSTEOARTHRITIS AS CHILDBIRTH CAN IMPACT ON THE CALCIUM STORES IN THE BODY AND CAN ACCELERATE THE CONDITION.

A SELECTION OF SILVER FOODS

SILVER SARDINES

WAKAME

DULSE

NORI

MONKFISH

GROUPER

SEA VEGETABLES

Sea vegetables are the highest digestible source of minerals such as potassium, iron and zinc. It makes perfect sense to include a varied supply of sea mineral-rich foods in your diet as they not only add flavour and contribute new tastes, they provide the body with vital minerals and nutrients such as:

- Iodine which supports the metabolism;
- Selenium which boosts the immune system;
- Calcium which promotes strong healthy bones;
- Natural iodine which is essential for normal thyroid functioning;
- Vitamin B12 which is great for providing energy.

Edible sea vegetables in Puerto Montt, Chile.

Dulse

Dulse sea vegetables have a strong and definite taste and grow in Ireland, Canada, North America and Iceland. They are useful in losing weight.

Nutrition
- Very rich source of protein
- Rich in Vitamin A and C
- Contains calcium and zinc

Good For
- Anaemia
- Prevention of osteoporosis

How Much To Eat
- A 10g (1/2 oz) portion
- Eat sea vegetables at least three times a week

Phytonutrients
- Carotenoids

TINA'S TIP

Massage dulse in water and drain immediately to retain minerals.

Wakame

This is a great sea vegetable for beginners as it tastes similar to green vegetables. The Japanese use it a lot in cooking and it forms the popular miso soup, which also contains fermented soya bean paste. Wakame can also be used in sandwiches as a great alternative to lettuce. Make sure to chop it up well, as it is quite chewy in texture.

Nutrition
- Protein
- Iron
- Calcium

Good For
- Boosting immune system
- Helping combat anaemia
- Helping reduce cholesterol
- Prevention of osteoporosis
- Aiding weight loss
- Helping maintain strong nails and hair

How Much To Eat
- An average 10g (1/2 oz) portion
- Eat at least three times a week

Phytonutrients
- Carotenoids

Nori

Nori displays positive anti-oxidant activity due to the fucoxanthins that are present. Nori is used to make sushi and is a welcome addition to any soup or rice recipe.

Nutrition
- Rich source of protein
- Zinc, iodine, selenium
- Calcium
- Vitamin B12

Good For
- Boosting energy
- Anaemia
- Boosting the immune system
- Healthy thyroid

How Much To Eat
- 10g (½ oz) portion
- Eat at least three times a week

Phytonutrients
- Carotenoids

did you know?

CANADIAN RESEARCHERS INVESTIGATING LOW BREAST CANCER RATES AMONG JAPANESE WOMEN PROPOSE THAT THE PROTECTION MAY COME FROM THE IODINE AND SELENIUM CONTENT IN SEAWEED.

SEA VEGETABLE CASE STUDY

This case study represents a group of men and women in business – ranging from finance and property to IT and design consultancy. The purpose of the survey was to establish the lifestyle and eating practices of the corporate, white-collar sector in the 21st century. The people interviewed had a varied age profile, from 28–48 years, and were a male/female mix. They also had varied sporting and fitness profiles.

TINA'S TIP

The ingredients for all the recipes listed in this chapter are readily available in larger supermarkets and the contributions they make to your health speak for themselves. Add small to moderate amounts to start, as the flavours can be a new experience so let your taste buds get used to them. Be adventurous and give sea vegetables a try – once you start: it will be hard to stop!

RESULTS A

Men and women aged 30–45 working in Financial Institutions.
Total number 200

FOOD	HOW OFTEN	DO %	DON'T %
Fruit	2–4 portions a day	17	83
Vegetables	3–5 portions a day	13	87
Seeds and nuts	Three times a week	22	78
Brown rice/quinoa/spelt/			
rice noodles/soya noodles	Three times a week	26	74
Sea vegetables	**Any time**	**0**	**100**
Fish	Three times a week	22	78
Biscuits, sweets and cake	Frequently	69	31
Exercise	Daily	65	35

RESULTS B

Men and women aged 22–55 years working in the Health Sector.
Total number 150

FOOD	HOW OFTEN	DO %	DON'T %
Fruit	2–4 portions a day	28	72
Vegetables	3–5 portions a day	29	71
Seeds	Three times a week	5	95
Nuts	Three times a week	23	77
Brown rice/quinoa/spelt/			
rice noodles/soya noodles	Three times a week	38	62
Sea vegetables	**Any time**	**0**	**100**
Fish	Three times a week	28	72
Biscuits, sweets and cake	Frequently	52	48
Exercise	Daily	60	40

RESULTS C

Men and women aged 18–23 years students at Third Level Colleges.
Total number 120

FOOD	HOW OFTEN	DO %	DON'T %
Fruit	2–4 portions a day	25	75
Vegetables	3–5 portions a day	12.5	87.5
Seeds and nuts	Three times a week	6	94
Brown rice and other grains	Three times a week	18	82
Sea vegetables	**Any time**	**0**	**100**
Fish	Three times a week	6	94
Biscuits, sweets and cake	Frequently	75	25
Exercise	Daily	68.75	31.25

RESULTS OF STUDY

The study highlighted the low number of people who regularly (three times a week) eat fresh fish and include sea vegetables in their diet. None of the people surveyed ate sea vegetables at all. When I asked them why, the answer was very simple – people didn't understand the significant contribution sea vegetables can make to their diet. They were also uncertain about how to cook them or what recipes they could use them in. From asking further questions in seminars and combining the answers with these statistics, it's very clear that adults need to learn more about sea vegetables to help improve their diets!

Fish Pie

SERVES 4

500G (1LB 2 OZ) SKINLESS COD
    FILLET

200G (7 OZ) SMOKED SALMON

400G (12 OZ) RAW KING
    PRAWNS – DEFROSTED

4 PLUM TOMATOES

50G (2 OZ) BUTTER

2 ¹/₂ CM (1 IN) PIECE FRESH
    ROOT GINGER – CHOPPED

50G (2 OZ) PLAIN FLOUR

425 ML (14 FL OZ) MILK

150 ML (5 FL OZ) DRY VERMOUTH

142 ML (4 FL OZ) CARTON SINGLE CREAM

3 TSP CHOPPED DILL

JUICE OF HALF A LIME

SALT AND PEPPER

FOR THE TOPPING

700G (1LB 9 OZ) SMALLISH POTATOES

GOOD PINCH SAFFRON

25G (1 OZ) BUTTER

Cut the cod into 2 ¹/₂ cm (1 in) chunks. Cut the salmon into strips.

Peel the prawns, leaving the tail section intact. Pat the prawns dry between sheets of kitchen paper.

Peel the tomatoes, cut them in half and squeeze out the seeds. Chop the tomatoes.

Mix the fish and tomatoes and put in a buttered 3 litre (100 fl oz) pie dish or other oven-proof dish.

Put the butter, ginger, flour, milk and vermouth into a non-stick pan and bring slowly to the boil, whisking all the time until the sauce is thickened and smooth.

Reduce the heat and simmer the sauce for 2 minutes; then season well with salt and pepper and remove from the heat. Leave to cool, stirring occasionally, to prevent a skin forming.

When it has cooled to room temperature, stir in the cream. Stir the dill and lime juice into the sauce. Taste and add more seasoning if necessary. Pour evenly over the fish.

Peel and slice the potatoes, then put in a pan with water to cover and add the saffron and salt. Bring to the boil, then cover and cook for 10–12 minutes until the potatoes are just tender. Drain well and leave until they are cool enough to handle.

Arrange the potatoes, overlapping, over the pie mixture. Melt the butter and brush over the potatoes. Cover the whole thing with foil or cling film and chill for up to 24 hours until ready to cook or eat immediately.

Monkfish with Mexican Salsa

SERVES 2-4

MONKFISH

675G (1LB 8 OZ) MONKFISH STEAKS

3 TBSP OLIVE OIL

2 TBSP LIME JUICE

1 GARLIC CLOVE – CRUSHED

1 TBSP FRESH CORIANDER

SALT AND PEPPER

SALSA

4 TOMATOES – PEELED AND DICED

1 AVOCADO – STONED AND DICED

HALF AN ONION – CHOPPED FINELY

2 TBSP CHOPPED CORIANDER

2 TBSP OLIVE OIL

1 TBSP LIME JUICE

TO MAKE SALSA: Mix the salsa ingredients and leave at room temperature for about 40 minutes.

Mix the oil, lime juice, garlic, coriander and seasoning together in a shallow non-metallic dish. Add the monkfish steaks to the dish. Turn the monkfish several times to coat with the marinade; then cover the dish and leave to marinate at room temperature or in the fridge for 30 minutes.

Then remove the monkfish from the marinade and grill for 10–12 minutes; turning once and brushing regularly with the marinade until cooked through.

Serve the monkfish garnished with coriander sprigs and lime slices and accompanied by the salsa.

Pan Fried Grouper on a Bed of Caramelised Leeks

SERVES 2

150G (5 ½ OZ) GROUPER FILLETS

2 TBSP OIL

2 FRESH CHILLIES

2 LIMES

LEEKS

3 LEEKS CUT INTO JULIENNE STRIPS

5 TBSP OF HONEY

SALT AND PEPPER

Make a marinade by mixing the oil, chillies, juice of the limes and the coriander together. Marinade the fillets for at least two hours.

Pan fry in a little olive oil; frying for about 8 minutes on each side.

Meanwhile, add the honey to the leeks and cook for about 4 minutes.

Serve the grouper on the caramelised leeks and accompany with a crispy green salad or a fine spinach salad.

Gilled Sea bass with Beurre Blanc and March Samphire

SERVES 4

1 SEA BASS, ABOUT 1 ½ KG (3 LB)

MELTED BUTTER – FOR BRUSHING

225G (8 OZ) FRESH MARCH SAMPHIRE

1 QUANTITY WHITE BUTTER (SEE THE

   FOLLOWING SECTION)

SEASONING

WHITE BUTTER

50G (2 OZ) SHALLOTS OR ONION –

   FINELY CHOPPED

2 TBSP WHITE WINE VINEGAR

4 TBSP DRY WHITE WINE

6 TSP FISH STOCK

2 TBSP DOUBLE CREAM

175G (6 OZ) UNSALTED BUTTER – CUT

   INTO PIECES

TO MAKE THE WHITE BUTTER: Put the shallots, vinegar, wine and fish stock in a small pan. Bring to the boil and simmer until nearly all of the liquid has evaporated. Add the cream and reduce a little more. Then remove the pan from the heat and whisk in the butter a little at a time until it is all amalgamated.

Preheat the grill to high. Brush the fish with some melted butter and season inside and out with salt and freshly ground black pepper. Grill the bass for about 10 minutes on each side.

Wash the samphire thoroughly, then pull off the fleshy leaves and discard the thicker stalks with their woody centres.

Bring a pan of unsalted water to the boil and boil the samphire for 2 minutes. Drain, set aside and keep warm. Serve the fish, whole and fillet, at the table on to four warmed serving plates.

TINA'S TIP

March samphire grows on sandy mud in salt marches and muddy seashores all around the British Isles and Ireland. It has a delicious fresh, salty taste and a firm texture. It is easy to use as it has unusual fleshy, light-green joined branches rather than leaves and grows little more than 23 cm (9 in) high. So if you have the opportunity, try and find some to serve with sea bass.

Carrot Dulse Salad

SERVES 2

2 CARROTS – SHREDDED

100G (3 ½ OZ) DULSE – CHOPPED AND RINSED

100G (3 ½ OZ) SNOW PEAS – SMALL JULIENNE SHAPE

2 TBSP BLACK SESAME SEEDS

3 TBSP ORANGE JUICE

1 GARLIC CLOVE – MINCED

Combine all the ingredients in a large mixing bowl and mix well.
Let marinate for 1 hour before serving.

TINA'S TIP

When cooking pulse vegetables like peas, beans and lentils, add a little fresh sea vegetable into the pot. This adds flavour to the dish and you don't need to add table salt to the food.

Silver Sardines and Black-Eyed Beans

SERVES 4

50G (2 OZ) PLAIN FLOUR

10 SARDINES – SCALED AND CLEANED

ZEST OF 2 LEMONS

LARGE BUNCH OF FLAT-LEAF PARSLEY – LEAVES ONLY ROUGHLY CHOPPED

3 GARLIC CLOVES – FINELY CHOPPED

3 TBSP OLIVE OIL

GLASS WHITE WINE (ABOUT 125ML/4 FL OZ)

2 X 400G CANS BLACK-EYED BEANS

250G (9 OZ) PACK CHERRY TOMATOES – HALVED

Season the flour and scatter over a large plate. Dip the sardines in the flour, one at a time.

Mix together the lemon zest, parsley and half of the chopped garlic and set aside.

Put a very large pan on top of the barbeque and heat until very hot. Add the oil, heat for a few seconds, then lay the floured sardines in the oil in one layer.

Fry for 3 minutes until the underside is golden, then turn over and fry for another 3 minutes. Lift out of the pan and onto a plate.

Fry the remaining garlic (add another splash of oil if you need to) for 1 minute until softened. Pour in the white wine, scrape any bits off the bottom of the pan with a wooden spoon and boil for 1 minute or until reduced by half.

Tip in the black-eyed beans and tomatoes; then stir until heated through. Season with plenty of pepper.

Then nestle the fish back into the pan. Take off the heat, sprinkle with the parsley mix and serve with plenty of crusty bread to mop up the juices.

Crispy Seaweed

SERVES 4-6 WITH OTHER DISHES

1 ¼ KG (2LB 12 OZ) BOK CHOI

850 ML (28 FL OZ) GROUNDNUT OIL –
    FOR DEEP-FRYING

1 TSP SALT

2 TSP SUGAR

50G (2 OZ) PINE NUTS – LIGHTLY
    ROASTED TO GARNISH

DID YOU KNOW?

Bok choi is part of the Asian cabbage family and has a mild flavour. It is available in all good fruit and vegetable shops.

PREPARE THE BOK CHOI: Cut the stalks from the stem of the bok choi and cut the green leaves from the white stalks. (Save the stalks – you can stir-fry them with garlic or use them in soup.)

Wash the green leaves thoroughly in several changes of cold water; drain well in a colander, then spin dry in a salad spinner or pat dry with kitchen paper. Roll up the leaves tightly and shred finely.

Heat a wok over a high heat, and then add the oil. When the oil is hot; deep-fry the greens in two or three batches. When they turn deep green – this will take about 30 seconds – quickly remove them, using a slotted spoon.

Drain well on kitchen paper and allow to cool. Mix together the salt and sugar; then toss the crispy greens in the mixture. Garnish with the roasted pine nuts and serve at once.

Silver Fish Kebabs with Mushroom and Sesame Seeds

SERVES 8

FOR THE KEBABS

450G (1LB) FIRM WHITE FISH FILLETS
(SUCH AS HALIBUT, HADDOCK, COD
OR MONKFISH) – SKINNED AND
CUBED

450G (1LB) SALMON FILLETS – SKINNED
AND CUBED

16 SPRING ONIONS – EACH CUT INTO 4

FOR THE SAUCE

50G (2 OZ) BUTTER

4 TBSP SOY SAUCE (LIGHT)

4 TBSP CLEAR HONEY

4 TBSP CIDER VINEGAR

2 TBSP SESAME OIL

2 TBSP LIGHT MUSCOVADO SUGAR

2 TBSP FRENCH MUSTARD

4 TSP FRESH ROOT GINGER – GRATED

2 GARLIC CLOVES – CRUSHED

FOR THE MUSHROOMS

675G (1LB 8OZ) CUP MUSHROOMS

2 TBSP SESAME SEEDS – TOASTED

MIXED SALAD LEAVES – TO GARNISH

450G (1LB) LONG GRAIN AND WILD
RICE MIX – TO SERVE

Place the sauce ingredients in a small pan and heat until the butter has just melted, then set aside.

Soak 16 wooden skewers in cold water for 30 minutes to stop them from drying out and burning during grilling.

Take two pieces of salmon, two pieces of white fish and four pieces of onion and thread alternatively onto each skewer. (The kebabs can be made ahead to this point, then covered and stored in the fridge for several hours until you are ready to cook them.)

Brush the kebabs on one side with the sauce before you grill them. Cook on a moderate heat for about 4 minutes on each side until the fish is tender; turning once and brushing again with the sauces.

Place the mushrooms on the pan for the last 4 minutes of cooking time and baste with the sauce. Strain the remaining sauce into a small pan and simmer for a few minutes to thicken slightly. Sprinkle toasted sesame seeds over the mushrooms.

Spoon a little of the remaining sauce over the kebabs; then place on a bed of rice on each serving plate. Garnish with salad leaves and serve.

Silver Truffles

MAKES 30

1 SHOP-BOUGHT MOIST GINGER CAKE 225G (8 OZ)

100G (3 $^{1}/_{2}$ OZ) PLAIN CHOCOLATE

85G (3 OZ) DRIED CRANBERRIES – CHOPPED

1 TBSP CRANBERRY JUICE, RUM OR BRANDY

2 TBSP COCOA POWDER – SIFTED

2 TBSP ICING SUGAR – SIFTED

1 TBSP GRATED PLAIN CHOCOLATE OR SILVER STRANDS

Crumble the ginger cake in a food processor. Then transfer to a mixing bowl.

Melt the chocolate in a pan over a low heat, and then add the cranberries and juice, rum or brandy.

Fold into the cake crumbs to make a fairly soft mixture. If it becomes too soft to handle, chill until firm.

Shape the mixture into about 30 small balls. While still sticky, roll some in the cocoa powder, some in icing sugar and some in silver strands. Chill until needed.

Colour Star Plan

GETTING STARTED

THE COLOUR STAR PLAN IS A WAY TO ENSURE THAT EACH DAY YOU (AND YOUR FAMILY) EAT A WIDE SELECTION OF FOODS FROM ALL THE FOOD GROUPS. EACH COLOUR GROUP WILL CONTRIBUTE SIGNIFICANT PHYTONUTRIENTS, TASTES AND FLAVOURS TO YOUR DIET. WORKING OUT YOUR COLOUR STAR PLAN EVERY WEEK IS A GREAT WAY TO BE SURE THAT YOUR BODY IS GETTING THE VARIED SELECTION OF COLOURED FOODS IT NEEDS TO THRIVE.

The colour star plan will show you what colour foods your diet is lacking. You can then have a look at the relevant colour chapter and the nutritional profile of the foods listed to find out what you should be eating and try out some of the recipes.

Working out your colour star plan starts with keeping a food diary for a week.

FOOD DIARY

Keep a weekly diary of all the foods that you consume on a daily basis. Include breakfast, lunch, dinner, snacks and all drinks, including alcohol.

	Breakfast	Lunch	Dinner	Snacks
Monday	Pear and Ginger Juice	Tuna Pasta Salad	Pasta Primavera	Taste Health Bar / Apple
Tuesday	Hot Lemon Water	Vegetable Burger	Fish Cakes / Glass of water	Apple / Nuts
Wednesday	Macerated Fruit	Alligator Sandwiches	Chicken Satay	Apricots / Orange / 1 litre of water
Thursday	Apple and Blueberry Muesli	Sardines and Black-Eyed Beans	Honey Chicken with Brown Rice	Small piece of dark chocolate / Apple
Friday	Apple and Pear Compote with Prunes	Monkfish with Mexican Salsa	Carrots and Green Salad with Garlic Potatoes	Handful of strawberries / 2 kiwis
Saturday	Pear and Ginger Juice	Vegetable Burger	Pasta Primavera	Fruit Platter
Sunday	Macerated Fruit	Alligator Sandwiches	Sushi / Glass of water	Handful of Blackberries

At the end of the week take a look over your planner. Count the number of red foods that you have eaten, the number of orange foods, purple foods and so on.

■ 13	■ 1	▥ 1
9	▨ 7	■ 2
2	□ 8	8
■ 2	1	5

COLOUR STAR WHEEL

The information from this table is transferred onto your Colour Star Wheel by making a dash on the appropriate colour line for each portion: 0 = not at all, 1 = 1 portion daily and so on.

Once each score is marked on the graph, they are joined together by lines. In an ideal chart, representing a week where you have eaten the correct balance of foods, these lines should form a star shape.

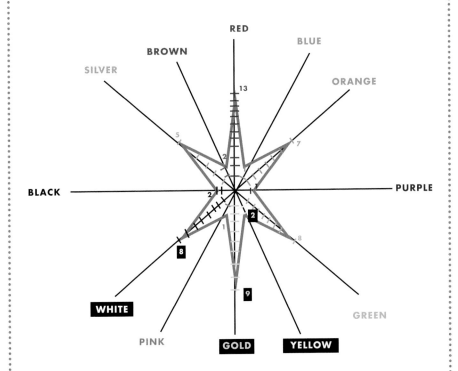

As time passes and you become more familiar with how the colour star plan works, it will become second nature to make each meal more colourful. It could be as simple as making some changes to the colour of bread you eat, for example, or including colourful fruits as snacks as opposed to biscuits, chocolate bars and sweets.

COLOUR STAR WHEEL

If you have made your Colour Star Wheel and it does not make a star shape, read on to find out ways to ensure that you have more colour in your diet in the future.

WHAT YOU NEED TO DO

1. Get out a calendar (e.g. Month: November).
2. Using these colours – red, orange, yellow, green, blue, purple, black, white, brown, pink, silver and gold – colour in one day on the calendar with each of those colours.
3. Ensure you (and your family) include foods of the colour outlined for that day into your diet. The chapters on each colour will give you ideas for foods to eat and list tasty recipes in each food colour group for you to enjoy.

Sample Month

Sunday	Monday	Tuesday	Wednesday	Thursday	Friday	Saturday
		1	2	3	4	5
6	7	8	9	10	11	12
13	14	15	16	17	18	19
20	21	22	23	24	25	26
27	28	29	30			

CALENDAR PLAN YOUR COLOUR STAR LIFE

January
Be adventurous
Boost physical energy
In season: peas, carrots

February
Be environmentally aware
Eliminate toxins and boost the immune system
In season: rhubarb, cabbage

March
Be confident
Lift your mood and emotional energy
In season: red peppers, yellow peppers

April
Be pretty
Springtime
Easter party
Skin, nails, hair
In season: aubergines

May
Be smart
Boost concentration and brain power
In season: broccoli

June
Be toned
Ideal weight
BBQ for the family
Summertime
In season: berries

July
Be active
Exercise
Live longer
In season: strawberries, blueberries

August
Be ambitious
Stabilise blood sugar levels
In season: tomatoes

September
Be a free spirit
Check cholesterol
In season: plums

October
Be relaxed
Autumn party
Hallowe'en theme
Chill out and relax
In season: courgettes, pumpkins

November
Be happy
Eat warm, sustaining foods
What is your tongue saying about you?
In season: celery

December
Be spontaneous
Christmas party
In season: broccoli, brussel sprouts,
carrots, cauliflower, celery,
pumpkin, red cabbage, onions

TO HELP YOU PLAN YOUR TABLE SHOWING WHEN FRUIT

FOODS IN SEASON BY COLOUR

	Red/Pink	Orange	Yellow	Green	Blue	Purple	White/Green
January	Eating apples	Carrots Swedes	Turnips	Brussel sprouts Butterhead lettuce Cabbage Kale Marrow Peas Cooking apples		Cauliflower Leeks	Mushroom Onions Parsnips Potatoes
February	Eating apples Rhubarb	Swedes Carrots	Turnips	Cooking apples Eating apples Butterhead lettuce Cabbage Spinach		Leeks Mushrooms Onions	Parsnips Potatoes
March	Eating apples Rhubarb Red peppers	Swedes Orange peppers	Yellow peppers	Cucumber Green peppers		Aubergines Leeks	Scallions
April	Red peppers Apples peppers	Carrots Orange	Yellow peppers	Broccoli Asparagus Cabbage Green peppers		Aubergines	Scallions Asparagus
May	Red peppers Apples peppers	Carrots Orange	Yellow peppers	Broccoli Asparagus Cabbage Green peppers		Aubergines	Scallions Asparagus
June	Berries Strawberries Logan berries Raspberries	Orange peppers	Yellow peppers Courgettes	Gooseberries Asparagus Broad beans Broccoli Butterhead lettuce	Blueberries	Blackberries Blackcurrant Aubergines Beetroot	Asparagus Cauliflow Celery Mushroor Scallions

COLOUR STAR LIFE, HERE IS A
AND VEGETABLES ARE IN SEASON.

FOODS IN SEASON BY COLOUR

	Red/Pink	Orange	Yellow	Green	Blue	Purple	White/Green
July	Red peppers Radishes Tomatoes Lollo Rosso		Courgettes	Cabbage Courgettes Spinach Cucumber Endives French beans Green peppers	Blueberries		Asparagus Cauliflower Celery Mushrooms Scallions
August	Tomatoes Red peppers	Swedes Orange peppers	Turnips Sweetcorn Yellow peppers	Broccoli Cabbage Spinach Green peppers		Aubergines Beetroot	Pears Cauliflower Mushrooms Potatoes
September	Tomatoes Red peppers	Swedes Orange peppers	Sweetcorn Turnips Yellow peppers	Spinach Green peppers		Plums Aubergines Beetroot	Pears Potatoes Cauliflower Mushrooms
October	Red peppers	Pumpkins	Yellow peppers	Courgettes Spinach		Plums	Pears
November	Tomatoes	Orange peppers		Cucumber Green peppers		Beetroot Aubergines	Celery
December	Eating apples Cranberries Red Cabbage	Carrots Swedes	Turnips	Cooking apples Brussel sprouts Cabbage Peas Kale		Plums Beetroot Aubergines	Cauliflower Leeks Mushroom Celery Onion Parsnips Potatoes

QUESTIONNAIRE ON EATING HABITS

This questionnaire has been formulated so that you can test yourself and identify the food groups that you need to either start eating more of or begin to ditch. Only by answering the questions honestly will you clearly see the food pattern in your life.

Tick yes or no beside your appropriate answer   Yes   No

1. Do you eat breakfast every day?
2. Do you consume the following drinks daily?
   a) black tea
   b) water
   c) coffee
3. Do you eat at least five portions of fruit and vegetables per day?
4. Do you eat raw seeds at least three times a week?
5. Do you eat natural nuts (e.g. almonds) at least three times a week?
6. Do you eat fish at least twice a week?
7. Do you use sea vegetables in your cooking?
8. Do you eat the following at least three times a week?
   a) rice
   b) quinoa
   c) oats
   d) buckwheat
   e) barley
9. Do you eat pulse vegetables (peas, beans and lentils)
   at least three times a week?
10. Do you eat the following nearly every day?
    a) biscuits
    b) sweets
    c) cakes
    d) white bread
    e) fried foods
    d) chocolate
11. Do you go grocery shopping with a list drawn up by you and/or everyone?
12. Do you cook your own fresh meals at least four times a week?
13. Do you sit down for dinner, without TV, radio or other distractions?
14. Do you exercise daily...
    a) on your own
    b) with a friend
    c) your partner
    d) your children
15. Do you drink more than the recommended alcohol amount per week?
    (14 units for women, 21 units for men)

QUESTIONNAIRE RESULTS

What has this questionnaire revealed about your eating habits?

For those boxes where you have ticked NO – go and check the varied foods featured in the individual colour chapters throughout the book. There are loads of nutritious and colourful recipe ideas featured for you to cook and taste.

Limit servings of processed, convenience and sugary foods so that they become occasional foods in your diet. It's very important to introduce colourful foods into your Colour Star Plan so that you feel gorgeous and vibrant.

For those of you that are eating up to:

6 servings of cereals per day of the golden grain variety as opposed to white breads, wraps and pastries,

5–9 servings of fruit and vegetables,

3 servings of fish per week,

3 servings of nuts and seeds per week,

1–2 portions of sea vegetables per week,

Congratulations and keep practicing the Colour Star Plan for success!

TINA'S TIP

Are you a nibbler? Are you always picking at something? When you prepare a meal have you nibbled your way through the preparation? When the time comes to dine have you eaten enough already? Remember your actions are only a habit that you can successfully take charge of and change.

Put a plate on your worktop area. Each time you reach out to eat or nibble something – even a piece of fruit or palmful of nuts – place the snack on the plate. Take a look at this at the end of the day. Even good, healthy whole foods have sugars and fats. So be aware of how much extra unnecessary food you are eating.

Case Study

THE MURPHY FAMILY

Ava — Aged 7

Ava is a fairly good eater, better than the boys at eating fruit. She will try anything but won't always eat it! She loves cheese, hates butter and milk but likes eggs. She eats fruit such as pears, apples, grapes and plums. She also eats a bit of salad or coleslaw and will occasionally eat yoghurts. Ava is good for eating chicken and other meats. She loves sauces like gravy or bolognese. She eats brown pasta and white bread and wraps. She even likes spicy food.
Note: Is prone to have slight eczema.

Mark — Aged 11

Mark is very bad at eating fruit; he can only manage an occasional banana or some grapes. He is a great meat eater. He also likes sauces. Mark loves all dairy products including cheese and milk; he also loves eggs. He is only ok with vegetables but will eat them. He doesn't mind peas, beans, celery, but complains about broccoli, spinach and other green vegetables. He never eats salads. Mark loves noodles, pasta and potatoes. Occasionally he eats brown bread, but mainly prefers white bread/wraps.

Raphael — Aged 15

Rugby player and conscious of his diet, Raphael is a good all-round eater and tries most things. He likes most of the food Mark likes, with the exception of cheese. He hates cheese topped on a lasagne or anything like that. He enjoys eating pasta, popcorn and all his carbs. He hates brown bread. He is good at eating fruit and vegetables and drinking plenty of water. Lately Raphael likes a bit of salad.

Case Study

Michael — Aged 44

Michael is an adventurous eater and will try anything. He is very good with his fruit intake and has muesli or fruit for breakfast. However his lunches are hit and miss; he can skip it, grab a sandwich or go the whole hog at the pub with chips, depending on how busy he is. He will happily eat beef but never lamb or pork, as they disagree with him. He eats a lot of chicken and pasta at home, but would often order fish or steak eating out. Michael has no allergies per se. He has a very sweet tooth and loves to snack. He drinks wine and the odd spirit, rarely beer. He occasionally drinks coffee but is mainly a tea drinker. Michael does little exercise.

Gabrielle — Aged 40

Gabrielle is generally adventurous with food. She likes to eat fruit and yoghurt in the morning. She tends to skip lunch due to her busy schedule, but will pick up a take-away cappuccino and pastry at least two days a week. She loves pasta and will eat this at least three to four nights a week. She likes to sit down in the evening. Chilling out in front of the TV is generally the time of day that really causes the trigger for Gabrielle to eat poorly. The ads on the TV prompt her to snack and she chooses foods from ice-cream to breakfast cereals, depending on her mood. Gabrielle wants to make lifestyle changes for herself and her family.

MURPHY FAMILY DIET ADVICE

I have studied all the Murphy family profiles and here are my suggestions:

Starchy Carbohydrates – Includes bread, rice, pasta, breakfast cereals, other grains and potatoes. Choose brown wholegrain bread wherever possible. Raphael does not like brown bread so he could try barley, buckwheat, rye, pumpernickel, spelt or rice bread or oat and rice crackers so that he varies the grain types in his diet.

Snacks – For family members who find mid-afternoon a challenging time, snack on a cracker with some tasty hummus or sliced tomato. Oat and rice crackers make a tasty snack for mid-morning or after school – Raphael could use peanut butter to give them flavour. This will boost his energy levels and ensure that after sports he will not have the urge to nibble on bits and pieces.

Pasta/Rice – As the Murphy family enjoy pasta and use the regular pasta made from durum wheat, they could be adventurous and taste the buckwheat type and alternate their choice when cooking. I advise them to use less pasta and more brown rice. Choose brown rice at least once a week and you can use other varieties such as basmati, wild and pilaff. Rice noodles and rice vermicelli are delicious and simple to cook. They can be added to stir-fries or mixed with fresh vegetables for a salad.

Breakfast Cereals – These are handy in the morning. I suggest, however, that they alternate their breakfast menus. I see Michael likes muesli but he may like to alternate the muesli with porridge for the winter months. Other cereals that are good include wheat and oat-based cereals.

Grains – Other grains should also be added to the family's diet. Quinoa is a brilliant grain and is the only one known to contain all the essential amino acids. I suggest that the family use quinoa flakes; they can add them to soups and pinhead quinoa can be sprinkled over potato wedges, adding a nutty flavour.

CASE STUDY &
COLOUR STAR FOODS

Potatoes – Mark likes potatoes. Boiled or baked potatoes make a really tasty sustaining meal when topped with beans. This is a terrific meal option for the whole family. Sweet potatoes baked or roasted offer an alternative flavour.

Vegetables – I know Mark is not mad about green leafy vegetables but he could eat other green vegetables instead – peas, mange tout and green beans will all be great for him. The good thing about green leafy vegetables is that they contain lots of iron which helps carry oxygen around the body and so helps energise us. Iron also helps remove toxins or poisons from the body so that the skin is fresh, immune system is boosted and our concentration is great. All root vegetables are good, including carrots, parsnip and turnip. As a general rule – eat the vegetables that are in season.

There are many ways of introducing these vegetables into your diet: stir-frying is a must and family and friends alike will adore it. Another option is to serve the vegetables with rice, in a tomato sauce such as primavera with pasta, in a tortilla wrap for fajitas or tortilla pizza. You could pile the vegetables on top of a tortilla wrap and grate some mozzarella cheese on top.

Vegetables can also be grated together – such as carrot and white cabbage mixed with some raisins and chopped orange; this will moisten the vegetables and help eliminate the use of mayonnaise. If you are using a

did you know?

THE BRILLIANT THING ABOUT CELERY IS THAT IT HELPS THE BODY ELIMINATE TOXINS. PEOPLE SHOULD TRY TO EAT CELERY IN COPIOUS PROPORTIONS, ESPECIALLY WHEN IT IS IN SEASON.

Soups, stews and casseroles are things that a family will love. Chicken casseroles, beef stews and all soups can have any combination of vegetables you like; pasta, rice, potatoes and grains like barley and quinoa can also be added. Chicken noodle soup is popular in many households. All these warm dishes help keep the body system warm over the winter months.

commercially prepared mayonnaise it contains a number of ingredients that are not necessarily good for the system. It is better to use this as an occasional food rather than a daily item.

Note for Michael – A cup of fresh soup in the middle of the day will boost your energy levels. It would be fantastic to have a cup or bowl every work day. This is most essential on busy days.

Stock Cubes – Kallo and Marigold are the only stock cubes I recommend as they are free from all artificial additives and preservatives.

Fruits – I encourage everyone in the Murphy family to eat apples, pears and plums. As these fruits are grown locally, they suit our digestive tract which is adapted for the assimilation of the nutrients. Local fruits are more attractive and often healthier for us when compared to tropical fruits such as mangos and pineapples. Exotic fruits are undoubtedly delicious but they are grown in warmer climates and have to travel a long distance to reach other countries. As a result, they are often treated with artificial substances to prolong their shelf life. Fruits that are readily available and grown locally are usually healthier for us. Keep exotic fruits to a minimum or stock up on them when holidaying in warmer climes.

Note for Mark – He might like to try cooked fruits as people sometimes find them more appealing and easier to eat. Why not bake a mixture of apples, pears and plums and add some crumble; use apple juice to moisten the dish. Use canned fruit only in emergencies as the fruit has undergone a process and some vitamins and minerals may be lost. Fresh is always best, especially if grown locally. Read your labels and try only to buy sugar-free brands.

Milk, Yoghurt and Cheese – All of these are good sources of protein and calcium. Meat, poultry, eggs, fish, nuts, seeds and green leafy vegetables are other good sources.

Note for Ava – She does not like cow's milk; this is absolutely fine, she can use rice or almond milk and this will also help calm any signs of eczema. Dairy foods can exacerbate skin and respiratory problems. It is a good idea for Ava to avoid the dairy group completely including all cheese – particularly in the winter months. For a treat she can have feta or haloumi cheese. In winter, the weather is damper and for those who produce more mucus and phlegm and have respiratory and skin challenges, the dairy group can often aggravate these conditions. So I advise that Ava keep this food group to a minimum or at least keep a monitor as to how the foods influence her system.

It is vital, of course, to include calcium-rich foods in your diet such as green leafy vegetables, nuts and seeds. Remember that 90% of calcium deposits are laid down before the age of 17 years. It is essential to include at least 3–5 servings of calcium daily to ensure that you are getting enough. If there is not enough calcium in your diet, the calcium will dribble out of your bones so that the body can have it and this will leave the bones weak and can lead to osteoporosis and brittle bones in later years.

Note for Raphael – He does not eat cheese but has many other calcium-rich foods in his diet such as yoghurts and milk that contribute to his calcium intake.

Meat, Poultry and Fish – The family all eat beef and chicken.

Beef can be stripped and used in stir-fries, minced for pasta sauce, cubed for stew or casserole or grilled as steak and burgers. I suggest that you include red meat once a week.

Chicken should also be included once a week. Use turkey crown for lunches or roast turkey as an alternative to chicken.

Try to introduce **fish** into your diet at least three times a week. It is easy to cook; pop the pieces of fish, cod, monkfish, salmon or whatever you like onto a baking sheet. Squeeze some fresh lemon or lime on top and cover with foil and bake for about 20–25 minutes. Tinned fish, such as salmon and sardines, make sandwich fillings. Fish cakes are another tasty and healthy option. Sushi is a must in the diet as it provides the diet with sea vegetables and a host of silver fish.

Nuts and Seeds – Natural almonds, hazelnuts, peanuts and Brazil nuts should be eaten as snacks three times a week. These foods make a significant nutritional contribution to the diet and provide a good source of protein and agreeable fats. Introduce all types of seeds; use them in salads, fruit bars or sprinkle on cereals or roast vegetables. A portion size is roughly the size of a clenched fist.

Avoid salted nuts such as peanuts and cashew nuts as the salt content is high and we only need 6g (¹/₄ oz) salt per day. This salt is present in many other foods in your diet and additional salt can lead to heart related illnesses.

Grains are very popular in Copacabana, Bolivia and are sold in all the markets, especially spelt and nuts.

Pulses – Beans, peas, mung, adzuki, lime, broad and chickpea are all fantastic. They are high in protein and make an excellent alternative to meat and meat products. I encourage everyone in the family to eat these at least three times a week. They can form a salad, be part of a dish or be eaten with rice. Adding a little seaweed such as dulse or nori will help give them flavour and provide you with iodine – a mineral that aids the metabolism.

Note for the family – The family need to start slowly when trying new foods – begin by choosing the vegetable varieties and then move on to the fish/meat selections. Only by trying and testing new foods will you see what works for you.

Sweets and Fats – Remember that it is fine to eat some foods from this food group but the secret is to be careful of which ones you have. Look for the codes! For example, with crisps – always read the labels. Carefully look at the ingredients before buying – all E-numbers are codes for additives, preservatives, colourings or stabilisers. Eat good quality dark chocolate and avoid the 5–10c bars and gums. Popcorn is a great snack, as is liquorice. Oat bars are a healthy and tasty snack but, again, always check sugar content. (For a healthy oat bar recipe, have a look at the Gold recipes.)

To curb a sweet tooth, taking a supplement called chromium can help. When a sweet snack-attack is in full swing do your best to eat some dried fruits, grapes or nuts. Drinking herbal fruit tea may also help with the pangs.

Note for the family – Watch out for the ingredient trans-fats or partially hydrogenated fatty acids. These are found, in copious proportions, in foods such as biscuits, cakes and pastries; so choose wisely. Trans-fats are added to foods to prolong their shelf life. They also contribute to the taste and are cheap to manufacture and therefore widely used. Trans-fats are particularly harmful to the body if you eat them frequently, as they raise cholesterol levels. (To read more about trans-fats turn to the The Colour Indigo chapter.)

DIARY

I took a flight from Caracas, Venezuela to Barranquilla, Columbia and onwards by car to Cartagena. It is a walled city, home to magnificent colonial structures. The streets create a labyrinth, where thousands of vendors bustle for custom, selling colourful fruits – sweet pineapples, mangoes, paw-paws, maracuya (a purple passion fruit), gooseberries, and guayabamanzana (a hybrid between guava and apple), mora-blackberry and guanabana. At the beach, the women carry large baskets on their heads, with a cornucopia of fresh and sweet smelling fruits which they use to make *jugos* or juice, as you have your toe nails painted or hair braided.

PORTION SIZES

The eyes play a big role in portion size when it comes to dining and "your eyes are bigger than your belly" is a familiar saying! Portion size is a habit. It is important to keep in mind that reducing your portion size will reduce your calorie intake.

Try to stick to the portion size guidelines in the next two pages. Trying to do this will heighten your awareness of the portion sizes you usually consume. Never make yourself finish what is on your plate, if you feel you've had enough.

Tina's Top Three Tips For Taking Charge of Portion Sizes

1. CHECK PORTION SIZES PER MEAL:
AN IDEAL ADULT SERVING FOR A MEAL WOULD BE 60–90G OF MEAT AND/OR FISH, TWO POTATOES AND 226G OF GREEN LEAFY VEGETABLES.
SEE THE NEXT TWO PAGES FOR SERVING SIZES FOR ALL FOODS.

2. PLAN YOUR MEALS AND YOUR SNACKS:
PEOPLE WHO ARE WELL-ORGANISED, SHOP IN ADVANCE AND HAVE WELL-STRUCTURED MEALS TEND TO BE HEALTHY, ENERGETIC AND, IF LOSING WEIGHT IS A CONCERN, CAN SUCCESSFULLY LOSE WEIGHT AND KEEP IT OFF.

3. EAT FOODS THAT ARE HIGH IN FIBRE WITH LOW ENERGY DENSITY:
FIBRE-FILLED FOODS FILL YOU UP AND, AS THE ENERGY IS RELEASED FROM THE FOOD OVER A PERIOD OF TIME, YOU WILL NOT HAVE LOW SUGAR DIPS AND CRAVE THE FOODS THAT ARE TASTY BUT HIGH IN CALORIES. SO WHEN YOU HAVE A SNACK ATTACK, CHOOSE A FOOD THAT IS HIGH IN FIBRE.

PORTION SIZES: THE MURPHY FAMILY

Ava – Age 7

Recommended To Eat Per Day

6–11 servings of starchy carbohydrates

3–5 servings of vegetables

3–5 servings of fruit

2–3 servings of milk, cheese and yoghurt

2–3 servings of meat, poultry, fish, nuts and pulses

Limit the intake of sweets and fats that are in biscuits and cakes.

Serving Sizes for Ava

Starchy Carbohydrates

Bread – 1 slice

Cooked pasta/rice – 113g (4 oz) cup

Breakfast cereal – 142g (5 oz)

Potato – 113g (4 oz) or three small potatoes

Vegetables and Fruit

Cooked vegetables – 113g (4 oz)

Salad – 240g (8 oz)

Cooked or canned – 71g (2 $^1/_2$ oz)

Fresh fruit – 1 piece

Juice – 125 ml (4 fl oz)

Dairy

Milk – 250 ml (8 fl oz) (Ava can use rice milk or almond milk instead of cow's milk)

Cheese, hard – match-box size

Yoghurt – 375 ml (12 fl oz) small pots

Meat, Poultry and Fish

60–90g (2–3 oz)

Eggs

1–2 eggs

Pulses

All cooked pulses – 113g (4 oz)

Nuts and Seeds

1 medium palmful (30g/1 oz)

Spicy Foods

Ava likes spicy foods but these can exacerbate eczema so she is better off avoiding them as much as possible.

PORTION SIZES: THE MURPHY FAMILY

Mark, Raphael, Michael and Gabrielle

From age 11 it's adult portions. The **'Recommended To Eat Per Day'** list for the four adults are the same as the foods detailed for Ava but it's important to watch portion sizes. For girls and boys under the age of 17 years it is also recommended that you have up to 5 portions of calcium-rich foods per day to help build strong bones.

Starchy Carbohydrates

Bread – 1 slice

Breakfast cereal – 240g (8 oz)

Cooked rice, pasta, noodles, quinoa – 113g (4 oz)

2 potatoes

Vegetables

Raw leafy vegetables – 240g (8 oz)

Chopped vegetables – 113g (4 oz)

Vegetable juice – 250 ml (8 fl oz)

Fruit

1 medium piece of fruit e.g. apple or pear or 2 x plums

Chopped fruit or canned (occasionally) – 113g (4 oz)

Fresh fruit juice – 250 ml (8 fl oz)

Dairy

Milk or yoghurt – 240g (8 oz)

Matchbox size of cheese x 2

Meat, Poultry and Fish

60–90g (2–3 oz) cooked lean beef, chicken or fish

Eggs

2 eggs

Pulses

Cooked pulses – 240g (8 oz)

Nuts and Seeds

Palmful of nuts or seeds

BREAKFAST IDEAS

Apple and Blueberry Muesli

SERVES 1

2 TBSP ROLLED OATS

80 ML (2 ½ FL OZ) FRESH APPLE JUICE

1 MEDIUM APPLE – GRATED COARSELY

50G (2 OZ) BLUEBERRIES

EXTRA APPLE JUICE (1 TBSP)

A COUPLE OF BLUEBERRIES FOR SERVING

blue

Combine the oats with the apple juice and place in the fridge until the oats soften.

Stir in the fruit.

Serve by drizzling the apple juice over the oat mixture and put extra blueberries on top.

Apple and Pear Compote with Prunes

SERVES 1

130G (4 ½ OZ)

   1 SMALL APPLE

180G (6 ½ OZ)

   1 SMALL PEAR

2 TBSP FRESH LEMON

   JUICE

55G (2 ¼ OZ)

   COARSELY CHOPPED

   PRUNES (SOAKED

   OVERNIGHT)

1 TSP FINELY GRATED ORANGE RIND

2 TBSP FRESH ORANGE JUICE

purple

Peel, core and chop the apple and pear into dice-size pieces.

Combine in a saucepan with the lemon juice and cook until softened.

Combine prunes, orange rind and juice in a saucepan and simmer until the fruit has absorbed the juice.

Serve compote warm or cold topped with prune mixture.

LUNCH IDEAS

Tuna Pasta Salad

SERVES 3-4

125 ML (4 FL OZ) CUP PASTA SHAPES

1 x 185G (6 $\frac{1}{2}$ OZ) TIN TUNA FISH IN BRINE

2 CARROTS - PEELED AND GRATED

1 SPRING ONION - FINELY CHOPPED

1 AVOCADO - HALVED AND PEELED

2 TBSP SWEETCORN

SALT AND PEPPER

Cook the pasta in a pot of boiling water until tender. Drain and place in a bowl.

Open the tin of tuna fish and drain the brine away.

Combine the pasta, tuna and other ingredients together in a bowl and serve.

Alligator Sandwiches

SERVES 4

4 LARGE, WHOLEMEAL SESAME ROLLS

FILLING

2 AVOCADOS - PEELED, STONED AND SLICED

ICEBERG LETTUCE LEAVES

SLICES OF TOMATO

4 TBSP ALFALFA SPROUTS

4 SCALLIONS (SPRING ONIONS) - THINLY SLICED

DRESSING

4 TBSP LEMON JUICE

2 TSP FRENCH MUSTARD

1 CLOVE GARLIC - CRUSHED

2 TBSP TOMATO PASTE

12 BLACK OLIVES - STONED AND FINELY
  CHOPPED

1 TBSP FRESH PARSLEY - FINELY CHOPPED

5-10 DROPS TABASCO SAUCE TO TASTE

SEA SALT AND PEPPER TO TASTE

Prepare the dressing ingredients by mixing them together into a coarse paste and set aside.

Halve and toast the rolls. Coat the insides with dressing and fill with equal portions of salad mixture.

DINNER IDEAS

Fish Cakes

SERVES 3

1 x 185G (6 ¹/₂ OZ) TIN TUNA FISH IN BRINE

3 COOKED AND MASHED SWEET POTATOES

1 SCALLION (SPRING ONION) – FINELY CHOPPED

1 ROSEMARY SPRIG – FINELY CHOPPED

silver

Blend the fish, sweet potato and spring onion together. Add chopped rosemary.

Use your hands to make even-sized ball shapes or use a star-shape cutter.

Place on a baking sheet and heat in the oven for 10–15 minutes at 180°C (350°F) or gas mark 5.

Garnish with parsley.

Pasta Primavera

SERVES 5

400G (12 OZ) PASTA – ANY SHAPE
  YOU LIKE

TOMATO SAUCE

1 X 400G (12 OZ) TIN CHOPPED
  TOMATOES

1 ONION – FINELY CHOPPED

1 CLOVE GARLIC – CRUSHED

HANDFUL FRESH BASIL

1 TSP CHOPPED OREGANO

1 TBSP OLIVE OIL

VEGETABLES

1 RED PEPPER – DICED

1 YELLOW PEPPER – DICED

1 COURGETTE – SLICED THINLY

10 BUTTON MUSHROOMS – SLICED
  OR QUARTERED

Sauté the onion and garlic in a saucepan and add the tomatoes and herbs. Simmer for 15 minutes to allow the flavours to develop.

Place the pasta into a pot of boiling water and cook for 12–15 minutes until tender. Drain and place into a large bowl. Why not check out buckwheat pasta for variety? (See The Colour Gold chapter)

Place the tomato sauce into a blender and blend for 1 minute.

Sauté the vegetables in a pan using olive oil. Combine the vegetables and pasta together in a bowl and stir in the delicious tomato sauce.

red

TINA'S TIP

This recipe has a better flavour and taste than any packet or jarred product and everyone will love it. The sauce is wonderful with any cooked pasta of your choice or spooned over well-seasoned meatballs.

Chicken Satay

SERVES 5

4–5 CHICKEN FILLETS, CUT INTO PIECES

PEANUT SAUCE:

2 TBSP PEANUT BUTTER (CRUNCHY)

1 TBSP PEANUTS

2 TBSP SOY SAUCE

1 TBSP BROWN SUGAR

1 TBSP LEMON JUICE

2 TBSP VEGETABLE OIL

DASH OF WORCESTERSHIRE SAUCE

100 ML (3 ½ FL OZ) WATER

gold

Put peanuts into a plastic bag and crush with rolling pin.

Put all the sauce ingredients into the saucepan and stir over a moderate heat to make into a creamy consistency. Add a little more water if necessary.

Preheat the grill. Thread the chicken pieces onto the skewers and brush all over with the sauce mixture.

Grill for 8–10 minutes, turning twice to cook through. Brush occasionally with sauce during cooking.

Heat any remaining sauce and serve with the satays. Serve with a fresh green salad and/or boiled rice.

SNACK IDEAS

Taste Health Bar

MAKES 14

200G (7 OZ) ROLLED OATS

25G (1 OZ) WHOLEMEAL FLOUR

25G (1 OZ) MIXED DRIED FRUIT

50G (2 OZ) SESAME SEEDS

100G (3 ½ OZ) BROWN SUGAR

100G (3 ½ OZ) BUTTER

3 TBSP HONEY

1 TBSP BOILING WATER

> These bars are fun to make, taste delicious and are great lunch fillers. They are also a great work snack, after school filler for kids or a sweet treat when you are have a coffee with friends.

gold

Preheat the oven to 180°C (350°F) or gas mark 4 and lightly grease a 20 cm (8 in) shallow tin.

Mix oats, wholemeal flour, fruit and sesame seeds in a bowl.

Melt butter, sugar and honey in a saucepan. Add this to the oats and mix thoroughly.

Turn into tin and bake for 15–20 minutes; until golden brown.

Remove from the oven. Cut into bite size pieces while warm.

Cool completely before removing from the tin.

Fruit Platter

SERVES 1

180G (6 ½ OZ) 1 PEAR,
    CUBED

130G (4 ½ OZ) 1 SMALL
    APPLE, CUBED

350G (12 ½ OZ)
    1 SMALL PINK
    GRAPEFRUIT, PEELED
    AND CUBED

100G (3 ½ OZ) RED
    GRAPES

Combine all ingredients in a bowl and serve.

Your Food Personality and Lifestyle Planning

WE ARE ALL COMPLETELY UNIQUE. IN MANY INSTANCES THERE IS NO ONE WHO KNOWS YOUR BODY AS WELL AS YOU DO YOURSELF; THE MORE YOU KNOW ABOUT YOUR OWN BODY, THE MORE IN TUNE YOU ARE WITH IT. THIS MAKES IT EASIER TO UNDERSTAND WHAT YOU NEED TO DO TO HELP YOU FEEL MORE RELAXED, ENERGETIC AND GENERALLY FRESHER AND BRIGHTER.

Have you ever wondered why some people favour salty snacks and others sweets or chocolate? After a meal would you prefer a cheese board or go straight for the dessert trolley to eye up a delicious pudding or would you decide that a freshly brewed herbal tea is just the thing for you?

Children selling coriander in Cusco, Peru

Observing and registering these characteristics can help you to understand your own individual food personality a little bit better. Recognising the foods that you have a craving for and the food rituals that you practice on a daily basis may, with some moderate changes, help you to renovate your current eating patterns.

The questionnaire on the next page will help you identify your own food personality. Answer the questions and discover what your food personality is today. It may change according to life situations, so please repeat this at least four times a year, ideally at the start of summer, autumn, winter and spring as these seasons may influence your eating patterns.

FOOD PERSONALITY QUESTIONNAIRE

✔

Q1 If your eating plan is erratic, what is the reason for this?

a. My life is just too busy to plan meals carefully every day.

b. I start off well, but the minute something goes wrong in my life I tend to turn to food for comfort.

c. I'm ok on my own, but family and friends encourage me to lapse at mealtimes and social events and I just go for it.

d. If the weight doesn't fall off immediately, I lose motivation and get bored with the routine.

Q2 Which statement best describes your attitude to food?

a. I spend my life battling with it – sometimes it's my best friend; sometimes it's the enemy.

b. I think of food as a treat, which can make me feel better when I'm down.

c. I love eating! There's nothing better than enjoying good food together with good company.

d. It's just fuel. I don't think about food that much really.

Q3 What do you typically eat each day? Pick the answer that best describes your daily eating habits.

a. I skip breakfast and sometimes lunch if I'm busy, and usually have a takeaway or a quick meal when I get home.

b. I often miss breakfast, but usually have a good-sized lunch and dinner to compensate.

c. Breakfast, lunch and dinner with snacks in between.

d. I don't have set meals, but snack throughout the day.

Q4 When you're craving something, what is it most likely to be?

a. Fast food, like pizza, burgers or noodles.

b. Something starchy and comforting like chips (fries), bread or pasta.

c. Something indulgent and rich like a scoop of ice-cream or a piece of cake.

d. Savoury foods such as meat or cheese.

Q5 How does stress affect the way you eat?

a. If I'm busy, I skip meals and fill up on snacks and caffeine beverages.

b. I tend to eat everything in sight as a way of helping me get through the busy time.

c. It makes me lose my appetite; it can be 5 pm before I realise I've hardly eaten since breakfast.

d. It doesn't affect it in any way – I just carry on eating as I normally would.

FOOD PERSONALITY QUESTIONNAIRE   ✔

Q6 In general, what do you do with your food after you begin to feel full?

a. Stop and leave what's left.

b. I don't often feel full.

c. Finish what's left – there's no sense in letting it go to waste!

d. I finish it and often have a second helping, even if I'm not actually hungry.

Q7 How do you prefer to do things?

a. Alone.

b. With one other person.

c. In a big group.

d. I enjoy both groups and solo activities.

Q8 Which statement best describes your personality?

a. Generally happy, but prone to stress.

b. Moody, emotional and sensitive.

c. Sociable and fun-loving.

d. I'm fairly relaxed and go with the flow most of the time.

THE RESULTS

MOSTLY As – THE STRESSED OUT STUFFER

You are a highly-strung personality. A busy schedule means that you tend to skip meals and grab quick snacks to keep you going. These snacks can be high in sugar and fat and are packed with empty calories that give you short boosts of energy. You are intense with everything you do, including your eating habits. You enjoy food and are prone to over-eat and tend to drink too much alcohol when stressed.

MOSTLY Bs – THE COMFORT EATER

You are a comfort eater – you 'pamper with a hamper'. You tend to be very good or very bold and engage in yo-yo dieting. You may prefer to snack on convenience foods but beware of these as they can be packed with hidden sugar that will only contribute empty calories to your diet. Instead, choose high-fibre foods with every meal – good choices include brown rice.

The next time things go haywire for you, reach for something unconnected to food to help keep your mind off the challenge; call a friend, take a shower or put on some funky music and have a 'boogie'. Learn to honour your body in all its magnificent splendour. Before putting anything in your mouth, ask yourself if you really want it, or ask your body if it wants it. Good nutrition and excellent body management are paramount to your well being.

MOSTLY Cs – THE SOCIAL BUTTERFLY

You are a social butterfly and love dining out. As your tastes and appetite varies from day-to-day, it is vital that you plan meals and stick to a regular pattern in dining times. Watch your tendency to miss meals or eat on the run.

TOP 5 TIPS TO HELP THE SOCIAL BUTTERFLY

1. Avoid heavy dressings and sauces – oil and vinegar with black pepper is the best for you. Soups, stews and casseroles are ideal choices for you. Eating warm soupy foods fit your nutritional profile and are easy to digest.

2. Too many nuts, seeds, sweets and dairy foods may cause digestive problems for you as the nuts and seeds can be too abrasive on the digestive tract and the dairy products may prompt your system to produce too much mucus. It is best to eat loads of fresh fruit and vegetables of orange, red and yellow colour.

3. Mid-afternoon can be a little stressful for you. Avoid scheduling important appointments during this time; work them into your morning instead. If you can, take a siesta after 2 pm for 40 minutes – this will pep you up, helping to refresh and re-motivate you for the rest of your busy day.

4. Be in bed by 10 pm generally as it will help keep you in a balanced, focused and centred space. It is a good idea to work your life schedule around this model, particularly during busy or stress-filled periods. Then when it's time to party, you will be up for it, looking and feeling glamorous and great.

5. Protein with every meal is the simplest tip and the best. Protein foods will help give you a feeling of fullness and make for a good option when dining out. Examples of protein-rich dishes include fresh fish or chicken with sauces on the side, as opposed to starchy pasta dishes with creamy sauces, or fried foods.

MOSTLY Ds – THE FOOD IS FUEL EATER

You are a 'whatever goes' type of person! You tend to be extremely busy with your daily activities and can do your 'food thing' without much planning or thought. You do not like to see waste and would rather clear your plate than throw anything away. This can have complications because you sometimes overeat without realising it and can end up eating more calories than you need. Your lack of interest in food could also cause you to miss out on vital nutrients.

TOP 5 TIPS TO HELP THE FOOD IS FUEL EATER

1. As you have a tendency to use food as fuel, you gobble down the grub and leave little time for flavour appreciation. Concentrate on developing your taste buds, fostering an awareness of different flavours. It would be a worthwhile exercise for you to write down the flavours or tastes you experience in each meal for a week.
2. Make a point of sitting down to dine, in a TV and mobile-free zone, rather than eating on the go.
3. Eat plenty of fresh fruit and vegetables.
4. Plan snacks wisely and choose snacks high in fibre. Keep them in your fridge, desk or press, so you have them close to hand.
5. Experiment with two new tastes and flavours a week for a month.

TASTE

It is important to truly taste the food you are eating as this will stimulate and promote healthy taste buds. You have six taste centres and each taste centre stimulates the body to function efficiently.

Sweet Taste: Sweet foods such as fruit, chocolate, pastries and ice-cream are good for the pancreas. It is advisable to only get your sugar from complex carbohydrates, which help stabilise blood sugar and keep your energy at an even level, as too much sugar will cause pancreatic challenges and blood sugar imbalance.

Sour Taste: Sour foods such as lemon, lime and rhubarb, support the liver. The liver processes everything you eat and drink, including nutrients and ingested toxins. Acidic foods rich in Vitamin C provide anti-oxidant protection for the liver.

Salty Taste: Sea vegetables and fish are a rich source of salt. This mineral nourishes the kidneys and maintains body fluid balance in the body.

Pungent Taste: Green leafy vegetables are examples of pungent flavoured foods that support lung function. They help clear congestion. Pungent flavoured herbs and spices such as ginger, cinnamon, rosemary and tarragon have a natural drying effect in the body. They prevent mucus build up, that can exacerbate sinus or chest challenges, and can help warm the body, especially during autumn and winter months.

Bitter Taste: This taste is a popular tonic for aiding fat digestion and assimilation. Bitter herbs are considered to be a tonic for the heart as they tend to nourish the heart energy system. Spring greens such as endives and sprouts are good examples.

Astringent Taste: This taste is the opposite to sour. Asparagus and spinach are good examples of astringent foods that support the lymph and sweat glands.

FOODS TO EAT TO BOOST ENERGY

Unrefined Carbohydrates

Spelt and Sprouted Wheat

Seeds – Sunflower and Pumpkin

Walnuts and Macadamia Nuts

Skinless Turkey

Fish – especially oily

Bananas and Dates

Live Pro-biotic Yoghurt

Oats

Apples, Avocados, Broccoli

Water

FOODS TO EAT TO BOOST CONCENTRATION

Essential Fatty Acids – Fish and Seeds

Organic Lamb and Beef

Brown Rice

Live Probiotic Yoghurt

Hemp Seed

Lentils

Carrots, Parsnip, Lettuces, Apples, Pears, Plums

FOODS TO EAT TO BOOST THE IMMUNE SYSTEM

Fish – white and oily varieties

Almonds and Pine Nuts

Seeds: Sunflower, Sesame Seeds, Linseed, Flax

Asparagus, Broccoli, Potatoes

Green Leafy Vegetables: cabbage, kale and spinach

Apricots

Water

FOODS TO EAT TO REDUCE STRESS

Celery – Raw or Juiced with Organic Carrot and Ginger

Complex Carbohydrates – Brown Rice or Quinoa

Almonds

Green Leafy Vegetables

Algae/Sea Vegetables

Cucumber

Garlic

Planning Your Lifestyle

Life is busy. Being organised and planning ahead are two fantastic ways to ensure that everything is in order and that things get done. Every once in a while you need to take a quiet few minutes, sit down, with a pen in one hand and a cup of tea or glass of wine in the other, and start to plan your month.

What do you want to do? Obviously there will be some things you know you need to do already – servicing the car, dentist appointments or to plan a birthday party for a friend. But it is worth planning out other activities as well. Perhaps you would like to start a new hobby, join a club, go on a holiday or find out about a new mortgage scheme and restructure your financial portfolio!

It is essential that we make specific time for these activities in our lives as time has a habit of disappearing. By making a plan, it is at least the first step towards making things happen in your life.

Without planning ahead, I never would have made it to South-America – one trip of a lifetime!

You may find, however, that you write something down and it does not happen in the month you want it to. Don't despair, just write it in again and if, over a few months, it does not come to fruition, shelve it. You will probably discover that you no longer desire such a thing or that it would be better to do it another time, when you will be able to do it with greater ease and efficiency.

Each month – who can I ask for help?

Each month as you plan your project(s), it makes perfect sense to jot down the name(s) of people who can help you so that your project will have the very best opportunity to succeed.

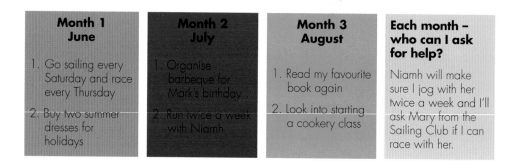

**Month 1
June**

1. Go sailing every Saturday and race every Thursday
2. Buy two summer dresses for holidays

**Month 2
July**

1. Organise barbeque for Mark's birthday
2. Run twice a week with Niamh

**Month 3
August**

1. Read my favourite book again
2. Look into starting a cookery class

**Each month –
who can I ask
for help?**

Niamh will make sure I jog with her twice a week and I'll ask Mary from the Sailing Club if I can race with her.

WEEKLY CHART

Everyone has a busy schedule these days so it's better to list the activities that must happen and then list those you want to happen. This will help you to manage your time more effectively and make sure you've done everything you need to do, leaving you time to enjoy yourself.

Putting your weekly activities into your plan will also help ensure that they happen.

Week 1

Date

May 5

Top Tasks

Go to the bank and look into mortgage options

Book six month check-up at the dentist

Week 2

Date

May 12

Top Tasks

Run a seminar on Wednesday, looking for 60 people to attend

Week 3

Date

May 19

Top Tasks

Fitness assessment at the gym and check membership fees

Go to the bank and look into mortgage options

Successful Outcomes

Seminar was a great success, with 64 people in attendance. I didn't get to the bank in Week 1 so I listed it again as a top task in Week 3 and made it to the bank to discuss my mortgage options.

Glossary

ANTI-OXIDANTS

Anti-oxidants are nutrients in foods that prevent oxidative damage to tissues. It helps the body eliminate toxins and protects it from potentially damaging free radicals.

CARBOHYDRATES

Carbohydrates are macronutrients, as are proteins and fats or lipids. They are divided into three groups: (a) sugars (b) starches and (c) cellulose (fibre). Sugar and starches are digested in the body by enzymes and are used to give energy and heat. Cellulose is found in plants and feeds beneficial bacteria in the intestine.

FAT

Fat is stored in the body as energy, as long as you take in more calories than you use up.

Essential Fatty Acids – the body cannot make Essential Fatty Acids (EFAs) so you must get them through the foods you eat.

Saturated Fats – solid at room temperature and found in animal sources or dairy produce.

Unsaturated Fats – oils at room temperature and found in vegetable foods.

Polyunsaturated Fats – a type of unsaturated fat found in foods such as sunflower oil and oily fish. Omega-3 and Omega-6 fatty acids are polyunsaturated fats. Omega-3 fatty acids are essential to human health. The best food source is fish.

Oil – Cooked oil, margarine and animal fat are inflammatory to the tissues. They impair brain function, harm the cardiovascular system and accelerate the ageing process.

Olive Oil Contains a range of phenolic phytonutrients which along with Vitamin E give the olive and olive oil it's well known anti-oxidant power.

Virgin Olive Oil Virgin olive oil is pressed from olives.

Extra-Virgin Olive Oil Extra-virgin olive oil is the richest in phenolic compounds.

Flaxseed Oil Flaxseeds are high in lignans, which boost the immune system.

MIGHTY MINERALS

Mineral	RDA	Functions	Sources
Calcium	1,000 mg	Prevents osteoporosis. Formation and continuing strength of bones.	Green Vegetables, Prunes/raisins/dates Apricots, Milk
Copper	1.2 mg	Works with iron to make red blood corpuscles	Olive oil, Nuts
Iodine	140 mcg	Needed for proper functioning of the thyroid gland.	Sea vegetables Seafood
Iron	14 mg (women) 8 mg (men)	Combines with oxygen to make haemoglobin which carries oxygen to every cell in the body	Seaweed Sea vegetables Dates and raisins
Magnesium	320 mg (women) 420 mg (men)	Functioning of certain enzymes. Transmission of nerve impulses.	Green vegetables Beans, Nuts, Peas
Phosphorus	540 mg	Bone formation.	Green vegetables, Dried fruit
Potassium	2,000 mg	Nervous system. Body cells.	Grapefruit, Oranges, Bananas
Zinc	7 mg (women) 9.5 mg (men)	Insulin production. Healthy sex organs. Natural resistance (immune system).	Garlic, Ginger Root, Oats Chicken

PHYTONUTRIENTS (PHYTOCHEMICALS)

Phytonutrients are nutrients found in the skins of several fruits and vegetables, and give these foods their colour, flavour and odour. The health benefits from phytonutrients are enormous.

Phytonutrients:

- Promote the function of the immune system
- Act directly against bacteria and viruses
- Reduce inflammation
- Are associated with the treatment and/or prevention of cancer and cardiovascular disease

Top 10 Phytonutrient-Rich Foods

Tomato	lycopene, beta-carotene
Sweet potato	beta-carotene
Citrus fruits	cryptoxanthin, oxalic acid
Broccoli	lignans, sulphoraphane
Blueberries	anthocyanins, lignans
Beetroot	anthocyanins
Garlic	limonene, quercetin
Flaxseed	lignans
Cocoa	flavonoids

Allylic sulfides – These are sulphur compounds that have been shown to induce enzymes that detoxify body cells.

Anthocyanins (flavonols) – These are water soluble and scavenge free radicals they encounter in tissues fluids. This is especially beneficial for athletes who exercise and generate large amounts of free radicals.

HYTONUTRIENTS (PHYTOCHEMICALS) *(continued)*

Capsaicin – This phytonutrient helps relieve nasal congestion and acts as an anti-inflammatory.

Carotenoids – These are the bright yellow, orange and red plant pigment found in vegetables. There are approximately 600 aturally occurring carotenoids found in plants but only 50 of these are found in the human diet. Carotenoids help the body eliminate ee radicals from the system and prevent disease. The two types of carotenoids are called carotenes (examples include beta-carotene nd lycopene) and xanthophylls (examples include zeaxanthin and cryptoxanthin).

Catechins – These are the major flavonoids in green tea and have protective benefits.

Chlorophyll – This is the pigment that gives green fruit its distinctive green colour. Recent studies have shown that, when eaten, ilorophyll is converted to compounds that may help to fight cancer.

Coumestrol – Coumestrol is a phytonutrient found almost exclusively in mung bean sprouts. It is a powerful phytoestrogen and boratory studies reveal it has anti-oxidant and anti-inflammatory abilities.

Flavonoids – These are the largest category of phenolic compounds and are responsible for the vivid red blush of fresh cherries nd the sharp bite of grapefruits. Over 4,000 different types of flavonoids have been identified and they are widespread throughout 'ant foods.

Glucosinolates – These include isothiocyanates, dithiolthiones and sulforaphane. One of their functions include blocking the nzymes that promote tumour growth.

Lignans – These are powerful phytonutrients that help prevent inflammation in the body.

Limonoids – Limonoids have shown to reduce the risk of the following cancers: Oral cavity, larynx, oesophagus, stomach, ancreas, lung, colon and rectum.

Lutein – Lutein and zeaxanthin constitute about half of all carotenoids in the retina and may protect against muscular egeneration. It is primarily used as a natural colourant and gives avocado and egg yolk their yellow colour.

Phytic acid – Phytic acid is seen as a phytonutrient and research has shown it can reduce the risk of colon cancer. Phytic acid revents the absorption of calcium by combining with calcium to form insoluble salts.

Phytosterols – They have a similar structure to cholesterol and both components compete for absorption from the intestine. hytosterols block the uptake of cholesterol and facilitate its excretion from the body.

Phytoestrogens – This is a type of plant oestrogen, with a similar structure to the female sex hormone. Their action in the body far weaker than the true hormone, oestrogen, yet they have biological effects in women, such as increasing the length of the enstrual cycle. Lignan is an example of a phytoestrogen.

Polyphenols – These contain rutin which strengthens and tones the walls of the smallest blood vessels and capillaries. It is eneficial for the treatment of high blood pressure.

Terpenes – These are the largest class of phytonutrients. Tarpenes function as anti-oxidants; protecting lipids, blood and other ody fluids from assault by free radical oxygen species.

Xanthine Alkaloids – These phytonutrients have a mild stimulatory effect on the nervous system.

PRE-BIOTICS AND PRO-BIOTICS

re-biotics and pro-biotics restore the balance of bacteria in the digestive tract.

Pre-biotics have profound effects on the health of the colon and its ability to sustain the health of the entire body.

Pro-biotics are cultures of various bacteria that have a favourable impact on colonic metabolism and helps your body resist nfection. Live yoghurt is an example.

PROTEINS

You need protein for growth and to repair body cells and also for hormone and enzyme production. Digestive enzymes break down proteins into smaller units or molecules called amino acids.

SALT

Salt consists of 40% sodium and 60% chloride. We need a little sodium in our lives as it helps to balance our body fluids. It is also important for proper nerve and muscle function. We are recommended to reduce salt intake to 6g per day.

1 level teaspoon salt = 2g sodium

2g sodium = 5g salt

Read the labels: Products with 1.25g salt per 100g is high in salt and should be avoided.

VITAMIN DEFICIENCY TEST

VITAMIN A	SOURCES
• Is your eyesight deteriorating noticeably? • Do you suffer from mouth ulcers? • Do you suffer from frequent colds/infections? • Do you have sinusitis, respiratory problems or excess mucus?	Beta-carotene: dark green leafy vegetables, including kale, Swiss chard, spinach, watercress, broccoli and parsley, and yellow-orange fruit and vegetables, including squash, cantaloupe melon, peaches and tomatoes; retinol: the livers of animals (calves' and pigs' livers), all dairy produce, eggs and oily fish.
VITAMIN B-COMPLEX	**SOURCES**
• Are you tired all the time? • Do you suffer from anxiety or nervousness? • Is your hair thinning, lank or dry? • Do you have dry skin, nails, or lips? • Do you suffer from depression? • Do you suffer from severe PMS symptoms?	Wholegrains (especially brown rice), cereals, pulses, nuts, yeast extracts, meat, fish, eggs, dairy produce, avocados, cream, mushrooms and broccoli.
VITAMIN C	**SOURCES**
• Do you suffer from regular colds or other infections? • Do you have poor skin texture or elasticity? • Do you bruise easily and are slow to heal? • Do you have arterial or venous problems, such as varicose veins?	Raspberries, blackberries, strawberries, citrus fruit, kiwis, mangoes, papayas, figs, potatoes, green peppers, broccoli, beetroot (beet) and sprouted vegetables, such as mung beans and alfalfa sprouts.
VITAMIN E	**SOURCES**
• Is your skin dry and inelastic? • Do you have different skin pigmentations over your body? • Do you have cardiovascular problems such as angina? • Do you bruise easily and are slow to heal? • Do you have signs of premature ageing?	All green leafy vegetables, including broccoli, watercress, spinach, parsley and kale, avocados (which have one of the highest vegetable levels of Vitamin E), brown rice, nuts and their oils, oatmeal and wheat germ.